D0893447

THE CITY

THE CITY

London and the Global
Power of Finance

Tony Norfield

VERSO
London • New York

First published by Verso 2016
© Tony Norfield 2016

1 3 5 7 9 10 8 6 4 2

Verso
UK: 6 Meard Street, London W1F 0EG
US: 20 Jay Street, Suite 1010, Brooklyn, NY 11201
versobooks.com

Verso is the imprint of New Left Books

ISBN-13: 978-1-78478-366-2
ISBN: 978-1-78478-367-9 (US EBK)
ISBN: 978-1-78478-365-5 (UK EBK)

British Library Cataloguing in Publication Data
A catalogue record for this book is available from the British Library

Library of Congress Cataloging-in-Publication Data
A catalog record for this book is available from the Library of Congress

Typeset in Minion Pro by MJ & N Gavan, Truro, Cornwall
Printed and bound by CPI Group (UK) Ltd, Croydon, CR0 4YY

For Alice and Lucy

Contents

List of Tables and Charts

Tables

Charts

Preface

The head of eurobond trading at Bank of America International in London was an intense and exacting man, not known for his sense of humour. So, as the new analyst in the securities dealing room, I had to be careful responding to the question he put to me: 'Where is value?' At first, I didn't know what he meant. He dealt in financial securities, and there is no 'value' in them, only a price that goes up and down for reasons I had not yet fully worked out. Surely, this wasn't an expression of existential despair. Did he want to chuck it all in and do something useful? No, he wanted to find a security that offered an attractive return, especially one whose price would not fall just after he had bought it. So I said, 'I'll have a look and get back to you in half an hour.' This seemed to placate him, although he would not have been pleased to know I had barely gotten to grips with the array of flickering grey-green numbers on the terminal screens.

That was in the summer of 1987, less than a year after the Thatcher government cut restrictions on UK financial markets with the 'Big Bang' reforms. Those reforms encouraged foreign banks, including Bank of America, to expand operations in the City of London, and enabled the City to benefit from an extended boom in world financial markets – a boom halted only temporarily by the October 1987 stock-market crash and by other market upsets. It was also the start of my career in finance that lasted nearly twenty years, and took me to three more banks, Japanese, British and Dutch, where I witnessed the inner workings of the financial markets. I worked in dealing rooms and travelled to forty countries to visit the banks' government, corporate and financial clients. Over time, the dealing room screens grew bigger, with multi-coloured prices and graphics, and the computers got faster and more sophisticated. But the search for 'value' was the same.

If the dealer found 'value', a portion of it would find its way into his (rarely her) bonus and into the bank's profits and dealing revenues. This was, and remains, the focus of City activity: making a good bet, or at least not getting caught out by the market. Many people conclude that the City is a casino, but the analogy is misleading. While the City does not turn away prospective clients who have more money than sense, its primary role is to manage financial deals for capitalist companies and governments. It is the financial nerve centre of the global system, not a betting shop, and this position also places it at the forefront when crises occur.

There was no small irony in my going to work in the City. I had decided some years before that organising society on capitalist principles was a bad idea, so the financial sector was not the obvious choice for me. My views hadn't changed. But needs must, and, letting discretion be the better part of valour, I kept my sense of self by injecting humour into the market reports I broadcast to the dealing rooms where I worked. Once, I even got a joke about US President George ('Dubya') Bush on the front page of the *Financial Times*. I said that Bush had a 'pronuncification' problem when he used the word *devaluation* instead of *deflation*, an error that led to some turmoil in currency markets.[1] Luckily, I managed to avoid extraordinary rendition.

This book is about how the global financial system works, and in whose interests. Although I give a number of examples from my personal experience, it is not my City autobiography. I will not distract the reader from my main objective with stories of agony and ecstasy in dealing rooms and the idiosyncrasies of financiers. Contrary to appearances, the City does not exist to launch a business elite into the upper stratosphere of wealth, although it can certainly do that. The real City story is that it plays particular roles for British capitalism, and that it could not do that unless it was also servicing a global system. So my focus is far from being just on the City of London. It is much more on how major companies and countries use financial operations to take control of the world's resources.

The City generates dealing revenues for the British economy from worldwide transactions and it offers easy access to funding for favoured corporations and governments. In doing so, it facilitates the global mechanism of finance and helps to centralise economic power.

Another aim of this book is to explain why it is wrong to counterpose finance to a more favoured, productive version of capitalism. Financial operations inevitably arise from capitalist market production, as one can see simply by considering what any company must do to obtain funds to buy goods or when making its regular payments, let alone when embarking on new investments. But more than this, a 'productive' company, especially a large one aiming to boost its market position, will also get heavily involved in financial dealing. Typically, this means merging with or taking over its rivals in stock-market deals, or using the equity and bond markets to increase its financial strength. My argument is that if you do not like 'finance' but have no problem with the capitalist market system, you ought to think a little more about that perspective, since the two are inseparable.

I would like to acknowledge those who helped bring this book to fruition, although I do not presume that they would necessarily agree with all, or even many, of the arguments it contains. Particular credit goes to Lucy and Alice, who read some earlier versions of the chapters, making valuable comments, and who also helped me envisage much more clearly those for whom I wanted to make these points. A number of people also read drafts of some chapters of this book and made useful comments, including John Smith, Andy Higginbottom and Maria Ivanova. Less directly, a longstanding friend, Susil, has been a persistent source of enlightenment in our many discussions. Apart from sharing little-known sources on historical developments and on how the world works today, he has offered valuable tips on writing clearly, not least by alerting me to the pleonasm virus and how to avoid it. Much of the research that culminated in this book was undertaken for a PhD course at the School of Oriental and African Studies, London University, which I completed in 2014 and during which Ben Fine was a very helpful guide. Finally, for more valuable encouragement than they might have realised, and for offering much more constructive, detailed and critical editorial advice than I had expected, I would like to thank my Verso editors in London, Rosie Warren and Leo Hollis.

London

September 2015

1.

Britain, Finance and the World Economy

This business of [being] a second-tier power – we are probably, depending on what figures you use, the fifth or sixth wealthiest nation in the world.

We have the largest percentage of our GDP on exports, apart from the tiny countries around the world, we run world shipping from the UK, we are the largest European investor in south Asia, south east Asia [and] the Pacific Rim, so our money and our wealth depends on this global scene.

We are a permanent member of the (United Nations) Security Council and I think that gives us [a] certain clout and [a] certain ability.

These mean we are not a second-tier power. We are not bloody Denmark or Belgium, and if we try to become that, I think we would be worse off as a result.

Admiral Lord West, Baron of Spithead, September 2011

With this angry statement at a British Labour Party press conference, Lord West, former head of the navy, caused a minor diplomatic embarrassment, followed by apologies to 'bloody Denmark and Belgium'. His outburst was blunt, and in stark contrast to the usual rhetoric on human rights and democratic values that characterises discussions of international affairs. Yet, although arguably a more obvious indicator of Britain's status as a major power, Lord West did not mention the UK's numerous military interventions. A military man himself, he might have noted Britain's participation in no fewer than five wars under the 1997–2010 Labour government.[1]

Just months before he spoke, Britain had added the bombing of Libya to a list that has not ceased to grow. Lord West is a forthright defender of British power – including putting himself on the front line, commanding a ship that was sunk in Britain's war with Argentina over the Malvinas in 1982 – and he would no doubt see militarism, covert operations and the use of political 'clout' as important tools for sustaining it. War, as von Clausewitz famously wrote, is a continuation of politics by other means, and politics, in Lenin's phrase, is 'a concentrated expression of economics'. There can be little doubt that Lord West also appreciates these links, although the main theme of his outburst was Britain's *economic* position.

In the same vein, this book focuses on the economic foundations of Britain's global status rather than on its military escapades. My expertise is in the former, not the latter, and particularly in the financial dimensions of British economic power, something also absent from Lord West's protestations. I worked for nearly twenty years in City of London bank dealing rooms, witnessing at first hand the major expansion of financial operations from the mid-1980s onwards. Unlike the soldier fighting in a war about which he may know very little, the basic mechanism of finance is clear to anyone who witnesses it from the inside, particularly to those who are more than a little sceptical about the benefits of capitalism.

Global finance is an integral part of the world economy today. Britain uses the financial system to gain economic privileges by appropriating value from other countries while appearing to do them a service. This examination of Britain's financial power also reveals how others use the system. Readers who may care little about what the Brits are up to might be surprised to learn how important UK-based finance is to the world economy, how it evolved and also where their 'home' countries fit into a network that encompasses the United States, Germany and France, Japan and China, the offshore tax havens and elsewhere.

World economic and financial power

Critics of modern capitalism usually focus on the United States. Often, especially in Europe, their argument ends up being pitched not against capitalism *per se* but against the *US domination* of it. This overlooks the stake in the system held by other countries and the consequent role they play in the oppression of others. Lord West, in contrast to such US-focused critics, was forthright in asserting British economic and political power. But, surprisingly, he failed to mention British ownership of many of the world's major corporations or the UK's leading role in financial markets as part of his evidence. These are the economic foundations of Britain's status.

In 2013, Britain had the *second* largest stock of foreign direct investments, worth $1,885bn.[2] This figure measures significant or controlling stakes in foreign companies and property. While the UK figure represented only 30 per cent of the total US investment stock of $6,350bn, it was larger as a share of the national economy. Data from a *Financial Times* table of the Top 500 global corporations in 2011 show a similar position. The UK was in second place behind the US, with thirty-four companies having a total market value of $2,085bn. The US had 160 companies with a value of $9,602bn.[3] Another survey shows that, of the world's top 100 *non-financial* corporations in 2013, ranked by the value of their foreign assets, twenty-three were US companies, sixteen were British and eleven were French, while Germany and Japan each had ten. The three biggest UK-based corporations held the second, sixth and seventh places: Royal Dutch/Shell Group plc, BP plc and Vodafone Group plc.[4]

These billions can be difficult to imagine – they have an unearthly quality compared with the money in your bank account – but they reflect real economic influence in the world. They show that while the US is clearly the most powerful country, there are also others with significant power.

Another United Nations report listed the top fifty financial companies in 2012, ranked by their geographical spread. Britain was still in second place to the US, having six compared to ten banks or other financial institutions in this top group. Britain's HSBC was present in sixty-five countries, while Barclays Bank was operative in forty-six.[5] Before the near-death experience of Royal Bank of Scotland and a few other UK banks in 2008, Britain was more closely tied with the US in global finance, even though foreign banks and institutions account for a large part of the City of London's business.[6] As for other powers, Canada, France, Germany and Switzerland each had four institutions in the top fifty; Italy, Japan and Sweden each had three. There can be no doubt that Lord West was correct in his assertion that Britain is a major world power, even if he omitted mentioning these other qualifications for that status.

The importance of British finance can be demonstrated in other ways. In 2013, the assets held by UK-based banks – a measure of the scale of their lending – were more than *four times* the value of UK GDP, or the annual national output. When the size of the equity market and debt securities, such as government and corporate bonds, was added, the total came to *eight times* GDP.[7] Only much smaller countries, such as Switzerland, Luxembourg and Ireland, have a bigger financial sector compared to their domestic economies, based on the particular niche they occupy in world markets. The UK – which is to say, London – is one of the world's leading financial centres and is the *most international* in its business reach.

The financial system is an integral part of the capitalist economy, not an anomaly that can be wished away. Rather than being like a cancer that surgery might remove to restore the capitalist body to health, it is more like a central nervous system: without finance, modern capital-ism is dead. Naturally, people get angry about the behaviour of banks and the public bailouts of financiers, but, to be effective, this anger must be supplemented with an understanding of what is really going on. Why do governments in the major countries continue to support the financial sector and how do financial operations help maintain economic power?

Three topics are covered in this book. The first is the nature of the economic relationships in global capitalism. A small group of pow-erful countries has a privileged position in production, commerce, investment and financial relationships compared to all the others. The second is the financial system. It does not sit on top of, or alongside, what almost all economic commentators call the 'real economy'; it pervades all economic activity. The third is the position of the British economy in the world, particularly Britain's external transactions and its flows of investment and business revenues. Each of these three dimensions adds to an understanding of the financial form taken by the world economy today.

The term 'finance' is often used in relation to particular financial institutions, especially banks, or to single out the 'financial' sector of an economy from the 'non-financial' sector. This book refers to banking and other financial operations, but it is important to note that the concept of finance is not tied to a particular type of institution, or to a separate 'financial sector'. All kinds of capitalist companies conduct important financial operations.

An example often given to illustrate this is the Ford Motor Company, when it set up Ford Motor Credit in order to offer its customers loans with which they could then buy Ford's auto products. Similarly, GE Capital is the financial services arm of General Electric. But what about the commonplace occurrence in which an industrial company takes over its rival in a stock exchange transaction, or buys an equity stake in its suppliers? Or the information technology firm whose investors and managers want to get the company bought out by Google or Facebook, so that they can become instant billionaires? These are not examples of producers who have inadvertently strayed from industrious activity into an alien world of finance. On the contrary, they are typical examples of how capitalism operates today.

Equally, it is not just private capitalist companies who manage financial deals, since government finance ministries and central banks do so too. Governments sell securities to private investors, whether companies or individuals, and to other governments, in order to raise funds for public spending and to manage the state debt. Central banks also oversee the operations of the financial system, determining the interest rates at which they will lend (or receive) funds, how much will be lent and to whom. This puts the state, and especially powerful states, in a key position.

Under imperialism – by which I mean the present stage of capitalist development, where a few major corporations from a small number of countries dominate the world market – access to finance both reflects economic power and is a means of retaining that power. While poor countries also have banks, and while their companies may also issue bonds and equities, their ability to gain privileges by way of the global financial market is equally poor. This is because they have to operate in a system run by the major powers, one in which they take the prices offered to them and have little say over the terms of the deal. Details of how the rich countries dominate the world's financial markets will be set out in later chapters.

There are some 200 countries in the world, but only twenty or so count as major players in world affairs, and even among those there is a clear hierarchy. As a rule, the rest must accept whatever changes in trade relations are imposed, bow to political pressures, and be wary of military intervention or other hostile actions. This also has implications for ordinary people. An old saying is that if you want to get on in life, the most important thing you can do is to make sure you are born to wealthy parents. From a global perspective, the best way to avoid being among the billions facing penury is to be born in a rich country. Then, if you have a job, the likelihood is that you will be able to spend as much on a morning coffee in Starbucks as the daily wage of the factory worker in Bangladesh who made the shirt you are wearing.

Understanding the day-to-day workings of the financial system in its international dimension is crucial here. Financial *crises* may hit the headlines, but they result from this regular daily mechanism and quite often distract attention from it. Above all, the financial system cannot be understood on a *national* basis. For example, the US dollar is the national currency of the United States, but it is also treated as 'world money' thanks to the international economic and financial power of the US. Decisions made in the US, especially those of the Federal Reserve on interest rates and credit policy, impact the global financial system. But world flows of finance also condition what happens in US financial markets. To a lesser extent, other major powers also have some influence, with the weakest countries condemned to being only on the receiving end.

Britain's invisible empire

From 1979 onwards the UK financial markets experienced a boom, exponentially so after the 'Big Bang' reforms of 1986 destroyed the previous cosy cartel of British financial firms. The volume of dealing grew dramatically and international banks flocked to the City of London. It is surprising, then, that there has been no substantial review of this from a radical perspective since the 1980s. The links between finance and Britain's international economic and political power have thus remained by and large invisible. There are three reasons for this.

Firstly, finance is often seen as something outside the realm of power: it is simply another line of capitalist business, while power is confined to the political sphere. But this perspective ignores the financial privileges of leading countries, which are quite distinct from their military or political strengths. As will be explained later, financial privilege is a form of *economic* power, and the countries that enjoy it use the financial system to draw upon the world's resources. Those that are important financial centres receive big revenues from international financial dealing, while companies based in the richer countries have greater access to investment funds and are in a stronger position to use their financial 'clout' to take over rivals and extend their economic influence worldwide.

Secondly, the dominant position of the US is usually seen as the decisive factor in world developments, or even as the only one. For example, during the 2003 invasion of Iraq, Britain was frequently viewed as being the 'lapdog' of the US.[8] There was little recognition that the British state might be acting in British imperialism's *own* economic interests. This happens a lot when the focus is on politics rather than economics.[9] While some writers do discuss Britain's role as an imperialist power, their analyses are most often conducted from a historical, political or diplomatic perspective, with little or no focus on the economic dimensions.[10] One exception, a major historical work entitled *British Imperialism: 1688–2000*, does offer detailed coverage of the economic aspects of Britain's relationships with the rest of the world, but, in its more than 700 pages, it reserves barely *eight* for the years after 1970.[11]

The third reason for the lack of comment on finance and British imperialism today is that the prominence of the financial sector is seen as a result of government policy-making, not as an outgrowth of imperialist economic power. Thirty years ago, some authors did discuss the historical evolution of finance alongside British power, but their principal concern was the relationship of the City to British economic policy – especially in debates over whether financial interests were affecting government decisions to the detriment of manufacturing industry.[12] More recent analyses have had a similar focus, whether they laud the City's operations as a successful example of how to provide competitive financial services in the world market, or whether they are critical of the City and how it supposedly dominates UK economic policy.[13]

Understanding finance and imperialism

Media stories are full of the deeds and misdeeds of financial dealers. News broadcasts are also incomplete if they fail to note the latest level of the equity market and the exchange rate: the FTSE 100 or the S&P 500, or what the dollar, euro or sterling is worth in the market today. But what kind of world works like this? Why should the lives of millions of people be influenced by the vagaries of financial market prices? This only looks normal, rather than weird, because we are used to it. Financial prices are (somehow) related to what is happening in the economy. The collapse of those prices can lead to economic disaster, while a boom will bring joy to the world, or at least to those who own its financial assets. What kind of economy is this? Every year may bring new improved electronic gadgets or breakthroughs in science and medicine, but year after year, decade after decade, the dysfunctional economic system that destroys lives and condemns productive individuals to unemployment remains in place. Improvements in knowledge do not change these relationships of the capitalist economy, the very relationships that lead to economic disasters.

The financial system develops as an integral part of capitalism.

For example, while financial operations include trading in company shares on the stock market, or in foreign exchange rates or interest rate derivatives, these things do not occur in a vacuum, or simply on a financier's whim. They are rooted in capitalist production and commerce. This book will show how these things happen, explaining the role finance plays for the major capitalist countries and their corporations, especially on a world scale. If this context is ignored, then finance will mistakenly be seen as simply 'what financial companies do'. This would greatly exaggerate the role of banks compared to other capitalist corporations and governments. Just as mistaken would be the political conclusion that, if only financial companies were better regulated or constrained by enlightened government policy, then capitalism could be turned into a viable economic system. The destructive tendencies of a social system dominated by production for profit should not be underestimated.

It would, of course, take more than one book to explain modern capitalism. This one focuses on explaining the *financial* mechanism that holds it together. Even so, putting this into a coherent story will require a number of chapters. It may be useful give some pointers here on the way the arguments will be developed, before reviewing what some other writers have had to say about these issues.

Firstly, I will deal mainly with the international aspects of finance. My approach stresses that finance is a feature of the *world economy*, and hence cannot be explained by starting from developments in, or policies enacted by, individual countries, when these are taken out of a global context. For example, most discussions of finance pay very little attention to revenues gained from *outside* the national sphere. But these revenues can be substantial, and they illuminate an importance dimension of finance. In 2013 alone, US *receipts* from investments in foreign companies, foreign equities and bonds, etc., amounted to $773.4bn. This was more than the entire economic output of Switzerland, as measured by GDP! US investment income *payments* on its liabilities – the investments foreigners made in the US – were $564.9bn, which was close to the GDP of Sweden.[14] So, the US had a *net* gain of some $209bn on its foreign investments, equivalent to receiving the economic output of the ten million citizens of the

Czech Republic. Put another way, US foreign investments brought in around $3 billion every working day, while they paid out only a little over $2 billion per working day. The scale of these US revenues is exceptional, but compared to the size of the economy the figures are not so different for some other key countries. In the UK, the most important revenues come from international financial dealing rather than from foreign investments.

Secondly, as suggested earlier, my stress on the critical importance of financial operations for modern capitalism means moving away from the common, almost exclusive, focus on the United States. America's dominant economic position means that it is understandably the centre of attention when it comes to finance. The US set the ground rules for the Bretton Woods world monetary system after 1944, designing it in a way that promoted its interests,[15] and US financial and economic power has remained strong, even after a series of crises in the 1960s that ultimately led to the collapse of the system in the early 1970s.[16] However, this focus often leads to the assumption that other capitalist powers are, at most, only minor accomplices in America's plans, ignoring how *their own interests* are also promoted by their actions. To the contrary, this book argues forcefully that UK policy has been conducted in British capitalism's interests.

Thirdly, although I will discuss some examples of financial crises, much greater attention is given to the regular, daily mechanisms of finance in modern capitalism. The latter is the more critical, decisive feature, although it gets far less coverage. It may be a single straw that finally breaks the camel's back, but it was the pile of previous straws that prepared the way. Because financial crises are often dramatic, this build up often gets overlooked, and the focus tends to fall on the evident symptoms rather than on what may be the more hidden causes. Such a perspective gives a very narrow view of imperial finance, disguising the fact that the financial system works each and every day to the benefit of the major powers. It does not require a crisis to do so, even if a crisis may present those powers with further opportunities, while its victims are left with little chance of escape.

Insights, conspiracies and policy contingencies

In his 1999 book *The Global Gamble: Washington's Faustian Bid for World Dominance*, Peter Gowan developed a sophisticated view of the role of imperial finance. His analysis was strong in several respects and I would agree with many of the points he made. For example, he showed how the US used its financial strength as a tool of state power, not least by forcing other countries to open up their markets to US financial institutions or risk being cut off from sources of funds.[17] He also offered an important insight in arguing that the aim of US financial policy from the early 1970s was 'to compensate for competitive weakness in its productive sectors through taking predatory advantage of its monetary and financial sector dominance'.[18] In other words, the US could use its financial power to compensate, in some respects, for its loss of industrial supremacy. One effect was that the more liberal financial regime established under US auspices from the 1980s meant that international crises often led to flows of finance into the US – both legal and criminal. Many countries, especially in Asia, that had faced financial crises in the late 1990s also feared renewed destabilisation, so they subsequently built up massive foreign exchange reserves as an insurance policy. In practice this meant that the revenues they earned from their trade surpluses were spent on buying US government securities.

These are critical points. Nevertheless, there are two problems with Gowan's analysis. Firstly, he views world financial developments only from a US perspective; secondly, he sees US power as being so strong that the US government is able to promote financial crises in order to benefit from them. Gowan does mention the UK's role in establishing the eurodollar market, but he sees this in terms of how it benefited the US, not whether there was any rationale in the policy for the UK. Yet the evidence shows that there was indeed a very strong rationale, as I will explain in Chapters 2 and 3. Similarly, because the UK does not appear as the main driver of global financial policies – and I would not claim that it is – Gowan characterised the City of London as operating 'principally as a servicing centre for the dollar currency zone and as a satellite of Wall Street'.[19] This conclusion followed from his one-sided emphasis, which prevented a fuller understanding of how the financial system develops out of the global capitalist market and is not controlled by particular states, not even by the US in what he called the 'Dollar–Wall Street Regime'.

This perspective led Gowan not only to see financial crises as being beneficial to the US, which was sometimes true, but also to argue that these crises were planned by the US government in advance.[20] While there is little doubt that the major powers do try to steer events in their favour, it is an overstatement to suggest that they can control the huge financial markets their policies have helped to foster. By contrast, this book argues that the privileged position of US imperialism in the global finance system means that it is more able to benefit from that system's operation in *both* good and bad times, *not* that it deliberately plans crises as a means of increasing its power. For example, while US-based hedge funds *did* bet against a number of Asian currencies in 1997, the bets were based upon the hedge funds' own assessment of the economic realities and the likelihood of crises. The hedge funds did not push viable economies over the cliff, nor were they encouraged to do so by the US government.[21] Still less is there any indication that US government officials had any special inside knowledge with which to tempt the speculators.

At the time of the financial crises in Russia and Asia in 1997–8, I was working in a City dealing room that had begun to trade in 'emerging market' securities and currencies. This was seen as the next big growth area for financial business, but these countries often had large trade deficits and had come to rely increasingly on inflows of foreign capital. Their vulnerability to a reversal of short-term inflows of funds was evident to many, even if few would have claimed to be able to calculate when the reckoning would occur, or how dramatic it would be. The systematic nature of crises in capitalism is a sign that they result from the workings of the capitalist system, not that they are the result of a conspiracy.

Eric Helleiner, a Canadian professor of politics, offers a more thorough account of the contemporary role of finance for imperialism, revealing the ways in which different governments, not only the US, have implemented measures to promote the financial system. He also has a more rounded view than Gowan's, stressing that these measures should be seen in the context of both the industrial *and* the national interests of the states concerned, rather than as resulting from the interests of one section of capital, the financiers. Helleiner notes, for example, how the dramatic growth in the overseas investments of US corporations from 1945 up to the 1960s led these companies to lobby politicians for the removal of restrictions on international flows of finance.[22] This was a critical factor behind the later shift to a 'free market' or 'neoliberal' ideology that is usually discussed nowadays in terms of the (unexplained) influence of financiers over government policy. Nevertheless, Helleiner's analysis sees government policy as being influenced by groups of intellectuals, rather than being a response to changes in the global economy. Instead of explaining more clearly how world developments were the driving factors behind what actually happened, he adopts the stance of a critical policy adviser, stressing how things *might* have been different.

Helleiner examines the key turning points in the expansion of financial markets from the late 1970s to the early 1980s, to illustrate how the economic stresses of the time gave UK, US and French policy-makers little choice but to allow financial markets to grow. The weakness in his argument lies in his conclusion that if controls on markets had been introduced, 'the globalisation trend would have been set back considerably'.[23] To suggest that financial controls could have been introduced contradicts the logic of the material he has previously used to explain the course of events! For example, France did try to impose controls, but was forced to reverse the policy in order to keep to its broader objective of remaining in a key position within European financial and economic affairs. The approach adopted in this book, by contrast, will be to use evidence from world economic trends to explain events and to place policy decisions in that global context.

Helleiner's arguments are especially unconvincing in relation to British finance. He claims that 'Britain supported liberalisation in finance because of its "lagging" hegemonic commitment to London's position as an international financial centre, a commitment derived from its past as a financial hegemon in the nineteenth century'.[24]

Britain was indeed a nineteenth-century financial (and economic) hegemon. But the British state's promotion of finance in the late twentieth century, and still today, can be explained by the fact that the UK financial system is a structural part of the international operations of British capitalism, underpinning the role of Britain as an imperial power. Far from Britain having a 'lagging' commitment to finance since the 1970s, British policy-makers had a very *forward-looking* view on how the existing status of the City as a global financial centre could be leveraged to its best advantage.[25]

The 'End of History' revisited

The role of the US in the world economy and global finance comes up in a different way in the work of Leo Panitch, Sam Gindin and their fellow authors, many from York University, Canada. Panitch and Gindin's book, *The Making of Global Capitalism: The Political Economy of American Empire*, is worth noting for its many insights but also because it displays some typical analytical weaknesses. Regarding the insights, they argue convincingly against those who underestimate how far other capitalist countries have bought into the global system dominated by the US. This point can be illustrated by how few examples there are of other major powers challenging US policy decisions. But Panitch and Gindin greatly exaggerate both the sustainability and the breadth of this consensus. A key point of the present book is how global developments, often first visible in the financial sphere, can destabilise relationships between the major powers. Their approach also pays too little attention to the *economics* of imperialism, especially in its financial dimension. As a result, they either fail to take into account the developing tensions, or else dismiss them as insignificant.

The weakness of Panitch and Gindin's analysis is that it is largely confined to the *political* sphere, concentrating on the power of the US Treasury and Federal Reserve in the world's financial system, either in direct negotiations with other states or via the IMF and the World Bank. They mention the resulting economic advantages for US corporations and financial and business services companies, but they report nothing to suggest what the scale of these advantages might be. The closest they get is to cite the widely known example of the final selling price of Apple's iPod, only a small percentage of which is made up from revenues paid to the China-based factory that produces them.[26] Similarly, in the financial sphere, while they note that the US has obtained easy funding for its external deficits owing to the international role of the US dollar – initially from Japan, then mainly from China – they pay little attention to how this acts as a significant *subsidy* from the world economy to the US, a privilege that results from US financial power.

By omitting or downplaying these factors, they ignore the economic substance of imperialism, especially as it relates to finance. If such factors are sidelined in relation to the US, the 'hegemon', then it is not surprising that they are also overlooked in relation to the UK. Panitch and Gindin's exaggeration of US power follows Gowan's view, noted earlier, that sees the City of London merely as a 'satellite' of Wall Street.[27] Major US banks *do* operate from the City and the US dollar *is* the principal currency traded, but this 'satellite' view ignores some key points. The UK enjoys significant economic gains from hosting the biggest international banking centre, and its own banks also take an important share of this business.[28] Furthermore, the nature of the UK banking and credit market is very different from that of the US. Far from US dollar LIBOR – the *London* Interbank Offered Rate for loans between banks in US dollars – being 'effectively the internationally "traded version" of the Fed's interest rate',[29] it is a rate that represents a financial market that *does not exist in the US*. For historical reasons,[30] the US has no equivalent to the UK's highly developed interbank money market for unsecured loans of different maturities in US dollars, let alone in other currencies. That is why there is no such thing as a 'NYIBOR' for New York, for US dollars or for anything else.[31]

Panitch and Gindin's political analysis also exaggerates the stability of US domination. Ironically, they trace the different historical phases of US power, but then suggest that the latest phase of US hegemony is one that will last *indefinitely*. This is a reincarnation of Francis Fukuyama's 'End of History' thesis, where (free market) global capitalism is the final stage of world economic development. Not surprisingly, Fukuyama's thesis was celebrated by Washington policy-makers.[32] But Panitch and Gindin do something similar, making many references to former US Treasury Secretary Robert Rubin's manage-ment of and influence on the resolution of global financial crises and posing the US as the world's 'chief financial architect'.[33] In this, they badly misjudge the security of the US position.

Many European countries are in a disastrous financial situa-tion and are unlikely to present any serious challenge to the US in the foreseeable future, but this does not mean that major European powers have not tried to do so in the past and may do so again. The currency turmoil of the 1970s following the break up of the Bretton Woods system – seen by Europe as a failure of US power – was the key stage in what later became the euro project, since it pro-duced chaos in European economic relationships, something that Germany and France were particularly concerned to avoid. It is not so unlikely that at some point defensive measures could be imposed by euro-based politicians against what they see as disruptive finan-cial markets, particularly those in which the US and the UK are heavily involved. While that would not necessarily be the first step towards a serious conflict between the major powers, it would go beyond simple economic rivalry between competing countries or companies.

Panitch and Gindin argue that there has been no inter-imperial conflict in the latest crisis, and that it has instead been characterised by *cooperation* among the main countries, led by the US. They claim that 'the conflicts that have emerged today in the wake of the greatest capitalist crisis since the 1930s are taking shape ... less as conflicts *between* capitalist states and their ruling classes than as conflicts *within* capitalist states'.[34] But this glosses over the recent problems in Europe, which are already destabilising political relationships between the major capitalist powers and giving support to more xeno-phobic and nationalist political parties. In Britain, for example, the Conservative government intends to conduct a referendum in 2016 or 2017 on whether the UK continues as a European Union member country unless it can renegotiate more favourable terms, and the UK

Independence Party, whose core policy is for Britain to leave the EU, received 13 per cent of the votes in the 2015 UK General Election.

History wakes up

China presents a far more important challenge to the US domination of the world economy and world finance than do the European countries. China's development is a striking example of how the changing balance of economic forces can create new political trends that upset the status quo, and which must be taken into account in order to understand the dynamic of the system. But Panitch and Gindin discount the possibility of any serious risk to US power from China, arguing that the Chinese economy is embedded in the US-designed structures of the world economy because, for example, it owns a huge volume of US dollar-denominated debt in its foreign exchange reserves that effectively cannot be sold. They are correct to note that there are limits to China's projection of power, yet they do so by questioning whether China has 'the capacity to take on extensive responsibilities for managing global capitalism',[35] as if that were the issue at stake! They fail to mention that the Chinese state has used its US dollar funds not only to recapitalise Chinese banks, but also for purposes that have riled US politicians, including overseas investments by state-owned and privately-owned Chinese companies in Africa, South America, the Pacific and elsewhere. In 2011, US Secretary of State Hillary Clinton argued for an increase in her budget on the following lines:

> Let's just talk, you know, straight *realpolitik*. We are in a competition with China. Take Papua New Guinea: huge energy finds ... ExxonMobil is producing it. China is in there every day in every way, trying to figure out how it's going to come in behind us, come under us ... I might also mention China has about a $600m development programme for these Pacific island nations. And what do we have in a response? Zero.[36]

One might think this merely a self-serving argument on Clinton's part, but there are many other indications that the US is all too aware of how China's growing strength represents a 'security' threat to its interests as well as an economic one. Since it was created in 2000, a special US-China Economic and Security Review Commission has provided the US Congress with an annual report on all the current issues. Its 2010 report covered US-China economic relationships, China's 'growing air and conventional missile capabilities', its activity in Asia (especially in relation to Taiwan) and examples of China's 'cyber attacks' on the internet. It pointed to the 'intensification of a number of troubling trends'.[37] Later reports have continued in the same vein, with the November 2013 report arguing that China's 'military modernization is altering the security balance in the Asia Pacific, challenging decades of US military pre-eminence in the region'.[38] These challenges to US hegemony cannot simply be dismissed as exaggerations by the US political and military establishment.

Chapter 9 will cover China's challenge to the US in the financial sphere in more detail, but it is worth briefly noting some important developments here. In 2014, Brazil, Russia, India, China and South Africa established the New Development Bank, otherwise known as the BRICS bank, funded mainly by China. Its headquarters is in Shanghai, the world's largest city and busiest container port, and mainland China's financial centre. The same year also saw the formation of the China-led Asian Infrastructure Investment Bank, which the US failed to prevent its political allies from joining. Furthermore, China's stock exchanges, including Hong Kong, Shanghai and Shenzhen, are already the *second largest* in the world in terms of market capitalisation and turnover. Contrary to Panitch and Gindin's view, this is not a basis on which one would expect China to be willing to remain subordinate to the US.

China's rise in the world economic hierarchy is relatively recent, but it is an example of how what can look like established, permanent relations of global economic and political power are more fragile than they might appear to be. This consideration also applies to the UK's changing position in the global economy.

'New Deal' and no deal

David Harvey offers another perspective on imperialism and finance, and his focus on the predatory aspects of imperialism is an unusual, and welcome, recognition of events in the world. Harvey's academic origins in geography led him to focus more than many others on the division of the world economy and the privileges of the imperialist powers, an important theme of the present book. In addition, his work shows how financial crises have wreaked havoc in developing countries from the 1970s, with pressures from the US, other powers and the IMF forcing them to adopt policies that have led to further depredation, as part of a process he calls 'accumulation by dispossession'.[39] Nevertheless, there are also some serious problems with his analysis.

Ironically, by focusing on *crises*, and how these can help the major powers take control of weaker countries' resources, Harvey's approach to the question of imperialism (and finance) ends up by calling for reform. For example, his book *The New Imperialism* concludes with the proposal that people should fight for a new 'New Deal' and a 'more benevolent imperial trajectory'.[40] This not only contradicts his earlier stated view that capitalism/imperialism is in the middle of a damaging crisis, it also represents a regrettable concession to imperialist policy. This political perspective seems to follow from his view that crises can be minimised by reforms to the capitalist system, a view that is consistent with the way he sidelines the crucial *regular mechanism* of capital accumulation by exploitation and financial appropriation. For example, he puts the issue of finance under the heading of 'dispossession' by focusing on crises, leading to the conclusion that a 'more benevolent' policy would ameliorate the impact of those crises. In doing so, he ignores the real mechanism of financial power, especially for the US and the UK – a mechanism that this book will spell out.[41]

There are a few other writers whose work I consider important for understanding the question of finance and imperialism today. One is the French Marxist scholar François Chesnais. He sees imperialism as being 'centrally related to the domination of a precise form of capital, namely highly concentrated interest and dividend-bearing money-capital', and he also stresses how 'financial assets generate legally protected claims on the current and future production and centralisation of surplus [value]'.[42] These ideas will be explained in later chapters, but they basically mean that capitalism today has taken on a largely financial form that dominates the production and distribution of social wealth. This is not to counterpose productive capital and 'finance' as respectively good and bad, but to recognise that countries with companies that are part of a global oligopoly *and* the large institutional financial investors of these countries are all 'partners in the global system of imperialist domination'.[43] This is a key insight and one that is also central to my own analysis. One difference of emphasis, however, is that while Chesnais tends to concentrate on the subordination of weaker countries by way of the high costs of borrowing imposed on them by the major financial centres, I consider this to be only a small part of the broader mechanism of value appropriation effected by the key financial powers in the world economy.[44]

The system

Without an understanding of the role of the financial system, the workings of the world economy and the relationships between countries remain a mystery. Still less can one comprehend why governments make policy decisions to protect finance, decisions which are often unpopular and alien to most people. The financial system is the means by which the corporations and governments of the rich countries control the world's resources. This is not to say, however, that they can control the *workings* of the capitalist world economy. The capitalist market system is beyond control, and capable of bankrupting even its most ardent supporters.

This book is not a study of what some academics have called 'financialisation',[45] nor is it an analysis of the 2007–8 financial crisis and its aftermath. Although I explain important dimensions of that debacle – from the role of financial leverage, to the privileged position of the US Federal Reserve in the provision of finance, to the options open to the City of London in the middle of the crisis in 2008 – this book is instead about how the financial system functions as a key economic feature of contemporary imperialism.

The US is the world's hegemonic power, but it is not pre-eminent in all areas of financial business. Chapters 2 and 3 explain how the global financial system evolved historically, in a process marked by both rivalry and cooperation between the US and the previous leading power, the UK. Other countries also played a part in this development after the Second World War, but the end result was that the UK was able to play a much stronger role in the world financial system than its economic status would have suggested. These historical developments also help to explain why Britain was reluctant to participate in the various European projects for monetary cooperation and eventual monetary union, and why it is in a quandary over EU membership today.

Having set out the evolution of the financial system, I continue in Chapter 4 with a closer look at the different types of financial institutions, the process of credit creation by the banks, and how the prices of financial securities are determined. Bank credit creation is often misunderstood, even in economics textbooks. It can also appear to break free from any link with economic activity, although there is always a reckoning at some stage. Similarly, the prices of financial securities look like they are driven only by speculation in the market, although these securities reflect the economic power of both financial and non-financial companies, enabling them to command astronomical sums of money.

Tracing the evolution of finance is important especially when the historical evidence contradicts widely held beliefs. But there is also a particular dynamic in the capitalist market that results in a small number of companies from a small number of countries enjoying privileged positions in the world economy, such that they dominate production, commerce and finance. This will be discussed in Chapter 5, highlighting the fact that my main focus is on the financial system – and not simply 'the banks' – since it is this that underpins the network of imperial domination.

The links between the financial system and the economy are analysed further in Chapter 6 by showing how profitability, a decisive signal for capitalism, is influenced by financial developments. For example, financial 'leverage', or borrowing, can change the rate of return recorded by capitalist companies. A country's position in the world economy will also change the way in which any data on profitability should be interpreted. This is particularly true for the US. Its privileged position means, among other things, that part of the profits recorded by its companies on domestic operations derive from its *worldwide* commercial and financial power.

Rounding off this theme, Chapter 7 undertakes a review of the different forms of financial privilege and how these work for different countries. The US has a special position, given that the US dollar is at the centre of international banking relationships and the US government can restrict who does business in dollars. But other countries also play a part in the global financial network and benefit from the parasitic game.

Chapter 8 returns to focus on the UK, detailing the operations of Britain's 'financial machine' and the flows of trade and finance over the past thirty years. Britain hosts the world's biggest *international* financial centre, with the largest volume of international loans, foreign exchange and derivatives trading. Such business is not as divorced from the 'domestic' British economy as many believe. For example, it brings in large revenues from around the world to help finance the huge gap between Britain's exports and imports of goods. The British system also acts as the world's financial broker, facilitating a myriad of deals, as well as helping to finance US deficits via tax havens.

Recent developments have seen Britain's financial machine run into a few problems. Foreign investment income has turned into a deficit and the growth in revenues from financial dealing has slowed down, while the UK trade gap has continued to widen. These developments have led the City and the UK government to seek new lines of business, both in so-called 'Islamic finance' and in new financial deals with China. But, as Chapter 9 indicates, the global environment for British finance is changing fast, and in ways that are not conducive to the continued, unchallenged domination of the Anglo-American system.

2.

The Anglo-American System

In 1925, Winston Churchill and John Maynard Keynes were at loggerheads. Their dispute was over the UK government's plan to once again tie the international exchange rate of sterling to gold, a policy that had been suspended at the outbreak of the First World War in 1914. This episode is of interest for illustrating how financial markets, and government policy towards them, cannot be understood from the perspective of the national economy alone. Churchill was then Chancellor of the Exchequer, taking advice from a number of policy experts. Keynes was one of these, but he was at that time best known for his blistering attack on the 1919 Treaty of Versailles, agreed by the victorious powers after the First World War. Keynes tore the Treaty apart in his book *The Economic Consequences of the Peace*, arguing that the damaging reparations imposed on Germany would lead to disaster. When Keynes lost the argument about returning to the gold standard, he published a pamphlet with a similar title, *The Economic Consequences of Mr Churchill*.

Keynes's pamphlet opposed the decision on the gold standard because of the *particular rate* chosen for sterling, which was the same as in 1914. Furthermore, Keynes argued that the current exchange rate was only about 10 per cent too high when considering sterling's value against the US dollar, although this was significant for some of Britain's industries, such as coal mining, which had already suffered from postwar economic setbacks. But what is striking about Keynes's pamphlet is that it covered only the domestic economic implications of the decision. It completely ignored the government's reasons for taking the decision and did not address the key issue: the fact that British policy-makers were worried about the US.

The higher exchange rate for sterling was a problem for the domestic British economy because it made British exports a little more expensive. However, the main problem for British trade was the postwar disruption of the global economy and finance, especially in Europe. In this context, while British policy-makers, like British industrialists, thought it would be difficult to adapt to the new gold parity for sterling, both thought it would be a cost worth paying in order to reap the benefits. There was widespread support for the view that a return to gold at pre-war levels would stabilise business conditions after the turmoil of the First World War and its aftermath. This would help to boost international trade and investment, and hence the British economy.[1] More importantly, there was an *imperial* rationale for the policy on sterling. Churchill made this point clearly: 'If we had not taken this action, the whole of the rest of the British Empire would have taken it without us, and it would have come to a gold standard, not on the basis of the pound sterling, but a gold standard of the dollar.'[2]

Britain's problem was that the First World War was largely a European war. The US had emerged largely unscathed and in a stronger international position. Hence the debate in British policy circles: should the government restore sterling as *the* currency underpinning global financial relationships, at the old rate against gold, in order to stress both that nothing had really changed and that international holders of sterling would not suffer losses on its devaluation, or should it recognise that the *status quo ante* was no longer attainable? In 1925, the former path was risky, but it looked to be far less of a threat to Britain's imperial position than the alternative. British policy-makers had reason to believe that their previous power could be restored, given the desolation elsewhere in Europe, particularly in Germany following Versailles, and despite their worries about Soviet Russia after 1917.

What Churchill had to say in his April 1925 budget speech announcing the return to gold is worth quoting at some length:

In our policy of returning to the gold standard we do not move alone. Indeed, I think we could not have afforded to remain stationary while so many others moved. The two greatest manufacturing countries in the world on either side of us, the United States and Germany, are in different ways either on or related to an international gold exchange. Sweden is on the gold exchange. Austria and Hungary are already based on gold, or on sterling, which is now the equivalent of gold. I have reason to know that Holland and the Dutch East Indies – very important factors in world finance – will act simultaneously with us today. As far as the British Empire is concerned – the self-governing Dominions – there will be complete unity of action. The Dominion of Canada is already on the gold standard. The Dominion of South Africa has given notice of her intention to revert to the old standard as from 1st July. I am authorised to inform the Committee that the Commonwealth of Australia, synchronising its action with ours, proposes from today to abolish the existing restrictions on the free export of gold, and that the Dominion of New Zealand will from today adopt the same course as ourselves in freely licensing the export of gold.

...

Thus over the wide area of the British Empire and over a very wide and important area of the world there has been established at once one uniform standard of value to which all international transactions are related and can be referred. That standard may, of course, vary in itself from time to time, but the position of all the countries related to it will vary together, like ships in a harbour whose gangways are joined and who rise and fall together with the tide. I believe that the establishment of this great area of common arrangement will facilitate the revival of international trade and of inter-Imperial trade. Such a revival and such a foundation is important to all countries and to no country is it more important than to this island, whose population is larger than its agriculture or its industry can sustain, which is the centre of a wide Empire, and which, in spite of all its burdens, has still retained, if not the primacy, at any rate the central position, in the financial systems of the world.[3]

The important lesson from this historical episode is that big events, especially financial ones, cannot be understood if we do not take into account the positions of the different powers. Going back on the gold standard in 1925 was a policy mistake in the sense that it lasted only until 1931. By then, large outflows of gold led to downward pressure on sterling's exchange rate and the gold parity had to be abandoned. Other European countries, including France, had devalued their currencies versus gold, making the sterling parity a bigger problem (although it is arguable that the French would have devalued by even more, had the British done so before 1931). However, British policy-makers had planned to use the gold standard as a means of re-establishing Britain's role in world finance, which was a key element of its economic power and influence in the world economy. After 1931, British policy changed course to establish much more direct, and protectionist, financial links with the Empire and Dominion countries. World trade and investment more generally during the 1930s came under the political control of the major powers with their different spheres of influence. Britain's effort to bolster its financial position eventually resulted in the Sterling Area, which lasted from 1940 until the early 1970s.

British or American finance?

The aftermath of the First World War was problematic enough for Britain. Much more difficult to manage by the close of the Second World War was the fact that the US stood out as by far the biggest economy in the world, with the most productive industrial capacity and the largest financial reserves. These strengths allowed the US to set the agenda and largely determine the outcome of the July 1944 Bretton Woods conference, held in a big hotel north of New York. Bretton Woods was a landmark event that established the financial institutions of the post-1945 world order and the rules for how the international monetary system would work. It signalled the transition from the broken, pre-war and formerly British-led system to one now dominated by the US. Henry Morgenthau, Treasury Secretary at the Bretton Woods negotiations, set out the US objectives clearly:

Now, to me it boils down to this ... that the financial centre of the world is going to be New York and we don't want to postpone this thing until another day where we may not be in as advantageous a position and maybe have them [the British] to get in a horse-trading position and maybe end up by having it in London.[4]

At this point, nobody really questioned the idea that the key decisions were going to be made by the US, so Morgenthau was able to ensure that the new International Monetary Fund and World Bank were based in Washington, DC. But New York did not quite achieve the domination that he had envisaged.

US-based financial markets were subject to more limitations than Morgenthau had anticipated, and this enabled the British to play a bigger role than might have been expected given the diminished position of the UK economy. During the 1950s and '60s, world economic and political developments also led British capitalists and policy-makers into a shift away from their dependence on Britain's colonial Empire and to seek other markets.

Achieving a *modus vivendi* with the power of US capital has for many decades been one of the most important objectives of the British state, and the UK is obviously in a subordinate position in this relationship. That became evident to UK policy-makers during the 1940s, when US governments made concerted efforts to undo the British Empire's protectionist policies as a *quid pro quo* for US financial aid. Britain's weakened position became painfully clear with the 1956 Suez crisis. The Anglo-French adventure against Egypt was stymied by US political opposition, especially when international investors began to sell sterling on the foreign exchange markets.[5] Without US support, Britain's lack of funds meant that it was unable to defend sterling's value in the monetary system, and it had to back down over Suez. This further threatened its already damaged status. Nevertheless, it would be a mistake to see the British financial markets as having simply become a 'satellite' of those in the US. In fact, the UK markets adapted to the political and economic realities of the post-1945 world in ways that built on their prior strengths. While this meant recognising US power, especially because financial dealing came to be focused on the dollar, it also generated lucrative and important business for British capitalism.

The Anglo-American relationship is an example of the complex system of cooperation and rivalry between the major powers. One consequence was that the City of London remained a major world financial centre – in many respects ahead of New York – despite the relative decline of the British economy post-1945 and despite sterling no longer being the principal currency for international trade and finance. Historical factors, and the interaction between financial companies and new developments in state policy, brought advantages to London-based international finance.

Relationships between capitalist companies, state policy and the evolution of the global market determined the form taken by global financial markets and explain how the Anglo-American financial system evolved. After 1945, British policy came to terms not only with its downgraded status but also with the reduced economic value of the British Empire compared to the opportunities that beckoned elsewhere, particularly in Europe. Nevertheless, the way in which British imperialism had interacted with the rest of the world had particularly strong financial dimensions, especially in trade finance and other dealing operations. So, despite strict UK government limits on the use of sterling for foreign investment, the City had the expertise to develop a business largely on the basis of using the new world currency, the US dollar. This put London in a favourable position, especially compared to the US-based financial system that not only had a huge *domestic* market as an alternative focus for its business, but which was also more constrained by official regulation. The growth of the so-called euromarkets from the late 1950s onwards is the clearest sign of this divergence between the US and the UK. These markets grew on the basis of the international expansion of capitalist business because they enabled major corporations to access large-scale funds, often of a size that was not available in their domestic financial markets. The euromarkets grew outside the control of individual governments, but the UK authorities fostered that growth as part of the British financial system.

Anglo-American financial relationships in transition

Britain's role in the post-1945 world economy was closely shaped by its relationship with the US, but this was far from being the special relationship of amicable, mutual support that Churchill had invoked. Churchill used the 'special relationship' phrase on a number of occasions, most notably in his 'Iron Curtain' speech in 1946 in Fulton, Missouri. In front of an American audience, the main thrust of that speech was not so much to attack the Soviet Union's erection in Eastern Europe of what western capitalists saw as an economic barrier, although it did do that. More importantly, Churchill's speech aimed to promote a *joint* Anglo-American domination of the world, with their combined power projected by way of a wide range of military bases, at the time largely run by the British, and nuclear weapons, controlled by the US.[6] Far from being a special friend of the British, however, throughout the 1930s and into the Second World War the US had used its economic and financial prowess to force political and economic concessions from the UK in return for financial assistance. In doing so, the US made a determined effort to supplant Britain from its formerly key global economic position.

Britain's dependence on US goodwill had already led it to end its alliance with Japan in the early 1920s. The US saw Japan as a threat to its interests in the Pacific region. The UK complied with US wishes, despite its gratitude to Japan for monitoring Britain's Asian colonies during the largely Europe-based First World War.[7] By the early 1940s, Britain's economic resources had been stretched to the limit as a result of prolonged war on a much wider scale than in 1914–18. This second major international conflict was conducted against three opponents in three theatres at the same time: Germany and Italy in Europe and North Africa, and Japan in Asia. Britain became heavily indebted to the US via the Lend-Lease policy and was forced to liquidate foreign assets, trading these for desperately needed US funds, while also offering the US military bases in Newfoundland (Canada) and the Caribbean.[8] By 1944, when discussions about establishing the International Monetary Fund and the World Bank culminated in the Bretton Woods agreements, the US had determined that its own interests demanded a postwar trade and financial system with the dollar at its centre, which would further undermine the international position of sterling and the commercial power of British imperial- ism. US officials rejected out of hand Keynes's pro-British proposal of creating a new international currency, 'bancor', which would have limited the power of American finance.[9] But the paradox was that Britain's financial position in the world economy was far from being fatally damaged, despite being bankrupt and heavily dependent on US credit.

Building beyond the Empire

Britain's status as the leading international power had clearly come to an end by 1945. Nevertheless, this did not stop the British govern- ment's attempts to shore up the Empire and make full use of colonial resources. This was met with disapproval from the US, because Empire protectionism limited the markets for US capitalists and the US was projecting itself to the world as being anti-colonial. In the immediate post-1945 period, however, the US became more con- cerned with the 'threat of communism' and the position of the Soviet Union in Eastern Europe and Asia. Hence it did not oppose Britain's efforts to restore its hold over its colonial possessions in Asia in the wake of the defeat of Japan. Neither was there any US opposition to Britain's post-1945 wars to revive Dutch and French colonial posi- tions in Asia, as part of its attempt to rebuild the *status quo ante*.[10] In the immediate postwar period under the Labour government, Britain used the troops of an enemy it had only just ceased fight- ing, Japan, in its colony-restoration projects in Asia! (A fact that has received little recognition aside from in the book by Bayly and Harper just cited.) More troublesome for the British Empire in these early postwar years were the Indian nationalists who wondered how their aim of achieving 'dominion status', or securing some independence from Britain, was consistent with Britain also using Indian troops to restore Europe's colonial empires. It took a peculiarly British audacity to have the gall to use a recently defeated imperialist enemy alongside its own colonial troops to fight anti-colonial popular movements. Despite this, as Cain and Hopkins note, these pro-Empire actions came to be accepted by the US because 'with the onset of the Cold War, American attitudes to colonialism softened. The British Empire finally ceased to be an obstacle on the road to progress and became instead a bulwark against the Communist menace.'[11]

This changed political situation also led to the US altering the policy view it had adopted at Bretton Woods, when it had argued that the British government must restore sterling's convertibility as soon as possible. The US came to realise that this was not feasible without leading to a collapse of sterling's exchange value against the US dollar, and financial repercussions elsewhere, given sterling's ties to a wide range of other currencies based on colonial and other financial relationships. Sterling devaluation eventually occurred in 1949, in the wake of a failed attempt to lift some restrictions on the ability to trade the currency in 1947. The 1949 devaluation reduced sterling's exchange rate from $4.03 (a rate set in 1940, after having been cut from $4.86) to just $2.80.[12] The evidently weak UK economy nevertheless meant that many restrictions on the ability to buy or sell sterling in foreign exchange markets continued until 1958.[13]

By that time, developments in the international economy had also begun to alter the British perspective on the value of the Empire, and this had implications for British finance. From the 1930s into the mid-1950s especially, Britain had shamelessly milked the colonies for their resources in order to bolster its poor financial position through what came to be called the Sterling Area. This happened in two ways.

Firstly, all Empire members had to deposit their international trade earnings in London, and were credited with a *sterling* amount at a fixed exchange rate. However, the colonies were not allowed to draw on dollar funds to pay for goods from the US, even though some had large dollar earnings from their commodity exports. Instead they were constrained to buy goods from Britain.[14] The white-settled 'Dominions', Canada, Australia and New Zealand had far more leeway to use dollar funds from the central Sterling Area pool held in London.

Secondly, Britain used colonial marketing boards to buy commodities from the colonies at below market prices, arguing that these were guaranteed and stable prices that would be a benefit to the producers. The lower prices were certainly a benefit to British consumers. In a May 1951 debate on the West African Marketing Boards, one Labour MP, the Rugby and Oxford educated barrister, Richard Acland, made the following comment as part of an apologia for this system:

> Firstly, the prices in the long-term contracts made by our Government were perfectly fair prices, there being genuine arguments at the time of the contracts to suggest that world prices for the crops might have fallen. But in fact that has never happened and the opposite has always taken place. To give an example: we are purchasing West African palm oil at £94 a ton, when the same oil on the free market has been fluctuating from £134 to £210 per ton.[15]

What a stroke of luck that no West Africans were listening! Just in case they were, he added that the amounts concerned were of no significance.

This exploitative attitude towards the colonies was by no means exceptional. In 1953, when in opposition, the future Labour prime minister Harold Wilson argued in Parliament that mineral resources in a wide range of British colonies could be developed to plug the gap between what Britain was importing and its ability to export: 'I do not think that anyone in the House would deny that the answer to all our dollar problems may well be found 200 or 1,000 feet below the soil in the Colonial areas.'[16] At Labour's Annual Conference in 1956, Jennie Lee – wife of Labour Party saint Aneurin Bevan – recognised that the Empire, then given the euphemistic title 'Commonwealth of Nations', might not persist, given many countries' demands for independence. She nevertheless noted the colonies' valuable contribution to the Sterling Area balances and concluded: 'We have to work for the day when there will be a higher standard of living here, a higher standard of living in the colonies, and when as free and friendly nations they will want us to be their bankers.'[17]

This outlook also led to the infamous Tanzanian groundnut scheme, a Labour government plan for the colonies to grow crops that would feed the UK but not cost any more US dollars. The scheme was abandoned in 1951 as an expensive failure. Much more evidence is available of the British Labour Party's attempt to put a 'socialist', concerned-for-development gloss on imperialist policies, but here I am more concerned with the changing mechanism of British policy.[18] By the end of the 1950s, the rapid recovery of the economies of Western Europe made the orientation of British trade and finance towards its Empire and the Dominions – or 'the Commonwealth' – look *passé*.

Maintaining a protectionist system to facilitate the former arrangements and ensure British privileges in the colonial markets was not a sufficient strategy when the rest of the world's economies were growing faster. Britain had benefited from the exploitation of financial resources in the Sterling Area – formally created in 1940, but informally in place from the early 1930s – when other members had surplus US dollar funds that were deposited in London. But in the 1950s 'an increasing number of Britain's colonies began to run deficits with the United States'.[19] This worsened in the 1960s. The Sterling Area's current account deficit with the rest of the world rose from an average annual £508m in 1958–61 to £754m in 1962–65,[20] figures that were a little over 2.0 per cent of UK GDP, while the UK itself had a modest current account *surplus* over this period.

The UK's current account surplus, when there was one, was usually insufficient to offset the outflow of long-term investment capital from Britain, or to help build up adequate foreign exchange reserves to offset any short-term outflows from sterling.[21] These Empire deficits thus added to Britain's own financing troubles, and they were an important factor in shifting the perspective of British policy-makers closer towards trade with Europe. However, at the time this was not enough to persuade them to participate in the European Economic Community (EEC) with the 1957 Treaty of Rome's founding six members – West Germany, France, Italy, Belgium, the Netherlands and Luxembourg. Such an alliance would have conflicted too much with the UK's existing trade and financial relationships with Commonwealth countries.

In 1960, Britain brought together a group of *non*-EEC countries to form the loosely structured European Free Trade Association (EFTA), in which members were free to establish individual customs duties in trade with non-EFTA countries. This was the first step in a series of developments that eventually culminated in Britain joining the EEC in 1973. However, its first application to join in 1961 was rejected by French president de Gaulle's veto in January 1963. Notably, this was the month after UK prime minister Macmillan had secured a nuclear deal with US president Kennedy on the supply of US Polaris missiles to the UK at a meeting in Nassau, capital of the British colony of the Bahamas. For de Gaulle, along with other European political leaders, this was a signal that Britain's political stance was not consistent with an independent (from the US) European project. British policy-makers would continue to have difficulties negotiating a relationship with Europe while protecting the wider interests of British imperialism.

Britain's financial position by the 1950s stood in dramatic contrast to its position half a century earlier. Before the First World War, the City of London was the main hub for the issuance of international loans, bonds and other securities, but by the 1950s its role had shrunk markedly. Between 1899 and 1913, Britain had a current account surplus averaging 5 per cent of GDP per annum: its large trade deficit in goods was offset by even larger revenues from services and investment income from foreign assets.[22] This financial strength enabled the City to act as a base for extending credit to the world economy, both via the funds accruing to wealthy families and domestic capitalists and by intermediating the funds placed in London by foreign capitalists. By the 1950s, the sale of foreign assets, the setbacks in world trade and finance resulting from two world wars, and the imposition of controls on financial flows to protect Britain's balances had more or less destroyed that comfortable position. In 1910 'around one third of all securities issued in the world were quoted on the London Stock Exchange, and foreign securities comprised around 60 per cent of all the securities listed in London'.[23] However, the sale of UK-held foreign securities during the war, and the restrictions imposed on overseas investment afterwards, limited the volume of international business emanating from British investors, while the maintenance of strict exchange controls until 1958 prevented non-British investors gaining easy access to the London securities market.[24]

By the 1950s, it was clear that Britain's previous role in the mechanism of global finance could not be restored. The weakness of the British economy, the reduced economic importance of Empire markets – a protectionist mainstay since the 1930s – and the pre-eminent position of the US in the world economy had put paid to that prospect. Some commentators have argued that 'financial capitalists' were in charge of British state policy, but the controls on the operations of financial companies based in Britain resulting from these economic conditions clearly contradict this view. The only valid point in this argument is that the earlier successful history of Britain as a financial centre meant both that financial service revenues *were* important for the economy and that this expertise could *potentially* be used in a different way to suit the new, post-1945 environment.

In this respect, a comment in the 1959 Radcliffe Report on the UK monetary system is relevant. The Report briefly discussed the declining role of sterling in international trade and payments, and the increasing importance of the US dollar, particularly in official foreign exchange reserves.[25] However, it expressed little concern about the future role of the City's 'substantial' invisible earnings if sterling's exchange rate were to become convertible. While this was thought likely to weaken financial ties between Sterling Area members, it did 'not demonstrate that these earnings would be perceptibly less if the settlements that now take place in sterling came to be made, under a different system of payments, in some international currency such as "bancor"'.[26] To refer in 1959 to Keynes's 1944 proposal for a currency called 'bancor', an illusory alternative to the real US dollar, was disingenuous. But the point being made in the Radcliffe Report was that the City was still a leading centre of international finance, one that was not confined simply to Commonwealth or Sterling Area business.

New York versus London

Morgenthau's 1944 ambition to make New York the financial centre of the world in place of London was not so audacious. The two world wars had greatly weakened British imperialism's finances, as was clear from Britain's extensive Lend-Lease debts and other obligations to the US. Before 1945 it was evident that the US was the world's major economic power, and the Bretton Woods financial framework had only formalised its financial power, with the US dollar as the numeraire of the system and the currency that was convertible into gold (between central banks). The importance of the US as a key provider of foreign credit had been evident since the First World War, and this position became more prominent after 1945. The surprising thing, however, was not that the US overtook Britain as the world's provider of capital, but that it did *not* overtake Britain as the world's centre for international banking. This point is worth dwelling on because it helps explain both the later relationship between the British and American financial systems and the basis for the renewed growth of British finance in the 1980s.

In 1945, and for several decades afterwards, US banks faced many legal restrictions on their activities following from the experience of the inter-war slump. These included limits on inter-state banking by bank corporations and the Glass-Steagall legislation, dating from 1933, which limited affiliations between US commercial banks and securities firms. This meant that, despite the global dominance of the US economy, the US financial system was in a much weaker position to overtake London's international role than it might have appeared to be. As one author noted:

> Given widespread perceptions of a direct link between the [1929] Crash and the severe depression that followed, revulsion at speculative financial excess was common and was voiced by the leading politicians of the Roosevelt administration ... Based on their considerable social and political power, isolationist American farmers, organised labour and industrialists ensured that New York could not be a WFC [world financial centre] at the heart of a reconstituted orthodox liberal world financial order during the 1930s.[27]

This impeded the development of New York as a rival to London. Despite the greater ability of US capital to provide funding for foreign investments after 1945, many of these flows to other countries took the form of direct investments by US industrial corporations and bank loans to foreign governments (influenced by the US state), rather than the shorter-term credit or issuing of foreign bonds and other securities in which London specialised.[28] London's international banking operations also had a wider geographical scope than those of the US, given sterling's previous international role and the UK's continued links with Empire and Dominion countries. After 1945, US moves into international markets were also restricted by Cold War political considerations. Britain was also anti-communist, but British capitalists could do business in communist countries without worrying about the kind of political repercussions that would have been faced in the US. As a consequence, even by 1957, sterling was still a major international currency and was used for financing some 40 per cent of world trade.[29]

The factors that favoured London as a leading financial centre are commonly taken to include the importance of English as a business language, the suitability of English law for commerce, the availability of a workforce with the relevant skills, a good communications infrastructure, and the 'economies of scale' that arise from the concentration of financial business in one location.[30] Yet none of these particularly explains the relative strength of London over New York, although there was some split of financial business in the US between New York, Chicago and other centres, including San Francisco. Another important factor often cited, one that *is* significant, is London's geographical location, lying both on the western edge of Europe, a major base for capitalist business, and between the Americas and Asia. This does indeed give London a clear advantage over New York, especially when one considers the regular business day, during which most financial decisions and communications are made. New York is cut off from Tokyo's and Singapore's regular business days and misses the European morning, whereas London can communicate with Asia in the morning, North and South America in the afternoon, and Europe all day.

Working hours can, of course, be changed or extended in any location, and many banks also run 'night desks' for trading. But in order to neutralise the time zone effect on international business, the hours would have to be changed not only for bankers in that location, but also for government and central bank officials, lawyers, accountants and corporate executives. This was, and remains, a disadvantage for New York's international financial business. The importance of these location factors was made very clear to me whenever I was in New York, and also when I witnessed the failure of the Sydney, Australia, office of the bank for which I worked to succeed as a financial hub for its Asian financial business. Although Sydney was politically favoured by the bank, the office dealers and sales people could not catch the important US afternoon trading session unless they came in early, which meant that they went home well before the end of the Asian trading day!

One would have expected London's purely 'historical' advantages to diminish over time, even if its geographical advantage and the convenience of its time zone remained intact. However, while New York's financial operations had grown rapidly by the early 1960s, with increasing volumes of foreign loans and issues of foreign securities, its potential to become the pre-eminent international banking centre was hindered by US government policies implemented both for domestic economic reasons and because of a concern to limit the outflow of capital from the US. Although still much bigger and more powerful than any of its rivals, the US was beginning to see its lead reduced as other countries recovered, particularly in Europe and Japan. Capital flows from the US began to outstrip its trade surplus and, by the early 1960s, the US dollar shortage earlier feared by analysts of the Bretton Woods payments system had been transformed into a dollar glut. Instead of the international payments system being strangled by a limited flow of dollars from the US, the system found itself burdened with an abundance of dollars, as US businesses used their currency to pay both for imports and for foreign investment. This fuelled the growth of an offshore pool of dollar funds held by foreign governments and companies. Konings notes that:

Concern regarding the stability of the dollar was widespread by the early 1960s, but the [US] Treasury opposed any proposals for fundamental reforms to the financial system and instead adopted capital controls. The latter, however, did little to reduce the outflows of capital associated with foreign direct investment by American companies.[31]

By 1960, and more evidently in the early 1960s, foreign holdings of US dollar assets had begun to exceed US government holdings of gold at the official price of \$35.[32] If the value of the US government's gold bars held in Fort Knox and in the New York Federal Reserve's basement in Manhattan was less than the dollar assets held by foreigners, then this raised the question: how much was the dollar actually worth? For example, if US gold holdings at \$35 per troy ounce were worth \$23 billion, but foreigners were owed \$25 billion and rising, then the dollar was looking overvalued against gold. This was a harbinger of the eventual demise of the Bretton Woods fixed exchange rate system in 1971 and of a rise in the gold price from the official \$35 level.[33] In the early 1960s the US authorities did not worry much about foreign *private sector* holdings of dollars. Only central banks could request an exchange of dollar assets for gold from US reserves. Later in the decade, however, this did lead to conflicts with the French government, who wanted some real gold shipped over, not just promises that America's bills would be paid in a certain number of dollars.

The most important of the US financial market regulations were 'Regulation Q' and the Interest Equalisation Tax. Regulation Q was imposed in 1933 and remained in force until the 1980s. It prohibited banks from paying interest on short-term 'demand' deposits and also restricted the interest rates banks paid on other types of account. The objective was to prevent the banks' competition for funds from weakening their finances. But it had two unintended effects. US banks began to develop other modes of competing for business, from expanding branch networks and services to developing new forms of financial dealing. Domestic US investment funds were also attracted by non-US locations that offered higher rates. The London-based financial market was in a position to attract such funds. The Interest Equalisation Tax of July 1963 was another US government measure restricting US financial markets. It aimed to discourage foreign companies from issuing dollar bonds in the US, and so reduce long-term capital outflows.[34] These factors boosted London's business at the expense of New York because they were the principal spurs to the growth of the 'euromarket' in London from the late 1950s.

There is one other factor behind the advantage of London-based banking over New York that is not often recognised: the structure of the US money markets. Although the US economy was several times larger than that of the UK, its banking system was fragmented, both along state lines and in terms of whether banks even belonged to the Federal Reserve System that from 1913 had acted as a lender of last resort. This led to some odd developments. For example, when the burden of the Fed's bank reserve requirements began to rise in the 1960s, US banks began to leave the system. From nearly 85 per cent in the late 1950s, 'the share of transaction deposits held by member banks had fallen below 75 per cent' by the early 1970s.[35] Many US banks did not even play much of a role in the *national* banking system, let alone internationally.

The Anglo-American euromarket

The growth of the euromarkets from the late 1950s onwards was dramatic, and has been the subject of many business books and journal articles. The relevant point here is how this market provided the basis for the expansion of London's financial markets from the 1970s. The euromarkets developed in two stages: firstly as a eurocurrency bank deposit and loan market from the late 1950s and then, from 1963, as a eurobond market.

The term 'euromarket' refers not to the *location* of the market for transactions in bank funds or financial securities – it may not be in Europe at all – but to the fact that this market normally lies outside the *regulation* of any national state authority. Banks anywhere can operate in the euromarkets if the national state authorities allow it. This kind of business is usually conducted with non-residents. For example, eurodollars are US dollar-denominated deposit accounts held outside US Federal Reserve jurisdiction, originally in European banks, and especially in London. The transfer of dollar funds between banks would still, however, have to be done through a bank *inside* the domestic US payments system.[36] The special status of the euromarkets does not mean that banks operating in them can do anything they like, and central bank authorities in the relevant locations will supervise them to some degree. But because their operations are considered to be with non-residents, their lending and borrowing, and dealing in securities, will usually fall outside the domestic monetary, banking or tax regulations that apply to residents.

For example, interest paid on euro deposits or coupons paid on eurobonds will normally be paid gross to the non-resident investor, with no deduction of national tax at source.[37] Similarly, a bank's eurocurrency exposures will not be subject to central bank credit restrictions that apply to dealings with residents. Eurocurrency deposits in US-based banks were also free from any Federal Deposit Insurance Corporation charge because the deposits are not repayable to customers resident in the US.

It might seem that these markets are *never* affected by any state regulation, but this is not the case. Every government can take a policy view on these markets, either to encourage them or to restrict the participation of local banks in their activities. Governments might also be concerned with what impact these markets might have on the domestic economy. Nevertheless, in their early years at least, the euromarkets developed spontaneously, as a function of what private capitalist businesses decided to do within the current framework, and sometimes the monetary authorities were only dimly aware of what was going on. But as the markets grew, they eventually became too big to ignore and government policy often responded.

Eurodollar deposits held by US banks did not initially attract reserve requirements from the US Federal Reserve. In other words, US banks did not have to hold back funds equal to a share of the size of the eurodollar deposit as they did with 'normal', domestic deposits. As a result, US banks could accept eurodollar deposits at a lower net cost because they did not have to place a portion of these deposits (as reserves) with the central bank at a zero interest rate, as they did with domestic deposits. This helped boost both eurodollar deposits and loans. But in October 1969 the US Federal Reserve imposed a reserve requirement at 10 per cent on *extra* eurodollar borrowings (not on the whole amount) as a means of limiting this new source of funds for US banks.[38] Nevertheless, since the euromarket continued to grow very rapidly after 1969, this suggests that reserve requirements were not a significant restraining factor, even if the earlier lack of reserve requirements might have been a spur to their growth at that point.[39]

The euromarkets clearly created room for 'regulatory arbitrage', in other words, for making deals that got around the rules imposed by different central banks and governments. But it was an arbitrage game that could only be played by those already working in a big financial market, one where dealing costs were not so high that they eliminated the benefit of engaging in these transactions. And London in particular was used to dealing in the large-scale funds that characterised the euromarkets.

The origin of these markets was closely related to the development of monopoly capitalism in the post-1945 period. In the US, credit restrictions had made it more difficult for companies to obtain the needed investment funds from domestic banks, so they looked overseas. In particular, US corporations had been expanding their foreign operations and this investment required financing. In the early 1960s, US foreign direct investment ran at a little below $3bn per year, but it had doubled to a rate of $6bn per year by the end of the decade, rising still further in the 1970s.[40] There was also an expansion of foreign direct investment from other major countries. This link between the growth of the euromarkets and the needs of large companies was made clear by the Governor of the Bank of England in a speech to bankers in Chicago in 1971:

> New procedures have been developed for meeting the needs of euromarket customers, typically big international corporations whose global credit needs cannot always be met from purely domestic banking systems. Among these are roll-over credits, floating rate notes and, more recently, an infant market in eurodollar commercial paper.[41]

He went on to add that 'the eurodollar market is now equal in size to the money supply of France'. The US dollar accounted for around 90 per cent of all currencies available in the euromarket in the 1960s,[42] but its share later fell as the size of the international pool of funds rose dramatically and as other currencies were added to the list. Total deposits in the euromarket are thought to have grown from about $1bn in 1960 to $57bn in 1970, and then to $1,050bn by 1983.[43] This vast expansion was based on the ability of banks operating in the euromarket to create credit in the same way as banks in the national credit system. They did not have to wait for new incoming funds to expand their lending.[44]

The euromarkets developed on the back of the demand for funding from large corporations and the flows of money-capital from big business and the wealthy. Some writers, such as Gary Burn, have argued that the 'creation of the euromarkets and an unregulated international financial structure was simply the reassertion of the interests of financial, as opposed to manufacturing, capital'.[45] However, such arguments ignore how major international corporations seek domination in the *world* market, usually with the assistance of their national states, and how 'manufacturing capital' typically conducts many financial deals itself. British corporations are big players in this respect, so it is wrong to suggest that there exists an economic gulf between 'the City' and 'manufacturing'. Such corporations were among those that needed the euromarkets to aid their global expansion when domestic money markets were not able to provide them with the funds they required. Burn is more correct in saying that 'this market also allowed the City's financiers to issue dollar liabilities and thereby share in the denomination rents and the privileges of seigniorage that had previously accrued exclusively to the US'.[46] However, even this point ignores the benefits for British capitalism as a whole through the balance of payments. The beneficiaries were not just the 'financiers'.

As one might expect, the Governor of the Bank of England lauded the euromarkets as a 'useful addition to our invisible earnings'.[47] UK balance of payments data show that the annual net foreign invisible earnings from financial services more than quadrupled between 1958 and 1970, to £439m, and doubled from 0.4 per cent to 0.8 per cent of

GDP. These revenues were very useful in helping to offset the persistent visible trade deficit during the 1960s. Whenever unemployment fell and demand in the British economy grew – in the 'go' phase of the economic cycle – imports and the trade deficit increased. This put downward pressure on the value of sterling in foreign exchange markets. In the policy set-up of the 1960s, a growing trade deficit meant that the government had to raise taxes and/or cut public spending to 'stop' the economy and cut the demand for imports. It was here that the valuable 'invisible' revenues helped offset the visible trade deficit and limit the impact of the 'stop-go' policies.

British capitalism, finance and official policy

It is common for otherwise perceptive writers to maintain that there is a fundamental conflict between finance and industry, a claim that supports their arguments for capitalist state policies to control finance and promote a sanitised version of capitalism.[48] However, the revenues described above – which took on greater prominence in later decades – and the broader economic benefits of City finance are a more solid foundation for explaining British government policy towards the financial markets than the idea that somehow a narrow social grouping, the 'City–Bank of England–Treasury' nexus, directed policy in a way that differed from the broader interests of British capitalism.

The City's ability to use the dollar and develop the new euromarkets depended on the at least passive acquiescence of the US and UK authorities. While the US Federal Reserve had shown some concern about the impact this might have on their ability to control credit in the US economy, the 1969 imposition of reserve requirements on extra US bank eurodollar deposits was the only real limitation on the market's growth that it came up with. Even these were eliminated by 1990. As for the UK, the Bank of England looked upon the market with great enthusiasm and was never opposed in this stance by UK governments. The development of the euromarket expanded the international role of the City and encouraged an increasing number of foreign banks to locate there, even when Britain's economic travails and balance of payments problems limited the international role of sterling. As the Governor of the Bank of England, in the speech cited above, went on to note:

> Absence of [restrictions] has been a feature of banking in London, though London is by no means unique in this respect. But London has provided freedom of establishment and banks of good repute have been welcomed – one result of which has been that the number of US banks with branches in London has risen from nine in 1963 to 31 today, not counting those multinational banks in which there are US interests. Such restrictions as we have found it necessary to operate have concerned the use of sterling – either domestically, or for use overseas, or for conversion into other currencies. Banking conducted wholly in other currencies has been free from restrictions, and in that sense the market has been extra-territorial.[49]

The euromarkets allowed the growth of City business outside of its previous focus on sterling, which had become a dead end. The new market was one step on from the City's use of other people's money to turn a profit – it was now specialising in using other countries' currencies too, particularly the US dollar! In doing so, it was expanding its role both for British and for international capitalist companies.

The financial institutions involved in the new euromarket business were not only British. London was attracting a wider range of foreign banks, in particular from the US. A Bank of England report noted that in 1963, 'three groups of banks together accounted for two thirds of the business done in the London market; these were the American banks and the British overseas and Commonwealth banks (each accounting for about 25 per cent of the total) and the accepting houses (rather less than 20 per cent)'.[50] US banks were the biggest foreign players in London, accounting for nearly half of the liabilities of foreign banks in the late 1960s.[51] By 1971, London had attracted some 160 banks from forty-eight countries.[52] The main role of the US banks in London was to service their international corporate clients with funds that were not so easily, or cheaply, available from the domestic US credit market.

. London was the international banking centre of choice not only because of the lack of 'restrictions', including no bank deposit reserve requirements on euromarket business, but also because London's money markets were highly developed and able to offer active trading in *unsecured* loans between banks. A bank's credit rating and its position in the market would determine how much, and for how long, other banks would be willing to lend to it with no security or collateral, but this was a key element of the wholesale interbank market established in London in the 1950s. There was no equivalent to this in the US, where bank funding was usually very short-term[53] and largely based on secured 'repo' borrowing – where cash was lent against a deposit of securities as collateral – or on *overnight* transactions in Federal funds held at the central bank.

One study of the evolution of the London money markets claims that, while the sterling money market developed initially through local authorities dealing with banks, it was the US banks in London that spurred the growth of the interbank market in the context of the new euromarket.[54] This is plausible, but the study does not mention the important fact that the US interbank money market had nothing to compare with the one-month, three-month, six-month, etc., standard period loans and deposits of the euromarket in London. While the bulk of eurocurrency business was shorter-term, some 30 per cent of bank deposits and 40 per cent of loans in the 1970s, for example, were for longer than three months.[55] This was because the London market had (and has) a large number of banks performing these wholesale market operations. That is why there is a London Interbank Offered Rate (LIBOR), which gives the interest rates for borrowing in this active interbank market in unsecured term loans, and why there is no such thing as a 'NYIBOR' for New York.[56]

Banking centres in Europe that might have become rivals to London, such as Paris, were eclipsed by strong Anglo-American economic and political links, and by domestic political events and policy decisions.[57] Above all, there was the more consistent promotion of international financial business by the British authorities, which included an implicit promise not to disturb financial interests with any changes in legislation. The British ruling class had honed a particular skill, learned from the experience of generations, of knowing when to upset, threaten or kill 'foreign Johnnies', and when to let discretion be the better part of valour and instead do a deal with them, especially when that deal was clearly in British interests.

These points were made clear to foreign financial businesses in direct discussion with Bank of England officials, likely over cups of tea in an impressive boardroom, and clear to everyone else through the Bank's published statements. For example, after noting the usual list of features favouring London, a 1989 Bank of England review of the City as a financial centre added that there was 'a degree of confidence among firms that regulations will not be altered without good reason and appropriate consultation'.[58] In 1996, the Governor of the Bank of England also spelled out that, apart from the usual domestic monetary functions of a central bank, its role 'concerning the effectiveness of the United Kingdom's financial services – is more unusual, *and perhaps peculiar to the Bank of England* which has a long-established tradition of encouraging the financial services industry in this country to meet the needs of the wider economy both domestically and as the world's major international financial centre'.[59]

Eurobonds and London's international role

The stability of capitalist property relations in the UK was a critical factor in the revival of the City, and something that the Bank of England could build upon in its promotion of London as a base for international financial services. There were no *événements* in London to rival those in Paris in 1968, notwithstanding the student demonstrations at the US Embassy in London against the Vietnam War, nor were there the equivalent of military plots to kill the country's political leader, as had recently occurred with France's President de Gaulle.[60] Big changes in policy that would harm the interests of foreign capitalists were very unlikely. This meant that the City's eurocurrency operations could also be put to use in funding another new business, in eurobonds, that began in 1963, the opening for which had been provided for by the Bank's 1962 decision to allow foreign securities denominated in foreign currencies to be issued in London.[61] The funds that buy such bonds usually come from investors outside the banks, but it is important not to ignore banks' own investments in eurobonds. Banks acting as dealers in particular issues, often as part of a syndicate, have to maintain a certain inventory for selling on to investors and will normally be committed to ensuring a two-way market (buying and selling) in these securities. This means that banks dealing in eurobonds will require short-term funding to run their positions, and funds from the eurocurrency market were the most suitable, being subject to the same *non*-regulation as the bonds themselves. This funding requirement was also true for other securities issued in the euromarkets, including floating-rate notes, where the interest rate paid on the security was set according to LIBOR fixing rates every three or six months.

London's role as the major eurocurrency banking centre also supported its position as the principal location for issuing eurobonds and other securities in the offshore market. While Regulation Q acted as a spur to the first market, the US government's Interest Equalisation Tax of July 1963 is generally considered to have been the major element in the growth of the eurobond market.[62] As mentioned earlier, this was a tax on US residents' purchases of foreign securities intended to reduce the US capital outflows into portfolio securities (direct investment, or a portfolio investment in 10 per cent or more of a company's equity, was exempt). The effect was to make it more expensive for foreign borrowers to issue securities in New York, and the business was attracted instead to London and other euromarket centres. At this point, the UK also had its tax disadvantages for foreign borrowers in the *sterling* domestic market – in the form of stamp duty – and in 1962 there had already been a discussion at the UK Treasury about whether to allow foreign (government) loans in US dollars to be issued in London, which would act to 'make the facilities of the London capital market more widely available and to mop up some of the very volatile eurodollars at present in London'.[63] The avoidance of tax is a key attraction of eurobonds: they are usually 'bearer' securities, where the coupon is paid to the holder of the security without any tax deduction.

Euromarket business in the City developed despite the continued weak position of Britain's balance of payments and its less than impressive economic growth performance. British capitalism was no longer the lender to the world that it had been in the period up to the First World War. Instead, the City's new markets were based upon the development of a new role: that of an intermediary. The City acted 'as a bridge between short- and long-term funds and as a conduit for international lending'.[64] However, this ability to attract money-capital from the rest of the world also enabled the City to help finance Britain's foreign investments. Banks based in London, British or otherwise, still earned fees from a company for issuing bonds to investors, and they also took a 'dealing spread', based upon the gap between buying and selling prices. These boosted the earnings of the City, especially from overseas.

By 1968, '60 per cent of the trading in eurocurrency bonds was in London, totalling $15 million per day and handled by a growing number of European banks and US brokerage houses'.[65] That should not be taken to mean that London was the centre of the global bond market, since most bonds, especially government securities, are issued, bought and sold on a domestic basis. This meant that financial centres such as New York and Tokyo had bigger bond markets than London, and the City could not compete with these larger economies as centres for raising funds. However, London still held a leading position for *international* issues and especially for cross-border trading. The international bond trading business grew dramatically over the next decades, and by the early 2000s 70 per cent of the total trading took place in London.[66] The international bond-market figures include both eurobonds and foreign bonds, the latter being issued in the domestic market by a foreign company or government. In 2010, the UK accounted for 13 per cent of total international bonds outstanding, second to the US with 24 per cent, but it was the location for 70 per cent of *global market trading* in international bonds.[67]

Nevertheless, London's position as the world's top international financial dealer was not secure. Although the UK had historical and political advantages, and although a number of potential rivals had limited their financial business with restrictive legislation, risks to London's status remained. In 1975, the UK was by far the biggest international banking centre, with 27 per cent of global business, twice the size of the next biggest, the US. Japan was only in seventh place among the major countries, with less than 5 per cent of the market.[68] Nevertheless, it later emerged as the main threat to London's position, as a result of Japan's large current account surpluses and growing foreign investments. There had been no international banking market in Japan before 1972, and its Ministry of Finance had restricted Japanese bank business. After 1972, however, it allowed Japanese banks 'to lend to non-Japanese entities and to participate in the international syndicated credit market'.[69] Alongside this, Japan's surplus funds also began to be lent directly from Tokyo, helping to make it a major international banking centre by the late 1980s. Japan's share of international banking had risen to 17 per cent by 1989, only a little below London's, and Japanese banks also accounted for more than 35 per cent of London's international banking business by 1987. This was not an overnight development, but it indicated how one power's market dominance might be threatened over time.

Fortunately for the position of UK-based financial operations, Japan's potential to become not only the world's major creditor country but also its major dealer and a leading financial power was undermined by its own financial implosion. From the late 1980s, under pressure from the US, Japan guided the value of the Japanese yen to higher levels in the foreign exchange markets. The yen-based costs of Japanese industry therefore rose in terms of US dollars and other currencies, making Japan's domestic industry less competitive in world markets. In response, the Bank of Japan tried to offset the impact by operating a very loose monetary policy (low domestic interest rates, encouraging bank lending) to keep growth going. Together with financial market deregulation, this fuelled a prolonged credit boom in Japan. Commercial and residential property prices rose sharply, leading to absurdities such as 100-year mortgages that would be handed down to one's children to pay off. When property prices crashed, a huge volume of bad debts undermined the capital ratios of Japan's banks. Having once been major creditors, Japanese banks were now viewed as big credit risks and ended up paying premium rates to borrow in the money markets.[70] Japan's share of international banking fell to below 10 per cent from 2000, putting it at less than half the UK's share. I witnessed the very early stages of this decline first hand, when working for a major Japanese bank in 1989–90, and observed the retrenchment of Japanese banks in the City of London and in Tokyo in subsequent years, as they cut back on loans and securities transactions.

London's status led banks from other European centres that were potential rivals, such as Frankfurt, to make the City their principal location for dealing. This occurred even when they had taken over London-based banks in an attempt to secure a bigger share of international financial markets, and even when the move to London had gone against national political sentiment.[71] For example, the largest Dutch bank, ABN AMRO, at which I worked until 2006, decided in the late 1990s to make London the centre for its European securities operations. But the bank diluted the political and economic impact of this decision by keeping the centre of its European foreign exchange dealing operations in Amsterdam.

Historical logic

The international expansion of industry and commerce, together with the need for larger-scale funds as capitalist operations grew, were the fundamental drivers behind the growth of international finance. In particular, the euromarkets developed to service the requirements of industry and commerce, not, as some might have it, because of the whims of financiers. The euromarkets were the first major means by which flows of finance found ways around official national regulations after 1945, but, as the evidence shows, this was encouraged by the UK authorities and was far from being impeded by the US administration. National controls on the movement of capital were later more formally relaxed in many of the richer countries, especially in the 1980s. This reflected not the power of bankers or international financiers over industry, but rather the demands from all kinds of capitalists for the right to invest wherever they wanted for the best return they could get.

This nevertheless helped to undermine the international monetary system established at Bretton Woods, based upon the quasi-permanent fixing of exchange rates. The changing balance of competitive power between the major countries, as the US and the UK became relatively weaker while (West) Germany and Japan became relatively stronger, put pressure on the monetary system through the 1960s and into the early 1970s. At the same time, the huge scale of financial flows now available via the euromarkets provided the ammunition to destroy that system. It is misleading to claim that this demonstrated the 'power of international finance'. Rather, the ways in which capitalism developed in new and ever more international directions gradually undermined the institutions that the 1944 political deal had put in place.

The UK adapted to its altered position in the world economy. Initially, the British government had attempted to restore the Empire after 1945 and to continue its flagrant exploitation of the colonies. But the Empire too was to become another unsustainable institution, in the face of some opposition from the US, but more significantly from those over whom Britain had once ruled. Equally, it was no longer clear to the British authorities that maintaining an Empire would deliver the economic goods as it had done in earlier times. World trade outside the Empire was now growing faster, with better economic prospects, and the financial balances within the Empire had turned negative. By the early 1960s, not only had a number of former colonies been successful in their fight for independence – although they still had strong links with British business – but British finance had begun to take advantage of the developing euromarkets and to switch operations to the US dollar. This initiated a process that would end up with the City depending far less on sterling for its business and much more upon transactions and financial intermediation. It was an important step for British finance on the road to where the City is today.

3.

Finance and the Major Powers

The 1970s was an extraordinary decade, both for the global economy and in terms of the changes in the financial relationships between the major powers. A steep fall in rates of economic growth and a sharp recession signalled the end of the postwar boom, with higher unemployment, inflation and government fiscal deficits. In the UK in the 1960s, an unemployment figure of 500,000 was considered to be a disgrace to the government in power; by the late 1970s, getting unemployment below a million was seen as a result.[1] Capitalist profitability had slumped in all major countries, leading to stagnant investment and low growth.[2] While the causes of the crisis were in dispute, it was inevitable that economic policy had to change. Everywhere the capitalist state moved to restrict the rights of trade unions and undermine working conditions. Such was the normal policy reaction to crisis. But an important new development from the 1970s was the final collapse of the Bretton Woods monetary system and the start of a new phase in global financial markets.

Different countries responded to the crisis in different ways, depending upon the options open to them, especially in how to handle relationships with their main rivals. The overall result was that the growth of international financial trading accelerated. Despite the relative economic decline of the UK from at least the late 1940s and of the US since the 1960s, both powers managed their positions through their ability to use the world financial system for economic support. This had implications for British policy towards the rest of Europe. The UK, with its significant *non*-European economic interests and its security and military alliance with the US, was reluctant to become an also-ran in the European power structure. Germany was bound to dominate the European economy, especially after the reunification of West and East Germany in 1990. British imperial interests also depended upon the UK having more control over its monetary and financial policy than a European-wide system might allow. Britain's positioning of itself between the US and Europe has led it into an uneasy relationship with European economic and financial developments, even to the point of questioning the UK's continued membership of the EU.

In this period, there were two major events in British financial policy. The first was the abolition of exchange controls by the Conservative government in 1979. This was not so much the result of free market ideology as of a desire to increase income from foreign investments. The second was the 'Big Bang' of 1986, a change in policy that aimed to boost the international position of London's dealing operations, even though it was obvious that many traditional City firms would be sold to foreign investors – a fact which itself contradicts the idea that there was a 'City–Bank of England–Treasury nexus' backing a British financial clique. Other major countries followed a similar trajectory, but the UK's policies were more systematic and built on an existing infrastructure to give UK-based financial operations a big share of a rapidly growing market.

Regime change

In August 1971, the US formally abandoned its obligation to convert US dollars into gold at the fixed $35 parity. That parity had been seen as the sign that paper money, or a promise to pay in terms of US dollars, was really worth something, in other words, a certain amount of gold. But US gold reserves had fallen to low levels compared to official foreign dollar holdings, a trend exacerbated by US military spending on the Vietnam War and the continuing outflows of capital from the US. The dollar began to depreciate against other currencies, and against gold, producing turmoil in financial markets.

However, despite flows of international investment funds away from the dollar, it still remained the basic international measure of value for the new, unstable system. Ironically, US financial power actually *increased* once the US had abandoned gold because no other major country was in a position to offer a serious challenge to it, or to establish an alternative to the dollar-based global financial system. In 1973, nearly 85 per cent of central bank foreign exchange reserves were still denominated in US dollars,[3] the bulk of international trade was denominated in dollars, and the US still had by far the largest capital markets in the world for issuing bonds and equities.

The continued financial power of the US – and the relationship of financial power to imperial power more generally – was demonstrated by the international flow of funds after the main oil producing and exporting countries, members of OPEC, began to increase oil prices in 1973. Although the price hikes are often discussed in the context of the 1973 Arab-Israeli War, a key economic backdrop was the previous weakening of the dollar, the currency in which the oil price was denominated. Oil prices had changed very little in dollar terms over many years, despite rising world inflation and large increases in other commodity prices in the previous decade.[4] The new oil price hikes now gave the oil exporting countries massive trade surpluses, while the US, Europe and Japan (and other countries) moved into bigger trade deficits. This was not such a problem for the US, since OPEC held its surplus revenues in US dollars, so-called petrodollars, which meant that when countries paid for their oil imports in dollars, it was unlikely that these funds would be exchanged for other non-dollar currencies. However, these dollars had been largely held in the form of bank deposits, which the US government now feared could easily be liquidated and moved into other currencies, thus putting more pressure on the US balance of payments and the value of the dollar in the foreign exchange market. Although currency values were no longer fixed and did not have to be defended as in the 1960s, there would still have been a problem for US economic policy if the dollar's value collapsed.

In response, US Treasury Secretary William Simon visited the Saudi Arabian Monetary Authority in July 1974 to sell them US

Treasury securities.[5] This was part of a more general deal with Saudi Arabia, the main OPEC oil producer, including lucrative weapons contracts for US companies and a US promise to give Saudi Arabia military protection.[6] By the end of 1977, Saudi Arabia accounted for 20 per cent of all Treasury notes and bonds held by foreign central banks, which at that time was astonishing for a 'developing country'. Following a US Commerce Department trip to Saudi Arabia, Saudi money was also invested in government-backed mortgage securities. Selling US mortgage debt to foreign investors had a long history well before the 2007–8 financial crisis!

Political and economic negotiations with the Saudis and other Middle Eastern OPEC states also kept the price of oil denominated in US dollars. The US supported Saudi Arabia's political ambition to secure a larger IMF quota (and enhanced IMF voting rights) at the same time as plans to shift the oil price from the dollar were dropped.[7] This was despite a June 1975 agreement between the OPEC countries to peg oil prices to a group of major currencies, not just the dollar, as a means of protecting themselves from falls in the dollar's value. That OPEC prices remained quoted in dollars was very important for the US government. If the dollar price were abandoned, the US authorities would have far less control over oil transactions because a major world commodity's price would have less connection with the US financial system, and there would be less reason for non-US companies and governments to use dollar accounts and to hold their funds in dollars.

Rising oil prices, and the increased deficits of oil importers versus the OPEC surpluses, were an important element in the greater volume of international financial flows in the 1970s. Between 1973 and 1974 OPEC's current account surplus rose more than tenfold, from $6bn to $67bn, despite a rapid increase of imports by OPEC countries. World recession helped reduce the surplus to zero several years later, but by 1979 another round of price increases raised the surplus again to $74bn.[8] The IMF attempted to manage a recycling of the OPEC surpluses to help fund those countries with trade deficits, although with limited success. A Bank of England study noted that the bulk of the new OPEC surplus revenues were mainly put into bank deposits and loans to developing countries, either directly or via the IMF. Nevertheless, many countries instead financed their trade deficits through the new euromarkets.

Between 1974 and 1979, OPEC countries had put a cumulative $84bn into eurocurrency bank deposits, providing further fuel for the expansion of the international credit system. By 1979, a little over half of the eurocurrency deposits were held in UK-based banks and nearly half of OPEC's total surplus from 1974–79 was invested in the UK and the US, each with close to 25 per cent of the total.[9] The UK could not attract OPEC money into its securities as easily as could the US, but its banking system's receipt of these funds was a clear sign that the UK had made the grade in terms of being a home for international money.

The other European powers had none of these advantages and received only a small share of OPEC surpluses. But, in response to the financial turmoil of the early 1970s, the original six continental European signatories of the Treaty of Rome tried to build a regional financial system as a shelter from the ups and downs of the dollar and the trouble it caused them. Their policies resulted in the Exchange Rate Mechanism (ERM), introduced in 1979, which aimed to limit fluctuations in European currencies against each other to avoid disrupting important trade and investment relationships. Even West Germany, the strongest country in economic terms, was buffeted by large financial flows out of US dollars that strengthened the Deutsche mark against the currencies of Germany's important European trading partners. The ERM was essentially a Deutsche mark bloc, with that currency the main reference point and with the Bundesbank, Germany's central bank, principally in charge of its direction. It did not do much to diminish monetary instability, but the ERM was an early incarnation of the later euro system introduced in 1999.

In 1970, the Heath government began negotiations to join the European Economic Community (EEC), and Britain became a member on 1 January 1973. But the UK still remained at one remove from the European project. The British government's rationale for membership rested on the importance of the EEC as a fast-growing trade bloc, a closer alliance with which would exert some competitive pressure on British industry through lower tariffs and the removal of other trade restrictions. The industrial policy of the Heath government – which it would later change as unemployment rose rapidly, threatening political problems – was to let industrial 'lame ducks' go to the wall and use the new EEC membership to force British industry to be more competitive in world markets.

The British state had little intention of participating in other moves towards European integration, particularly those in the financial and political spheres. In Britain during the 1970s, and for a long time afterwards, the EEC was referred to as 'the Common Market'. This indicated the difference of perspective from that of the founding members, in whose view the EEC was not just an 'economic community' but also one that, as the preamble to the 1957 Treaty of Rome put it, was 'DETERMINED to lay the foundations of an ever closer union among the peoples of Europe' (no emphasis added!). Even the moves towards closer UK–European trading relations were opposed by a significant minority of the British public because of the threat to established economic relationships with Commonwealth countries, in particular in relation to Australian and New Zealand agricultural products that would be affected by the EEC's Common Agricultural Policy. The UK's EEC membership was also inconsistent with the continued operation of the Sterling Area, but the latter's benefits for British imperialism had by then become questionable, not least due to the threat of the former colonies' sterling balances, held in London, being sold for other currencies. The Sterling Area was eventually dissolved during the 1970s, and a UK referendum in 1975 endorsed EEC membership by 67 per cent to 33 per cent.

The EEC membership decision was one sign that British policy-makers recognised that things could not go on as before. The UK's economic problems had resulted in a sharp rise in inflation, a then record current account deficit of 4 per cent of GDP in 1974, a slump in the value of sterling on foreign exchange markets, and the need to negotiate a series of loans from the IMF. In September 1976, the Labour Chancellor Denis Healey had to abandon a trip to an international finance ministers' meeting and return from London's Heathrow airport to apply for another loan. The IMF granted him $3.9bn on

condition of £2.5bn cuts in government spending.[10] While the spending cuts were in line with changes in government policy that were
already under way, the political embarrassment of being humbled
so publicly was something that no UK government would want to
risk again.

British imperial strategy and the pound

Britain's weak economic position relative to other major powers
conditioned its policy responses and set the context for the development of UK financial markets from the 1970s. But why did Britain
not take part in the euro project when this became the main economic and political project for Europe's major powers from the 1980s
onwards? At first sight, the economic case for British membership
of Europe's Economic and Monetary Union (EMU) looked compel-
ling. Continental Europe was a major trading partner for the UK and
the location for much British overseas investment. However, Britain
also had a much wider range of *non*-European interests than did the
main continental powers, and in particular the strong political link
with the US. Britain relied on the latter to protect its non-European
interests, even at the expense of having to concede ground to the US
where it was not in a powerful enough position to act on its own, as in
the 1953 Anglo-American coup against Mohammad Mossadegh, the
democratically elected prime minister of Iran. Britain has depended
on the US for its nuclear weapons systems since the Polaris deal in
1962, and has maintained close cooperation with the US in military
policy and spying activities.

   This latter form of UK–US cooperation became more widely known
following the revelations in 2013 by Edward Snowden, a former US
National Security Agency official. Much of the media furore over
spying concerned access to *personal* communications, but the inter-
ceptions by British and American spies were clearly focused on major
business and political targets. They did not set up a hugely expensive
spying infrastructure in order to dredge through billions of telephone
calls and emails from Joe Public.

British policy-makers came to realise that they did not have the power to operate as they wished in the international arena. That is of course always true in so far as it is necessary for any power to judge the potential response of others to its actions. But after the Suez crisis in 1956, it became clear to the British that any major initiatives with international repercussions could not succeed in the face of US opposition. A possible alternative for Britain would have been to establish closer links with other European powers. But until the late 1950s, UK policy-makers saw little reason to become more closely involved in European affairs, given Britain's Empire and its other interests in the world. This had been most clearly expressed by Churchill, who in 1946 called for a 'United States of Europe', but one that did *not* include the UK. In later years, the opinion on Europe was a little more evenly balanced, but British policy still came down firmly on the side of an alliance with US imperialism. The point was reinforced by its former 'Dominions' – the white-settler countries of Canada, Australia and New Zealand – now being in the US sphere of influence.[11] These factors meant that British governments of either party did not see a strategic advantage in joining the European project beyond their involvement in its narrower economic dimensions.

One simple measure of the difference between the UK's perspective and, for example, that of Germany and France, can be seen in the different geographical patterns of trade, as illustrated in Table 3.1. Exports to the rest of the EEC/EU have been important for the UK, but less important than for Germany and France. UK exports to the US and Canada, Japan and other non-European developed country destinations have also tended to be more important for the UK than for Germany and France. However, the UK and France have a similar share of exports going to developing countries, one that is bigger than Germany's. The ties the two powers still have to their former colonies largely explain this, and in particular the significant exports of military equipment from the UK and France as major weapons producers. The data for 1980 and 1990 indicate the trade patterns before the discussion of closer European financial ties really got under way in the 1990s, and they also reveal the economic backdrop to those discussions. Changing rates of growth in the demand for imports in

Table 3.1 UK, Germany, France – patterns of trade, 1980 and 1990 (% of total) *

	1980	1990
UK, merchandise exports		
European Union	51.8	57.5
US and Canada	11.2	14.4
Japan	1.3	2.5
Other non-European developed countries	4.9	3.6
Developing countries	23.4	16.1
Germany, merchandise exports		
European Union	60.6	62.6
US and Canada	6.8	7.8
Japan	1.1	2.6
Other non-European developed countries	2.4	1.8
Developing countries	16.9	12.5
France, merchandise exports		
European Union	55.7	63.3
US and Canada	4.8	6.8
Japan	0.9	1.9
Other non-European developed countries	1.3	1.0
Developing countries	23.6	17.6

Note: *Selected regions only.
Source: UNCTAD, 2002, Table 3.1A, pp. 57, 58, 68

the different countries have an impact on these export numbers, but the relative importance of the different geographical areas for the UK, Germany and France stays much the same.

The political divergence between the UK and the core European powers became clear in the negotiations over the Maastricht Treaty in 1992, which turned the EEC into the 'European Union' (EU). The British strategy was to avoid any aspect of the 'ever closer union' that would restrict its freedom of manoeuvre. The UK prime minister John Major negotiated an opt-out from the commitment to join the future euro project, the Economic and Monetary Union (EMU), and from the social and employment elements of any Europe-wide legislation.[12] The latter gave British capital a freer hand to downgrade employment conditions. EU foreign and defence policies were also made matters of inter-governmental cooperation and agreement, rather than policies that might be imposed upon the UK.

In addition to Britain's ties to the non-European world system, an important factor in the UK's rejection of EMU membership was the crisis that occurred after Britain put sterling into the currency management system of the ERM in 1990. The decision to join the ERM was a largely tactical policy move by the Conservative government, designed to allow a reduction of UK interest rates while maintaining some stability for sterling in the foreign exchange markets. The plan came to grief, however, when the economic pressures of German reunification led the Bundesbank to raise domestic interest rates, causing problems for other ERM countries, like Britain, whose economies were in a weak position. Two years after joining, and having spent many billions from the foreign exchange reserves in a futile attempt to defend sterling's value against the Deutsche mark, Britain exited the ERM.

The UK's policy of handling these issues in a tactical, piecemeal manner undermined support from the other key European countries – Germany in particular. The lack of British loyalty towards the European project meant there was little appetite in 'Europe' for supporting Britain if it got into trouble. The German government and the Bundesbank, especially, saw no reason to go out on a limb to back up sterling's position within the ERM. At this time, I had regular discussions with a Bundesbank official at the German Embassy in London. He made it clear that he thought sterling was significantly overvalued in the ERM at the central rate of DM2.95, a view with which I agreed. He was especially annoyed that this rate that had not been discussed with Germany before Britain's ERM entry in 1990.[13] The ERM fiasco forced the Bank of England to raise interest rates twice *in one day* to defend sterling – an unprecedented move – and then to reduce them again once the game was up and sterling exited the system. It was politically embarrassing, but the UK's economic recovery after the 1992 collapse of sterling endorsed the popular view that Britain was better off outside the European project.

Before the euro crisis in 2010, the decision on Britain's potential membership of the Economic and Monetary Union was often considered only in narrow economic policy terms. Would there be an advantage in joining a single currency system, given that Britain would then have much less control over its currency and monetary policy? The decision is better understood, however, by considering Britain's interests in the world system, not by judging only what might be better for the domestic economy. A book published in 1997 by a Conservative ex-minister, entitled *Our Currency, Our Country*, pressed home the point.[14] It focused on the risk of political pressure from the two major European powers, Germany and France, in particular Germany, who could undermine the flexibility of UK policy. Once inside EMU, Britain's freedom of action would clearly be constrained.[15]

British policy-makers' reluctance to board the euro train stemmed from these concerns, in particular about the role of Germany at the centre of the system. Members of the Germany-aligned group included the Benelux countries plus Austria and Finland, each fellow creditors, while others depended on Germany's role as the paymaster of the European system, providing the biggest contributions to the EU budget. British worries grew following German reunification in 1990, and they were also shared by France. While the latter had been a long-term ally of Germany in European policy, it had seen its position undermined with the spread of capitalism into what it feared was to be a German-dominated Eastern Europe after the fall of the Berlin Wall in November 1989. A UK Cabinet Office report of a meeting in January 1990 between the UK prime minister Margaret Thatcher and French president François Mitterrand brought the point home sharply. It described the concerns each leader had about a Germany on the verge of reunification:

> President Mitterrand said that he shared the Prime Minister's concerns about the Germans' so-called mission in central Europe. The Germans seemed determined to use their influence to dominate Czechoslovakia, Poland and Hungary. That left only Romania and Bulgaria for the rest of us.[16]

It is in such confidential meetings that imperial interests and concerns are more openly expressed. In the plan to open up a wider range of countries to exploitation within the orbit of the EU's major powers, those receiving the less attractive cuts were not happy.

These factors help explain the 1997 Labour government's '5 Economic Tests' for deciding if and when the UK should join EMU. The five conditions made the decision not to join look like an economic one, based upon cyclical and structural differences between the UK economy and the euro area, differences that might be overcome at some stage. More realistically, they should be interpreted as a deliberate sidestepping of the bigger issue of whether the UK was politically aligned with Europe or with the US.[17] 'Leaving Europe', or distancing Britain further from any influence over European policy, would not have been a sensible decision for the British ruling class as it would have weakened its position vis-à-vis both continental Europe and the US, not least by losing its role as an intermediary between the two. But joining EMU would also have meant sacrificing some important aspects of Britain's political and economic flexibility, including compromising its close links with the US. Prime Minister Tony Blair, like most other UK political leaders in recent decades, had a clear conception of the need for an alliance with *both* the US and Europe.[18] This middling position may appear to be an unstable, merely tactical, or even a thoroughly unprincipled stance. But it reflects the strategic reality in which British imperialism finds itself, and which it must still manage today.

The most important economic point, however, is that EMU membership would have threatened the *financial* dimensions of British power, since these might not have been sustainable within a euro-based monetary system dominated by Germany. While one may question whether the '5 Economic Tests' constituted a serious economic assessment, it is notable that the fourth test, listed ahead of the one concerning 'Growth, stability and jobs', constituted a strong defence of the City of London as a financial centre. It read as follows: 'Financial services – EMU must improve the competitive position of the UK's financial services industry, particularly in London.'[19] This reflected a contemporary concern that EMU might undermine the City's business if Frankfurt, the home of the European Central Bank (ECB), became more important as a financial centre. That did not transpire, but the City's well-being – still more, its *improved* well-being – was a major issue for the Labour government. This shows how much financial business was, and remains, central to the economics of British imperialism, no matter which political party is in power.

Being outside EMU, the UK government was free to decide on its own rescue operations during the recent financial crisis. In particular, the Bank of England was able to introduce a policy of 'quantitative easing' independently of any decision by the European Central Bank. Between 2009 and 2012, the Bank bought a massive £375bn of UK government bonds and pushed official interest rates down towards zero.[20] While the ECB also cut interest rates and bought huge amounts of government bonds from weaker countries in crisis, including Greece and Spain, the countries receiving assistance had strict economic policy measures imposed upon them. It is difficult enough, even for a major economic power, to manage the capitalist market. Having learned the lessons of 1976 and 1992, British politicians saw the risks of being constrained by a policy framework largely determined by the interests of other states, so EMU membership was not going to be on the agenda.

State policy on financial markets from 1979

Different types of finance, from foreign exchange deals to bank loans and issues of bonds and equities, emerge from the way capitalist business develops. A government's policy towards financial markets will influence this process, especially in determining whether certain kinds of dealing are to be allowed or whether they are restricted by law. This has been especially important for the ability of capitalists to deal across national borders. After 1979, government policy in all major countries turned in favour of an expansion of financial markets, helped by the elections of Margaret Thatcher in the UK and Ronald Reagan in the US. That said, it would be an exaggeration to claim that the policy changes after 1979 were *qualitatively* different from what had happened before. They are more accurately viewed as being further developments of earlier moves. By 1974, the US had removed almost all the controls on international capital outflows, partly due to its new-found freedom in not having to defend the dollar's value and partly on the expectation that OPEC oil revenues would be invested in US securities.[21] Before 1979, several other countries had followed the US in cutting back capital controls, including Canada and Germany. The collapse of Bretton Woods in the early 1970s had also brought about a boom in financial market activity. For example, the value of outstanding international bank loans rose by two-thirds between 1977 and 1979 to exceed $1,000bn, and it was in the 1970s that major US exchanges began trading in financial futures contracts on US government bonds and currencies.[22] By 1979, the euromarkets had also already passed their teenage years. Nevertheless, 1979 is a useful starting point for discussing two significant policies affecting the UK financial markets: the abolition of foreign exchange controls and the 'Big Bang' reform of the London Stock Exchange.

One of the first moves of the incoming UK Conservative government in 1979 was to abolish the existing controls on foreign exchange markets. It was able to do so with little risk of a collapse of sterling's exchange value because the UK's North Sea oil production and net exports had begun to increase sharply. Removing exchange controls was seen as a way of enabling *more* capital outflow from the UK. This was intended as a means of limiting the likely upward pressure on sterling's exchange rate from the oil export revenues, but the key point was to get more income from foreign investment. As Geoffrey Howe, the Chancellor of the Exchequer at the time, explains in his memoirs:

[Exchange controls] had cost us dear. Our overseas assets and investment income had fallen as a proportion of national capital and gross national product very sharply. Overseas investment income in the 1970s was down to under 1 per cent of GNP. The invisibles account looked like going into deficit. The financial markets were being stifled. Competition was stunted. Pension funds and institutions were being prevented from getting the best return on capital.[23]

Evidently, the best return on capital was from overseas. A boom in foreign direct and portfolio investment from the UK followed the abolition of exchange controls, with net outflows rising from an annual rate of close to 1 per cent of GDP in 1978–80 to nearly 4 per cent in 1984–6.

The UK's deregulation was part of a general trend among the leading capitalist powers towards coming to terms with the latest developments in financial markets. Many tried new ways of managing domestic monetary policy, including controlling consumer credit, but they all had to take into account their financial relationships with other countries. Not all opted for the same policy initially. France tried a version of 'Keynesianism in one country' under President Mitterrand in 1981, hoping to reduce unemployment with a boost in government spending. But it was soon forced to abandon the policy, having failed to get support from other European powers.[24] France's retreat reflected not so much the importance of global financial markets as the very limited ability of any country to operate in isolation from the world economy. Stringent controls on the movement of capital and on financial markets might have been a policy option for France, although not one that could be used if it needed to borrow from capital markets or if it wanted to have some political influence over the developing European Monetary System. Furthermore, its companies would have faced restricted access to the sources of foreign finance that the expanding euromarkets were providing.

For the US, the UK and Japan, a key motivation for lifting capital controls was to boost their own financial markets and gain a bigger share of this growing business. By 1981, the US authorities had become more favourably disposed towards the euromarkets, passing laws to establish 'offshore' International Banking Facilities that were located in the US but, by running a separate set of accounts, would be free from most national 'onshore' banking regulations.[25] Japan also set up its own 'Japanese Offshore Market' from 1985. By the end of the 1980s, the major capitalist countries had eliminated most forms of capital control. One indication of this was shown by the narrowing gap, down to zero in most cases, between the interest rates paid for 'onshore' versus 'offshore' interbank deposits.[26]

Financial business boomed as a result, not only in the volume of eurocurrency lending and borrowing, but also in eurobond issuance and trading and in the large-scale buying by foreign investors of government bonds and equities.[27] The key financial centres' access to foreign capital was not without its problems, however. In the US, for example, despite a growing current account deficit, by 1985 a large influx of funds into US securities led to a big rise in the value of the dollar on the foreign exchange markets. This threatened to make the US deficit much worse by making its exports more expensive, and to cause political trouble as domestic companies complained about their waning competitiveness. It took official guidance by the 'Group of 5' powers – the US, Japan, West Germany, the UK and France – in the Plaza Accord to help prompt a reversal in the dollar's exchange rate. The much stronger link between national financial markets was also strikingly demonstrated in the 1987 *global* stock market crash, an event triggered by a dispute between the US and West Germany over monetary policy and interest rate levels.

With other countries developing their own international financial markets, the City's leading position was looking increasingly insecure. A key UK government concern in the early 1980s was thus to improve the competitiveness of London, especially vis-à-vis the much larger New York stock market. This meant getting rid of the financial cartel in London that had been in place for decades. Far from the Thatcher government being 'pro-City' and backing a clique of wealthy financiers, its objective was to promote the City as an expanding business area for British capitalism as whole. It decided that the previous insular forms of protection were now unviable. This led to the 'Big Bang' reforms of 1986, which made it easier for financial companies to join the London Stock Exchange, abolished fixed commissions on buying and selling securities, and ended the established division of labour between jobbers and brokers.[28] The relatively small size of the London-based jobbers (financial companies that advanced money to hold shares for sale) and brokers (who matched buyers and sellers for a fee) was a problem: if they wanted to compete internationally, they had to grow to a much bigger scale.[29]

The 'Big Bang' reforms led to the influx of many more foreign financial companies into London, especially those restricted by their own government's rules on the scope of their activities back home, as was still the case even in the US and Japan. The result was that more of the City's operations were taken over by foreign financial companies, boosting London as a profitable base for doing business, and allowing the City to attract inflows of foreign money-capital into the UK more easily.

Some critics of the Thatcher government's policies on finance argue that its view was short-sighted because it ignored the importance of the UK's manufacturing industry and in any case failed to boost the role of the City or to increase net income from foreign investments.[30] Particularly in the years immediately after the 'Big Bang', it was not clear how selling off UK financial companies to foreign investors could be counted as a major policy success. But this analysis misses the point about what was really going on.

Even with the build-up of North Sea oil and gas export revenues and a domestic recession that cut imports, the UK's current account position only briefly moved from deficit to surplus in the early 1980s. It was soon back in deficit again. The British economy was looking uncompetitive, but this did not lead to any government initiatives to raise productivity. Earlier failed attempts to boost industry by Labour and Conservative governments from the late 1960s onwards did not set a precedent for success in the 1980s, so other ways of generating revenues had to be found. The Thatcher government's policies made more sense as a capitalist strategy than most critics admit. By making moves to boost the City's business – and earnings from foreign investment – the Thatcher government placed a bet that looked to have better odds than any others on offer, especially given the international status of the City.

Other major capitalist powers were also pursuing a similar strategy, particularly in the European Union. In 1986, all member governments of the EU signed the Single European Act, the first major revision of the Treaty of Rome and one that aimed to create a 'single market' by 1992. The scope of this single market was not restricted to the products of industry and regular services. It also included the removal of capital controls and a 'free market' in *financial* services within the EU. A number of these policies had already been operative since the late 1970s. By 2012, their impact could be seen in the fact that 5.3 per cent of total employment in EU member states was in financial and related professional services, and that 5.5 per cent of the EU's GDP was accounted for by financial services.[31] The UK was well above the EU average on each measure, at 7 per cent for employment – 2.1 million people – and 7.9 per cent for GDP. There were also exceptional figures for some smaller, financial-service-oriented EU countries such as Luxembourg: 17.9 per cent and 23.5 per cent, respectively.

Finance and the major powers

Aided by sympathetic governments, the UK financial markets remained in a strong global position, even though government policy was more focused on removing controls or allowing certain types of financial dealing rather than providing a direct boost to the financial businesses concerned. Among other things, this policy stance supported the development of the euromarkets. As noted in Chapter 1, it makes no sense to argue, as Helleiner does, that Britain supported liberalisation because of 'its "lagging" hegemonic commitment to London's position as an international financial centre' or that it was 'locked into a policy of openness that dates from its hegemonic days.'[32] British policy clearly had a forward-looking objective of boosting revenues from overseas via expanded City operations. It was not based on nostalgia.

Table 3.2 gives some data for comparing the position of UK financial markets with those of other major powers – the top five of the 'Group of 7' – in the 1980s and 1990s. Comprehensive data for global financial markets do not exist for the whole of the period from the 1970s, and before the mid-1980s surveys were very patchy. Nevertheless, the table offers sufficient evidence for concluding both that UK-based markets punched above their weight *and* that their position was under threat from developments elsewhere.

Firstly, consider the data for international banking, which consists of making loans to and taking deposits from outside the national territory. The UK had the highest share of this market, but its lead fell back after 1980. This was partly due to the BIS data including offshore tax havens for the first time from 1983, although there were (and still are) strong British financial links with these areas that attract vast international funds. In addition, the UK's share at 20 per cent in 2000 was still twice as big as that of the second placed power, the US. However, as noted earlier, the rapid expansion of Japanese banking had become a competitive threat by 1990, before Japan's financial crisis set in. Germany's position in international banking also strengthened, and did so more persistently than Japan's. Eventually, Germany overtook Japan's share of business and came closer to the US position, another indication of its potential threat to UK-based financial business by the late 1990s and one factor behind the UK government's worries about German competition.

Table 3.2 Financial market shares of major powers, 1980–2001

	1980	1985	1990	1995	2000
Banking – % of international global assets/liabilities outstanding by location*					
UK	27.0	23.7	17.8	17.6	20.1
US	13.4	15.3	9.6	9.2	10.0
Japan	5.0	7.3	14.9	12.3	8.3
Germany	5.5	3.4	4.7	6.9	9.1
France	10.8	6.9	7.1	7.8	6.3
FX market – % turnover by location (April)			**1989**	**1995**	**2001**
UK	–	–	26.0	29.3	31.8
US	–	–	16.0	16.3	16.0
Japan	–	–	15.0	10.3	9.0
Germany	–	–	–	4.8	5.4
France	–	–	3.0	3.8	2.9
FX market – % turnover by currency traded (April)**			**1989**	**1995**	**2001**
GBP	–	–	15	10	13
USD	–	–	90	83	90
JPY	–	–	27	24	23
DEM (EUR in 2001)	–	–	27	37	38

Notes: *Data for end-year. **Two currencies are involved in every FX deal, so the sum of the shares for all currencies is 200%.

Sources: Bank of England and BIS reports, with author's calculations

Other data in Table 3.2 are for the foreign exchange (FX) market. From the 1980s, the share of global FX trading in London increased steadily and remained well ahead of all other financial centres. This was despite the volume of trading in sterling (GBP in the table) being only the fourth largest in the global markets, well behind the US dollar and also behind the Deutsche mark (DEM, later the euro) and the Japanese yen (JPY). This was another sign that the City had consolidated its position as the main centre of international financial dealing, one that did not necessarily relate to the UK domestic economy nor depend upon the use of sterling, and one in which the main institutions doing the deals were as likely as not to be owned by foreign banks.

The rising importance of the euro in global foreign exchange – and in other financial markets, including bonds, equities and financial derivatives – presented another possible threat to the UK's position. Yet in many respects the euro financial system, although developing apace from the late 1990s, showed little sign of establishing a single financial centre to rival London. Greater unification of the financial services sector within the EU and a common currency for euro member states encouraged banks to centralise their dealing operations. Yet despite the European Central Bank being based in Frankfurt, these operations were commonly centralised in London – and if not there, then it tended to be in the home country's business centre, rather than Frankfurt, unless the bank was German. Even after the introduction of the euro, German banks, like others, conducted most of their securities business in London, which remained the key financial centre. Since London offered good communication links to European clients, this often meant that a bank's main sales teams were also located in the City.

National political differences within the euro area meant that there was far less impetus than might have been expected towards the creation of a single, dominant centre of financial market activity. There is a single currency, but a multiplicity of states. Politically and economically this makes the euro *less* than the sum of its components. Notably, in the aftermath of the 2007–8 crisis and the problems with Greece and other member countries, reports suggested that the previous integration of euro banking markets was being *reversed*. If a bank had euro assets in France and euro liabilities in Spain, it could not have complete confidence that the assets and liabilities would be treated in the same way by any supra-national authority. European banks began to match their assets and liabilities on a *national* basis.[33]

Gravity and the global system

As was argued in Chapter 1, it is a mistake to treat the UK financial markets as simply being 'satellites' of the US markets. To use a more accurate astronomical metaphor, the relationship is better described as a 'double planet' system: rather than the UK simply orbiting the US, each country's financial market exerts a significant 'gravitational' pull on the other, even though the pull of the US is obviously larger. More than that, the centre of gravity for the global system is determined by the balance of power among *all* the major capitalist countries, a balance that will shift over time as their relative power changes.

Reckoning on its position within the global hierarchy, the UK will accommodate US demands, but it will also pay close attention to its own interests. The UK's dependence on the US in military and security matters does not mean that British policy is determined by the wishes of the US administration. On the contrary, it will occasionally be in direct conflict with them. For example, given its desire to restrict China's growing financial role in Asia, in March 2015 the US administration rebuked Britain for joining the Asian Infrastructure Investment Bank.[34] This new China-led financial institution will rival the US-dominated IMF and World Bank, further undermining US power and influence in the Asian region, but it gives the UK a means of developing its own relationship with China. There have also been occasions when US policy shifted in favour of the UK becoming more closely involved with European developments, but the UK nevertheless persisted with its 'mid-Atlantic' policy.

The authority of the British state, not only over its national territory, but also in relation to other powers and, in particular, over the rules for managing financial obligations in the City, has been critical

for London's international role. It was this authority that supported
the renewed role of the City in the post-1945 world, when Britain
was no longer in a position to be the world's major creditor. But the
British state did not create the new postwar financial markets, neither
the UK government nor the Bank of England. The prime movers were
clearly private capitalist companies. To that extent, I would agree with
part of Gary Burn's thesis on the euromarkets, which argues that they
were not directly established by government policy. However, Burn
could not be more wrong in arguing that the City represents a pre-
industrial financial clique now 'restored' to its role of controlling the
British economy.[35] This view ignores the impressive performance of
the British ruling class faced with the realities of post-colonial economic competition in the increasingly harsh world market with
which successive UK governments have had to deal.

Such a view also sets up a false conflict between 'financial' and
'industrial' interests. These branches of capitalist business are closely
intertwined, as is most clearly seen in the way that even industrial
companies are heavily involved in financial operations and remain
highly attentive to their own stock market values, financial risks
and access to market liquidity. This is not to argue that a bank is the
same thing as an industrial company, since they each have a different economic function and a different relationship to the exploitation
of labour. However, they are close *partners* in that exploitation. The
main difference is that the financial companies facilitate the operations of those more directly engaged in production, taking a cut from
their business revenues, as will be explained in more detail in the
following chapters.

4.

Power and Parasitism

Bruno Lafont, the head of France's Lafarge, one of the world's biggest cement producing companies, was downbeat in March 2015. His company's merger deal with its Swiss rival, Holcim, would go ahead on less favourable terms than expected, and his own status was somewhat diminished as he would be only co-chairman in the new group. 'The project is much stronger than individuals', he told the *Financial Times*.[1] The project was to create the world's largest cement producer, operating in more than seventy countries and almost twice the size of its nearest competitor, based in China. Even the biggest companies come under pressure from market forces, against which individuals do not count, even rich and powerful ones, when survival is at stake – although such individuals are happy to set aside their personal wishes when they are compensated sufficiently. Mergers and acquisitions enable a further concentration of the market into the hands of fewer producers, but this particular company merger had run into trouble. A year earlier, it was planned as a merger of equals to save on costs. Then Holcim's finances began to look better than Lafarge's, boosted by a jump in the value of the Swiss franc versus the euro on foreign exchange markets. So, instead of their respective shares being exchanged on a one-for-one basis in the merger, it was now to be ten Lafarge shares for only nine Holcim shares to complete the €41bn deal.

This is a 'concrete' example of how financial markets affect economic power. Financial developments can rapidly alter the relationships between major corporations and how they consider their role in the world market. The financial system grows out of the needs of the capitalist market, and it is also a means by which the major countries and their corporations try to maintain their privileged economic status. Finance is both a necessary part of capitalism and a way for rich countries to draw income from the rest of the world economy. Furthermore, a large number of people in the rich countries, not just 'the 1 per cent', hold wealth in financial securities and receive income from them.

The creation of credit and the role of financial securities are two of the most fundamental aspects of capitalist finance. Both appear also to allow capitalist wealth to run beyond the bounds set by what the economy actually produces. Furthermore, financial dealing is *not* confined to financial institutions, as shown in the Holcim-Lafarge merger deal. While some companies, like banks or hedge funds, specialise in financial dealing and investment, *all* major companies are tied up in these deals, aiming to consolidate their economic power. Allowing for the different status of different countries in the world economic system, all forms of international finance, and even commerce, can also be seen as parasitic on the value created elsewhere.

Money-capitalists and financial institutions

Capitalist producers need financial services. They are required to help with buying and selling, to operate a payments system, to provide working capital, to get foreign exchange for international trade, to obtain funds for long-term investment, and so forth. Commercial capitalists focus on the buying and selling of commodities, like the retail giants Wal-Mart, Carrefour, Tesco and Aldi. The money-dealing capitalists, like Visa, MasterCard and American Express, specialise in managing the different kinds of money circulation that arise from this commercial function. Money-dealers handle payments for commercial and industrial capitalists, including foreign exchange dealing and the discounting of commercial paper. While commercial capitalists exchange money for commodities (buying or selling), money-dealing capitalists usually exchange one form of money for another kind of money, whether cash for a money-market security (e.g. a commercial bill) or one currency for another. They can also offer (as with credit cards) short-term loans to facilitate purchases.

Both commercial activities *and* money dealing are necessary for producers of commodities to keep their businesses going, although the former play no direct part in the actual *production* of the commodities. Both types of capital get a profit by taking a cut from all their transactions (buying at lower than market selling prices, taking a commission, using bid-offer spreads on deals, etc.) to share in the new value produced by others. This also means that not simply their profits, but also the wages of the people they employ, and the costs of the buildings, materials and technology they use, are funded by this value they extract from the productive sphere.

They can maintain this position in the market only if they do a more efficient job in buying/selling and money dealing than the industrialists could manage by themselves. If they did not, then the industrial company could decide to perform this function independently. In recent decades, many apparently industrial companies well known for their products (for example, Apple or Dell in the technology sector) have gone even further than this by producing almost nothing themselves. Instead, they employ other producers to do it for them, while they manage the branding, advertising and sales. By contrast, commercial capital or money-dealers rarely move directly into production. However, it is common for commercial capitalists to have supply-chain links with producers, as for example when Wal-Mart and others employ industrial companies in China, India and elsewhere to make goods for them on demand.

Interest-bearing capital

Under capitalism, the *money-dealing* function evolves into something called *interest-bearing capital*. Here, money is not exchanged for other forms of money or commodities, but is advanced as money-capital to the 'functioning capitalist' who then uses it to produce surplus value and later returns the money back with interest to the person or company that advanced it.[2] The money-capitalist advancing the money does not need to pay much attention to production: it is just money lent out and more money being repaid, as if by magic. The concept also includes advances of money to buy company shares (which pay dividends), and to buy government and corporate bonds that pay interest.

Money-capitalists are not just bankers lending money to companies. They include rich individuals who buy bonds and equities, those on the boards of directors of the major corporations, the managers of investment funds and other financial institutions. They use not just their own money, but also many forms of *borrowed* money. Money-capitalists also include the so-called oligarchs of Eastern Europe and other *nouveaux riches* who have often 'risen without trace' after being in a political position to secure economic favours that can include being gifted, or getting at low cost, the ownership of formerly state-run companies. These people do not have to rely upon financial institutions like banks to tell them where to invest their money, although they will often use banks to execute a deal.

The key point is that interest-bearing capital is an advance of money-capital to those *within* the circuit of the production and circulation of commodities, from those *outside* it, whether banks or others. The former are the productive, commercial and money-dealing capitalists already mentioned. This distinction between the different ways in which capital is invested does not imply that 'financial capitalists' are a different group of people or a different class in society. All big capitalists tend to become money-capitalists. The active capitalists using their own funds in their own enterprise, as depicted in the cartoons of the fat, cigar-chomping, nineteenth-century industrialist whom Marx nicknamed 'Moneybags', have little relevance in today's financial markets.

Interest-bearing capital can also be examined from the perspective of the financial institutions involved in advancing money and receiving it back with interest. These institutions are often involved in *both* commercial money dealing and in advancing money-capital as an investment. A brief description of these institutions might be useful to provide some background for the analyses offered in this book.

Banks

A large part of bank business consists of managing the payments of clients, shifting funds from one account to another. This function has landed many banks in trouble with regulators when it turns out that their clients include drug dealers and money launderers, as in the case of the $1.9bn fine imposed by the US government on Britain's HSBC in 2012.[3] Banks also take in deposits from customers and make loans, about which more later. Their dealings in short-term money-market instruments (certificates of deposit, commercial paper, etc.) and foreign exchange dealings (in spot, forward and swap deals) for industrial and commercial companies can be placed under the heading of 'money-dealing capital'.

However, banks managing deals of this kind also take on market risk of their own, and this usually involves them taking bets on the market ('proprietary positions') that have little to do with customer business. In that case, the money-dealing capital label is no longer really applicable. Bank foreign exchange deals, for example, are conducted mainly with financial institutions, far less so with industrial and commercial companies, and these operations are mainly transactions related to interest-bearing capital. Many of the fines imposed on international banks in recent years have been related to bank dealers' manipulation of the interest rates or exchange rates involved in these transactions. This has some similarities with price fixing by big corporations in other markets, although it takes a very different form.

A bank advances interest-bearing capital when it makes longer-term loans to a company for investment. Banks might also advance money to companies when buying their newly issued bonds and equities. If the bank is only buying an *existing* security in the market, one that has already been sold by the company, then the company receives no new cash; it is just a transaction with another investor. But when banks buy or sell securities, then they make a dealing margin and might also profit from a rise or fall in the price of the security. These revenues come from *dealing in* interest-bearing capital. If a company needs funds for ongoing operations, then it would normally use a bank overdraft or other short-term borrowing for cash-flow purposes, which is an advance of money-dealing capital by the bank.

Brokers

Brokers get a fee for connecting the buyers and sellers of currencies, securities or commodities, and sometimes for giving advice on the market. Fees may be calculated as a small percentage of the value of the deal transacted. Important parts of the broking operations of modern capitalism also take place on the exchanges – stock exchanges, commodity exchanges or futures, and options exchanges. The exchanges also charge fees for these transactions. Broking activity is also incorporated into bank operations, where sales agents contact clients to see what business they would like to do with the bank, in foreign exchange and money-market instruments or in buying and selling financial securities. In these cases, the gap between a bank's buying and selling prices is one way in which it can make a profit on the deal. This business might be considered as money dealing, but in reality the bulk of it does not involve offering commercial dealing services to industrial or commercial corporations, but rather dealing in forms of interest-bearing capital such as equities and bonds.

Asset managers

BlackRock in the US is the world's biggest asset manager. It has a huge $4.6 trillion in assets, with offices in thirty countries and clients in 100. Asset managers, including so-called hedge funds, control large sums of money, mostly invested in company shares and in bond securities issued by governments and companies, but they also invest funds in real estate and commodities like oil, copper, corn and soybeans. They do so as managers of *other people's money*, and usually with investment mandates (instructions) that are chosen by the investor, for example to invest in European or North American equity markets. They sell their financial services for a fee that is usually taken as a percentage of the value of assets held, not based on the return from those assets (which could be negative). However, the hedge funds also take a share of the profits received from the fund's investments. All asset managers advance money-capital on behalf of others, although this still gives them a social power because they usually have some discretion over where the money goes. For example, even if a fund were constrained to invest in European equities or US corporate bonds, then the asset manager would usually be able to decide on which particular company equities or bond issues to invest in. Their fees are for a service provided to money-capitalists and their operations should also be considered as coming under the heading of interest-bearing capital.

Insurance companies

The US company Berkshire Hathaway is by far the world's biggest insurer, measured by the value of its shares, and it regularly hits the financial headlines for its sizeable investments in the equity of corporations that it thinks have a commanding position in the market. Its largest investments are in other US corporations, such as IBM and American Express, with most of its key holdings in other financial companies. Insurance companies take in payments for providing financial services and invest these revenues in financial securities and other assets to generate the funds to pay for claims from policyholders. Individuals or companies may hold the policies. Insurance companies can be viewed as performing commercial, financial services, but there is also an overlap with operations of interest-bearing capital since they are investing in financial securities.

There are different types of insurance. For example, a policy may be taken out on the assets of a company or on the life or personal property of a worker. In the former case, the insurance premiums should be considered as a deduction from company profits and the policies' payouts simply a redistribution of profits between different companies, taking into account the deduction taken from these profits by the insurance company itself.[4] In the latter case, the workers' insurance premium payments can be considered to be part of their wage if they are a normal part of living costs, while the policies' payouts are a repayment compensating the worker or his or her family for the loss of property or for death. In this case, workers' savings have become 'metamorphosed into capital' as they are returned to the control of capital by the insurance companies – and also by pension funds, considered next.[5]

Pension funds

Insurance companies may also be pension funds, as in the case of the UK's Aviva, which has more than 30 million customers in sixteen countries. The biggest pension fund in the Netherlands, ABP, is the world's fourth largest, despite being based in a relatively small (but rich) country. It manages pensions for nearly three million public sector employees and has almost $400bn of assets. Like insurance companies, pension funds can be seen as both operating in commercial financial services and as advancing interest-bearing capital.

Pension funds use regular incoming payments to invest in a variety of assets and use the revenues obtained from these to pay pension incomes. On a much larger scale than insurance companies, they have the power to allocate money-capital to different financial assets – government bonds, corporate bonds, the equity of different companies – or to property, or anything else that might appear to offer an attractive future return. As in the case of the premium payments made to insurance companies, these companies control the pension savings of individuals. Especially from the early 2000s, pension funds began to invest in commodities via the futures market, which was one factor behind the sharp rise in a wide range of.commodity prices.[6]

The kinds of companies discussed above are all specialists in financial operations, but within the general concept of finance used in this book, I include *everything* that arises from the evolution of money dealing, both the pure money-dealing capital forms (where money is exchanged) *and* where money is advanced as capital in terms of direct loans or through buying bonds, equities, etc. Many apparently 'non-financial' companies do these things too, but there are some specific functions that *only* financial companies can perform.

Bank credit creation

Most people know that banks 'make money', but this is usually under-stood to mean that they register big profits. Few realise that the phrase is *literally* true: banks *create money* in their credit operations. This topic is often poorly covered by Marxist writers, who can give the impression that banks merely take in deposits from a myriad of people and companies and then lend *this* money out to others. In other words, they see banks acting only as middlemen with *existing* sums of money.[7] Banks do take in deposits, but the credit creation process is even more important and highlights one way in which command over society's resources does not have to depend directly upon value production. Money being printed by a *central* bank is something people are more used to hearing about. For example, the US Federal Reserve is the monopoly issuer of US dollar currency, as are other central banks with their own currencies, and a $20 bill costs only 10 cents to produce. Yet, the vast bulk of what we call money is *created* in quite a different way via the banking system.

This happens through banks making loans. For example, a bank creates money by making a $200,000 mortgage loan to a property buyer, or a $50 million investment loan to a company, and credits their bank accounts with the funds. These funds in the borrower's account should be seen as *fictitious deposits*, since they are created out of thin air by the bank and do not depend upon how much actual cash the bank has at its disposal at the time. After the property is pur-chased or the investment expenditure is made, those credited funds end up in the sellers' bank accounts, and are then balanced against the transactions that other banks have with the first one.

A simple example will make this process clearer. Assume that Jack arranges a mortgage loan of $200,000 with Bank Beavis so that he can buy a property belonging to Jill. Bank Beavis then credits the account that Jack has with them for the $200,000. But Jack does not withdraw all these funds as cash and then hand over the notes to pay Jill for the property. Instead, he transfers the funds from his bank account to the account that Jill has with Bank Butthead. To do this, his bank will use the interbank payments system for the transfer, so that his account will be debited $200,000 and Jill's account will be credited for the same.[8] Since Jack did not walk out of Bank Beavis with $200,000 in notes, his bank did not need to have that sum available in cash. Bank Beavis will have an obligation to pay Bank Butthead $200,000 as a result of this transaction, but it will also be processing many thousands of other incoming and outgoing payments. Its net position might be such that it has a surplus of funds on that day, or a deficit. If Bank Beavis has a deficit, then it can then borrow funds from other banks, including Bank Butthead, or it can get allocated short-term funds from the central bank's regular market operations.

Transactions between banks will often more or less balance out. On any given day, the interbank payments system will process many billions of dollars, euros, sterling or whatever in both directions: from Bank A to Bank B and others, and then back again to Bank A. In 2011, CHAPS, one of the UK's interbank payment systems, was transferring more than £250bn *per day* in payments between banks. If the total flows for individual banks do not balance, the banks with surplus funds usually lend them out to those with deficits.[9]

How does this extra $200,000, or any of the other funds created by banking operations, tally with the production of value in the economy? Wouldn't economic life be much easier if all you had to do was to use the credit that the bank has just created for you? There is a catch, of course.

The catch is that while money creation in the banking system offers flexibility – you do not need to have already earned the money you spend today – there is still a potential reckoning with the production of value. It is a *potential* reckoning because the timing is not pre-determined. Depending on your status in the world economy, the reckoning might be a long way off.[10] The link between value production and what credit creation enables you to buy is not really broken, only stretched – and the risk, especially for a weak country, is that the stretched elastic will snap back.

If a central bank just printed money that went into circulation –
those \$20 bills mentioned earlier – eventually the demand created
would cause inflation if there were no extra output. In any case, the
extra output would not occur unless it was profitable for capitalists
to produce it. The banking system's creation of credit is different, but
it can also lead to problems. A bank's loans count as its 'assets', but
they are only really assets if they get paid back and do not become
losses. Those receiving the loans are debtors who have to repay the
money with interest, and their ability to do this depends upon the
creation of value. The more a bank expands its loan assets, the greater
the risk that potential losses on those loans will eat into its capital and
reserves, eventually making it bankrupt. As it begins to face losses, it
will find it harder to access the monetary system because other banks
will be reluctant to lend to it, something that usually happens before
the bank's customers realise the problem and decide to get their
money out. In the case of the UK's Northern Rock crisis of 2007, the
interbank deposit market was closed to Northern Rock well before
the bank's worried customers queued anxiously outside its branches
or tried to use internet banking to transfer their funds elsewhere.

The process of credit creation is critical for the capitalist system's
expansion of financial assets and is a unique feature of banks as financial companies. Importantly, this process is supported by the central
bank – the state-backed institution that oversees the operations of the
private banking system and provides liquidity to it. Credit creation is
not limited by the deposits of spare cash arising from the circuits of
industrial and commercial capital, or by the savings of individuals, as
accounts of this process often claim. For a while, credit creation can
also appear to be completely independent of capitalist production.

Financial securities and economic power

The reader may already feel a little unsettled about the extent to which
bank credit creation stretches the link between what an economy produces and the funds available to buy things. If so, I would recommend
taking a deep breath before reading on, although be comforted that

there is a method in this madness. Bond and equity securities have different characteristics that determine each type of security's price and the role it plays in the capitalist system. They are both summary measures of wealth and a means by which the rule of the capitalist market is expressed and enforced. These securities are often influenced by the banks' creation of credit, but they go far beyond bank loans and can be used by money-capitalists to extend their ownership of and control over society's resources. They can make wealth seem to appear from nowhere, both promoting and reflecting capitalist power.

A useful way to understand these securities is to start from the advance of money for investment in a productive operation, for example an investment in buildings, machinery, software, raw materials, and so on, and the money set aside to pay the wages of employees. Say that the sum of such an investment amounts to $100 million. In principle, one can point to the value of the items bought by the capitalist that add up to that amount. Then, surely, the company is 'worth' $100 million? Well no, probably not, and not just because the company does not actually own its employees. If the company is quoted on the stock exchange so that the ownership stakes in it are sold as shares, its value will be determined by what it is expected to earn in future years and also by how attractive the security looks for investors who might buy it. Capitalist production is *not* about possessing goods or even producing goods, but about making a profit. If the company fails to make a profit, the expenditure of $100 million will have been a waste of money and the value of its shares would fall to reflect only the scrap value of its assets. But if it looks like making high profits in future, and especially if investors – even stupid ones – are interested in buying it, for whatever reason, then the market value of the company's shares would rise.

If the value of all the company's shares happened to be exactly $100 million, the same as the capital invested, then that might seem to be 'correct'. But even if that were the case, there is still something strange going on here. The capital does not exist *twice*, once as the invested assets and again as the value of the shares in the market, but they do have a *separate* existence. The shares entitle their owner to a portion of the company's profits and a claim on the company's assets, but they are traded as securities in the financial market and their price has little to do with the value of the invested capital. This led Marx to describe securities as *fictitious* capital.[11]

The fictitious nature of such capital is most evident in the case of government securities. At least with company securities the shareholder has, in principle, ownership rights over the assets of the company, so that even if it earns no profits and its share value collapses, shareholders might still get some money back from the sale of the assets (minus any company debts). But with government debt, for example US Treasuries or UK gilts, the securities' price is not based on *any* existing capital asset, only on the ability of the government to service and repay its debts. The sum of money the security can fetch on its sale does not reflect the value of *any* invested capital at all.

What are these securities worth in the financial market? The banal answer is: whatever someone is willing to pay for them. But that raises the question of how calculations are made to decide on their prices. One key factor in these calculations is that the financial market makes a judgement on the future payments from the security. Another is the need to allow for the fact that receiving, for example, $5 million from an investment in one or two years' time will be worth less to a money-capitalist than receiving it right now. How much less will depend on prevailing market interest rates, so that the expected future earnings are discounted, or reduced in terms of what they are worth today. In the case of our example company above, if its profit expectations are high and interest rates are low, then its stock market value could be much more than $100 million.

A simple example will illustrate how the price of a financial security can change dramatically with the level of interest rates. If you own a security that will pay you $5 every year, and prevailing interest rates are 5 per cent, then that is the same return as if you were investing $100 at 5 per cent per annum (because 5 per cent of $100 is $5). If the level of interest rates then went down to 2 per cent, the price of your security would rise sharply to $250, because the $5 you receive is now equivalent to $250 being invested at a 2 per cent annual interest rate. Or, if interest rates rise to 10 per cent, then the price of your security would drop to $50, because you could invest just $50 and get a payment of $5 every year.

In practice, the calculations are more complicated than this because allowance must be made for all the future cash flows associated with the different kinds of security, including any principal repayment, and the rate at which all these cash flows are discounted. But in general, lower levels of market interest rates will tend to raise financial security prices and vice versa. Since 2008, the sharp reduction of global interest rates has been an important factor in helping some recovery of equity prices, despite the continued weak state of the world economy. Another complication in determining security prices with any confidence is that they are also influenced by the hopes and fears of capitalists in the financial market about the size of future revenues.

The flexible noose

Higher security prices increase the wealth of the owners of fictitious capital, even if nothing has changed in the economy at the level of production. Although the security's price will reflect views about future production, profit and potential revenue to some extent, even that relationship is greatly affected by levels of interest rates. In any case, how can production or profits that *do not yet exist* generate wealth *now*? Nevertheless, this is a capitalist market reality. When billions of dollars are wiped off the value of shares in a stock market slump, the disappeared wealth may have been 'fictitious', but it was nevertheless once an asset that could have been cashed in, belonging to whoever owned these securities.

The owners of financial securities have an economic power that manifests itself in several ways. Firstly, the owner of an equity security has some power over a company's decisions, at least if more than a minimal portion of shares are owned and those shares come with voting rights. Owners of significant shareholdings are often invited onto the board of the relevant company, receiving serious money for negligible work in addition to their dividend income from the shares they own. Secondly, the owner of a debt security is a creditor of a company or government, and has a legal right to be paid back, or must be asked to agree to any deal among creditors to forgive a portion of the debt owed. If a company cannot repay its debts, the creditors can usually seize its assets as compensation, and legally the debt holders have higher priority in being paid back than do the equity holders. If a government cannot repay its debts, then the holders of the debt securities – usually backed by their states – often have a decisive role in determining what policies are to be imposed in order to benefit the creditors. Thirdly, even if security owners have no such economic or political power over companies or governments, they still have a liquid asset that can be sold for cash on the market. This is a form of command over social resources that comes from having monetary wealth. One peculiarity of fictitious capital is that, while it usually takes the form of *previously invested money-capital* committed for months, years, or, as with equities, indefinitely, it is still a relatively liquid asset and can be turned back into money at any time. It can be sold, used as collateral for loans, or used as a means of payment in other deals.[12]

This also means that financial securities do not only reflect capitalist market sentiment about future revenues; they can also be used as a means of enforcing capitalist market discipline. If a company's investment policy or commercial decisions do not tally with what the 'market' wants – in other words, what the aggregate of capitalists demands – its shares will be sold, the price of any bonds it has issued will fall, and it will find it more difficult to get new funds. Similarly, government policies that do not sufficiently favour capitalist interests usually lead to a fall in the price of government debt, and investor selling of equities, bonds and the currency will also hit the exchange rate. The markets for financial securities are a development of the famous 'laws of supply and demand' for commodities, and demonstrate most clearly what the capitalist system wants and what it will accept.

Financial securities also have striking effects on the dynamics of capital accumulation because they are a part of the credit system that goes beyond simple bank loans. By issuing shares or bonds to attract new funds for investment, companies can grow to a scale formerly impossible for capitalists using their own money. The use of financial securities also features heavily in company mergers and acquisitions, as with the Holcim-Lafarge deal noted at the beginning of this chapter. This kind of system reproduces both monopolies and 'a new financial aristocracy, a new variety of parasites in the shape of promoters, speculators and simply nominal directors; a whole system of swindling and cheating by means of corporation promotion, stock issuance, and stock speculation'.[13]

Although surplus value, the source of profit, comes from the exploitation of workers by all forms of *productive* capital, the revenues that owners of fictitious capital or the lenders of money get do not have to come *directly* from productive capital. The credit system obscures value relations – for example, apparently 'money creates money' – so the owners and controllers of financial assets of all kinds may pay little attention to whether the returns on those assets are claims on industrial capital, commerce, the financial sector, the government or even individuals. For example, Collateralised Debt Obligations (CDOs) played a key part in the explosion of financial asset holdings ahead of the financial debacle in 2008. These were securities with a claim on future residential mortgage payments. When borrowers could not keep up with their mortgage payments, CDO prices collapsed. This suggests that ignoring the productive foundations that are the source of interest payments can lead to a few problems! Nevertheless, this is another characteristic feature of contemporary finance.

Appreciating the wider dimensions of fictitious capital and money-capital also means recognising that it is not only the 'financial aristocracy' that benefits from the revenues. A much broader stratum of society in the richer countries benefits too, although on a smaller scale, as is shown by the widespread ownership of financial assets in the rich countries (to be discussed at the end of this chapter).

The financial form taken by modern capitalism is not confined to financial institutions; it includes all types of capitalist companies, intertwined with the role of the state domestically and internationally. Capitalist individuals, companies and states express their economic power principally via their *financial* power, and especially in terms of how far they are able to marshal and control social resources. Fictitious capital – the tradable financial security – is the common element in all the main aspects of modern finance. But fictitious capital is not solely owned and controlled by 'financial sector' capitalists. Industrial and commercial companies, often those favoured by critics opposing 'finance', also use these securities to consolidate their market power.

Take, for example, the flotation of Facebook shares in 2012. This raised $16 billion for the company, and Facebook paid less than $200m to the banks organising it (bank fees are usually between 1 per cent and 4 per cent and this was at the low end of the range). This flotation turned *all* the shares, not just those newly issued, into assets priced on the market and at the time this gave Facebook a market capitalisation in excess of $100bn.[14] As a result, Mark Zuckerberg and the original founders/owners accumulated tens of billions of dollars in new financial wealth. The market value of the company soared exponentially beyond any money they had invested in its operations. Not only this, the shares sold were mainly *non-voting* shares. Despite owning only 18 per cent of the company after the flotation, Zuckerberg had three times the voting rights – 57 per cent – and thus remained *personally* in control of it.[15]

Having been elevated into the higher realms of financial security calculations, in 2014 Facebook was able, with little or no input from investment banks, to acquire WhatsApp, a company that it judged to have a key position in an area important to its future growth. A 'mere' $4bn of the total $22bn payment to buy WhatsApp was paid in cash, with the rest in Facebook shares, illustrating the role of share valuation as a means of payment.[16] The Facebook valuation of WhatsApp also showed the importance a monopolist puts on market position, as compared to the standard equity market valuation method taught in business schools, or any calculation of discounted future revenues. WhatsApp registered a trading *loss* of $139 million in 2013, rising to a loss of $232 million in the first half of 2014!

Since capitalist society's assets take the form of financial securities, they can usually be bought, sold and transferred with ease. This facilitates the concentration of economic wealth and power, especially through company mergers and takeovers, which helps a small group of powerful capitalist companies to dominate the world economy. It reflects the way in which the productive capabilities of humanity are distorted in an increasingly dysfunctional capitalist system.

Finance and the rule of capital

Few writers after Marx have done more to analyse the role of finance in modern capitalism than Rudolf Hilferding. His book, *Finance Capital*, published in 1910, was a powerful examination of contemporary trends, considered by many at the time to be the 'fourth volume' of Marx's *Capital*. It is worth looking at some of Hilferding's ideas, because explaining where I think they are mistaken helps to clarify the role of finance today.

Hilferding's concept of 'finance capital' contains a number of confusions. While he does not simply argue that banks invest money in industry and end up controlling the economy, his many comments on the banks' financial power and investments do support this narrow interpretation. Even when he notes the lower dependence of industry on bank funds in England, because 'the public does directly what is done by the bank [in Germany]' when purchasing industrial shares, he immediately adds that: 'An ever-increasing part of the capital of industry does not belong to the industrialists who use it. They are able to dispose over capital only through the banks, which represent the owners [of this capital].'[17] In England's case, at least, the banks were far from being the key owners or the main representatives of capital. However, Hilferding extends the idea of the banks being in control by arguing that 'with the increasing concentration of property, the owners of the fictitious capital which gives power over the banks, and the owners of the capital which gives power over industry, become increasingly the same people'.[18] So, the class of fictitious capital owners who control the banks closely overlaps with the class of those who own industry. And because it is the finance capitalist who 'increasingly concentrates his control over the whole national capital by means of his domination of bank capital', the banks are placed at the centre of the process.

But this is wrong. Hilferding appears to be distinguishing a 'fictitious capital' ownership of the banks from a 'capital ownership' of industry. But the owners of *industrial* companies are the owners of its equity capital, usually in the form of quoted financial securities that *are* fictitious capital.[19] Furthermore, the owners of fictitious capital in industrial companies do not have to secure this ownership *indirectly* by owning fictitious capital in banks. Hilferding may be referring to owners of *bank deposits*, which he says banks use for industrial investment. But this not only confuses fictitious capital with bank deposits, it also ignores the banks' ability to create their own deposits and implies that money-capitalists never use their own bank deposits to buy shares in industry. Hilferding correctly focused on fictitious capital as a key feature of monopoly capitalism, but in doing so he elevated the banks, which are *dealers in* as much as *owners of* fictitious capital, to a position of having complete *power over* capital. For this reason he could argue that 'taking possession of six large Berlin banks would mean taking possession of the most important spheres of large-scale industry'.[20]

Hilferding's view of finance capital is usually criticised on the basis that it did not apply to the UK, the most prominent imperialist power at the time. Large British companies did not depend upon bank finance for long-term investment since they were profitable enough to finance themselves for this purpose – helped by captive Empire markets. Hilferding was well aware of the different relationship between banks and industry in the UK, where the banks mainly provided financial services to UK companies.[21] Nevertheless, his view did appear to apply well to Germany (his main example), and also to the US, France, Russia and Japan. The first two countries were second and third, behind Britain, and the remainder were numbers four to six in Lenin's list of the top imperialist powers in the early twentieth century.[22] Five out of six was not a bad mark, but Hilferding's method of analysis was mistaken.

Hilferding's concept of finance capital is defined from the perspective of the *national* economy, rather than that of the world economy. He argues that the monopolisation process results in a block of capital, 'finance capital' managed by the banks, the owners of which favour a powerful state that can implement their wishes at home and, especially, abroad.[23] Hilferding does take the international capitalist economy into account, but he does not relate the form taken by 'finance capital' to the position that each country has in the world market. This is why his concept does not include Britain, and also leads to a one-sided understanding of what was going on elsewhere.

With Britain being the first industrial country and in control of a huge commercial Empire, UK-based capital was under far less pressure to form cartels and trusts, or to develop strong links between banks and industrialists in order to compete against rivals. In 1905, well before the global pre-eminence of US corporations, there were already far fewer very large British companies than American ones.[24] Much of the export of capital from the UK was in the form of trade finance, bank loans and bond investments that facilitated the export of British commodities. The situation was different for capitalists in countries that were more recent entrants into the world market. Even so, their formation of trusts, etc., did not necessarily imply that the banking arm of any given group was in control. Japan's *zaibatsu* (Mitsubishi, Mitsui, Sumitomo and Yasuda) were examples of a closely linked group of companies, with intra-group cooperation and cross-shareholdings between heavy industry, light manufacturing, insurance, trading and banking. The bank was important for mobilising capital in these groups, given its role in the credit markets, but it did not necessarily run the group: it depended on business from the other companies as much as they depended on its funds and financial services. In the case of the US, although J. P. Morgan's business portfolio seemed the quintessential bank-dominated form of finance capital, his rival Rockefeller had financial operations that grew out of the huge profits from his monopoly of the oil business.

The main problem with Hilferding's argument in this context is that his notion of 'finance capital' misrepresents how the rule of capital is expressed. In particular, his focus upon the banks exaggerates their role and leads to a political view that the capitalist economy could be tamed if only the state controlled the banks. Although in very different circumstances from those he may have envisaged in 1910 when *Finance Capital* was published, Hilferding became Germany's finance minister for several months in 1923 and again in 1928–29. His attempts to exercise state control were consistent with his theory of the capitalist economy: he thought monopolistic trends in capital accumulation would, or could, lead to an 'organised capitalism'.[25] This view also has some resonance today, but it does not take into account how monopolists cannot control the capitalist market even within a single country (Hilferding's main focus), let alone on a global scale. For example, competition is not eliminated in markets dominated by a handful of big players. They may not compete much on price, but they will use advertising, patents, deals with suppliers and retailers, buying out rivals, etc., as means to consolidate their market positions. Even the biggest companies eventually come under pressure from existing or new rivals. What for years might look like a cosy cartel can then become a fight for survival.

Financial parasitism

There is a strong relationship between finance and 'parasitism' in Marxist theory, as developed by Hilferding and Lenin. Given that the financial sector is not productive of value and mainly trades currencies and interest rates along with the creation and trading of financial securities, it seems to make sense to cast 'finance' as being parasitic on the productive sector of the economy – not forgetting that the source of the profits made in the latter is the exploitation of productive labourers! However, it may seem surprising that Marx did not raise the issue of parasitism when discussing the money-dealing or commercial capitalists, since they buy and sell the commodities of the productive capitalists or take a dealing margin. They produce no value and their costs and profits are deductions from the total social value produced. Are they parasitic too?

Marx's view was that money-dealing and commercial capital were *not* parasitic because their operations facilitated the productive circuit of capital, enabling the buying and selling that helped the productive apparatus function in the capitalist market system. By contrast, interest-bearing capital is not only unproductive, it is also *outside* the circuit of producing, selling and buying commodities, and instead has a distinctive M – M' circuit: advancing money and getting more money back, with no regard for what happens in between. For example, even though a bank's loan of funds for investment will obviously have an impact upon the accumulation of capital, it is the industrial and commercial capitalists who are involved in the production and circulation of commodities and the money-dealing capitalists who facilitate the circulation process. Since the bank's advance of money-capital as interest-bearing capital is outside that circuit, the deduction of interest from the profits of that system can be seen as parasitical. The capitalists advancing the money-capital in this way make up the social stratum of parasites in Marx's sense.

The large owners and controllers of money-capital, including the top executives of corporations, can be seen as the upper stratum of this 'financial aristocracy'. In lesser degrees of nobility beneath them are the senior executives of banks, top brokers, asset managers, and managers of insurance companies, pension funds and hedge funds, among others. In my own experience of financial institutions, the status of each was directly related to its size, but it was always the case that the pure brokers – those who merely matched up the buyers and sellers, taking on no market risk of their own – were at the bottom of the hierarchy. Without too much exaggeration, it can be said that while the brokers took the bankers for a drink in a City bar, the bankers took the asset managers, fund managers and corporation executives to the Wimbledon tennis tournament or Premier League football matches. The bank clients claimed that their business jollies and weekends away to attractive destinations were justified by them attending an 'important' conference to listen to people like me talk about the financial markets.

The dealers in the banks, the 'risk takers', saw themselves as the real workhorses, delivering the profits. The brokers were, at best, seen as a necessary evil, only required to line up clients for the dealers if their own sales people could not manage it. Meanwhile, the dealers' opinions of the economists in the dealing room varied from the obscene to the temporarily grateful, depending on how the latest piece of

advice had cashed out. If an economist actually took on some personal dealing risk, as I did on occasion, but which was very unusual
in banks, then there was a certain credibility to be gained from being
willing to 'put your money where your mouth is' and take the pain of
a potential loss on a deal done.

Marx's analysis in *Capital* described interest-bearing capital as
being parasitic, rather than money-dealing capital, although there are
many hybrid forms of the two types. However, this perspective does
not take into account the reality of an imperialist world economy,
based upon a hierarchy of economic power between different countries. This is not such a surprise, given that Marx had still to complete
his analysis and that he was writing in the third quarter of the nineteenth century, before several important economic trends had fully
developed. All forms of financial operation can potentially assist in
the transfer of surplus value *from one country to another* and so contribute to increasing the power of the dominant countries. I would
consider this to be a form of parasitism, one that follows from considering the structure of the world economy, but involves a different use
of the term from Marx's own.

Global parasitism, investment, trade and finance

Lenin sees parasitism as a defining aspect of imperialism considered
as a stage of capitalist development. But his use of the term is both
narrower and broader than Marx's:

> Monopolies, oligarchy, the striving for domination and not for freedom,
> the exploitation of an increasing number of small or weak nations by a
> handful of the richest or most powerful nations – all these have given
> birth to those distinctive characteristics of imperialism which compel
> us to define it as parasitic or decaying capitalism. More and more
> prominently there emerges, as one of the tendencies of imperialism, the
> creation of the 'rentier state', the usurer state, in which the bourgeoisie
> to an ever-increasing degree lives on the proceeds of capital exports and
> by 'clipping coupons'.[26]

Lenin's focus is on the *international* dimension of parasitism, whereas in *Capital* Marx had developed the concept only in relation to the capitalist system as a whole, considered as a unit. For Lenin, a distinguishing feature of parasitism is that an imperialist country's bourgeoisie increasingly 'lives on the proceeds of capital export' *and* the revenues from 'clipping coupons' from investments in other countries. The proceeds of capital export would include the profits of foreign investments in industrial and commercial enterprises. The revenue from 'clipping coupons' referred to the practice at that time of cutting the coupons from bond certificates that had been purchased and presenting them to a bank for payment. Only this latter form directly corresponds with Marx's concept of parasitism. But Lenin, following an earlier analysis by Hobson, made the further distinction of stressing the growing importance of *foreign* payments on capital advanced.[27] The available evidence backed this view. In the 1899–1913 period, the UK had a huge inflow of net investment income averaging 6.8 per cent of GDP.[28] In addition, net services income, including that from shipping, insurance and financial dealing, was a lower, but still very significant, 4.3 per cent of GDP. Even if the foreign payments made to the UK were not all *interest* payments, they included surplus value produced in *other* countries.

The focus on revenues from foreign loans and investments was probably more valid a century ago than it is today. In the contemporary global economy there are important *additional* items of foreign income for rich and powerful countries. One stems from the capacity of major corporations to use their monopoly power to 'outsource' production to poor countries where labour costs are much lower, even allowing for possibly lower productivity.[29] Another source of revenues is derived from international financial transactions. The latter will be detailed in Chapter 8 for the UK, but a number of other countries also benefit from this kind of operation, and other types too, as discussed in Chapter 7.

Lenin's argument was neither that the bulk of all the interest or other money received by money-capitalists or rentiers came from foreign countries, nor that *all* the foreign countries involved were weak and dominated by the major powers. Interest-bearing capital

is advanced worldwide. A 'rich and powerful' versus 'weak and dominated' country division occurs nevertheless, to the extent that the
weaker countries will tend to have smaller, less developed economies
and financial systems, with a lower volume of funds to lend out, so
they are usually more dependent on borrowing funds from elsewhere.
However, rich countries also lend funds to other rich countries whose
domestic financial systems may not provide what their capitalists
need. An international division of labour is thus bound to develop
in the sphere of financial operations as much as in industry and
commerce.

In terms of finance, this global division of labour includes not
only the purely interest-bearing forms of capital but also the money-
dealing forms. The more powerful a country's industrial and commercial relationships in the world economy, the more likely it is that
its money-dealing capital operations will grow – along with insurance, foreign exchange and trade finance. These, in turn, spur the
growth of interest-bearing capital, especially as capitalists become
wealthier. The largest financial institutions will also tend to be located
in the richest countries. Pension funds and insurance policies are far
more prevalent there than in poorer countries, while there will also
be a larger group of wealthy people who can invest in funds with asset
managers, do deals through brokers, or who have significant money
deposited with banks. For example, in 2014 the US had some *14
million* residents with wealth in excess of a million dollars, compared
to barely one million in China, where the population is more than
four times larger.[30]

If companies in a particular country have an advantage in providing financial services, this will be linked to their ability to tie these
services together with advances of money-capital. The early strength
of the City of London in providing long-term investment finance,
mainly through its flotation of bonds but also its issuance of equities,
was very much dependent upon London-based financiers being able
to maintain a liquid market in these securities. Stock exchange jobbers
could borrow short-term funds to finance their holdings of equities
and bonds, and could hope to sell out of their positions when necessary with less risk of capital losses. The Bank of England supported

that market as the cash provider to the banks and discount houses.[31] An international dealing mechanism was put in place as a result of the commercial financial operations established by City practice, and that practice grew out of the power of the British Empire.

Imperialism's relationship to monopoly is often viewed in terms of the large industrial and commercial corporations that are linked to the major powers. But the same thing also happens with companies in the financial sphere. Being bigger can also mean being able to provide services or capital at a lower cost, or at least being in a more influential market position. The ability to secure a larger scale of operations depends not only on the national market, but also on the international market, and here the position and power of the national state is a vital factor. As capitalism expands to create a world market, the operations of financial companies expand alongside those of commerce and industry. In this, too, they receive support from their national base – if only in the national currency to which they have privileged access via the home central bank. Access to the home currency is commonly their area of advantage over banks and financial institutions in other countries.

For example, a US bank setting up in France will do so initially in order to service US companies doing business in France. It will have access to euro currency operations and European Central Bank finance, directly or via the Banque de France, since it is accepted as part of the local monetary system, but it will have no advantage in euro finance compared to local French banks and may not even be allowed to take euro deposits from non-corporate residents. Normally, it will also have less capacity to fund euro operations than the principal French or euro-based banks, since Europe is not its home territory, nor the site for the allocation of a large share of its capital. However, the typical US bank will often be able to offer better (larger-scale or cheaper) access to US dollar funding and financing operations than French banks, both to US companies *and* to other companies, because of its links with the US banking system and the funding operations of the Federal Reserve. In the same way, this will be true for banks of other nationalities setting up in a foreign country offering financial services in their own national currency.

Financial companies have an advantage in expanding their foreign operations when *their countries* enjoy a dominant position in global trade and to the extent that international transactions are denominated in their own national currencies. The financial power of an institution rests on its having privileged access to credit markets and the ability to undertake large-scale transactions. But these aspects of economic power are *external* to any particular company in the sense that they do not depend simply on its own capabilities. Rather, they depend more upon the economic power of the states to which they belong.

This form of economic power is different from the power of a state to make favourable trade and investment deals with other countries. It operates far less overtly and appears to others simply as the fact of having to use the prevailing infrastructure for conducting (financial) business. To do otherwise would be like trying to travel from city A to city B without using the connecting roads, railways, ports or airports.

Financial power, or the lack of it, becomes most evident in a crisis, as a number of Asian countries, including Indonesia, South Korea and Thailand, found in 1997–98, and as others have discovered both before and since. In the case of South Korea, for several years before 1997 it saw a huge flow of international funds into its currency and securities, since these offered higher yields than elsewhere. When the bubble burst, the earlier fund inflows exited and the country's currency, financial markets and economy sank, making it dependent upon external financing. The IMF imposed drastic policy changes, causing the economy to collapse further and opening it up to more foreign investment. In the euro zone, Greece has experienced a similar vulnerability since 2010, despite being the member of a privileged club. Greece's chronic and large deficits on its external current account and in its public sector finances were funded easily in the good times, but could no longer be supported when the financial markets turned after 2008. Greece has since witnessed the destruction of its economy and mass unemployment, with its GDP dropping by a quarter between 2008 and 2014.

Despite the significance of such crises, my focus here is on the day-to-day operations of the financial system. Crises invariably leave some countries in charge and others as mere supplicants hoping they can do a deal. Those in charge of the financial mechanism retain their access to large-scale funds, through the banking system or via the stock market, especially in the currencies used for international business transactions. In this way, among others, an imperialist country can appropriate value from other countries via the financial system, as will be detailed further in later chapters.

Who reaps the returns?

Financial securities are often seen as mysterious things, far removed from everyday life and existing only for financiers, 'banksters', oligarchs and other usurpers of social wealth. But *many millions* of people, from a surprisingly wide section of the population, own equities and bonds, especially in the rich countries. As one might expect, the richest people own the bulk of equities, bonds and other securities. But many other people also own them, both directly and, more commonly, via savings plans, investment funds, endowment policies and pension schemes.

US Federal Reserve data for 2013 reveal that the slogan of the Occupy Movement of 2011–12, 'the 99 per cent versus the 1 per cent', is more than a few percentage points adrift when it comes to economic divisions, at least in terms of *financial assets* owned. Ownership of equities and bonds also means receiving income from dividends and interest payments, not simply having the wealth they represent. The data show that 93 per cent of the US families in the top 10 per cent of the income distribution owned equities, both directly and indirectly via investment and pension funds. That is close to 29 million people! Half of those were in families that had equity holdings of more than $281,700.[32] For the next level down, in the upper 80–90th percentile of the income distribution, the median holding of equities was $69,000, and this sum fell just as sharply lower down the income ranking.

Less detailed reports are available for the UK than for the US, but there is a similar pattern of wealth distribution in the form of financial assets owned. In 2005, 15 per cent of the UK population, or around nine million people, owned equities either directly or via mutual funds.[33] Other data show that UK individuals *directly* owned 11.5 per cent of the value of UK equities at the end of 2010, worth £204.5bn, excluding any holdings via investment funds, etc.[34] While the median net financial wealth of UK households in 2010–12 was estimated at just below £6,000, including cash savings, bond and equity holdings minus financial liabilities (but excluding mortgage debt), there were many households with significant assets. Most financial wealth is held in the form of bonds and equities; only a small proportion is in the form of cash deposits.

In 2010–12, a quarter of all households in Britain had zero or *negative* net financial wealth, in other words, net debts. Just over half the households had net wealth of zero to £50,000, while 9 per cent had from £50,00 to £100,000. Twelve per cent of households had more than £100,000.[35] So, of a UK population of 64 million, around seven million people (including children) were living in a household with more than £100,000 net financial wealth. In the UK at least, rather than '1 per cent versus 99 per cent', on the basis of financial wealth it is instead: a quarter of the population is broke, half has little and the remainder is doing OK, or very well.

These figures *exclude* equity and bond holdings that individuals have via pension funds. In the UK, pension fund assets make up 39 per cent of total household wealth compared to just 11 per cent for financial wealth. Property wealth makes up *another* 39 per cent. Although the distribution of pension assets is similarly skewed in favour of the wealthy, as in the US, the diversity of pension assets makes it difficult to give a representative figure.[36] This will nevertheless amount to a further stake in the revenues flowing to financial assets, and to property, for a significant proportion of the UK population, as elsewhere in the rich countries. This provides a clue to where the direct economic interests of a key segment of the population lie, and a material basis for its political outlook.

Finance as a normal part of the system

Two features of capitalist finance stand out: credit creation by banks and the formation of fictitious capital as financial securities. These appear to break the link between the production of value in the economy and the resources at the command of capitalists. However, this is not so much a link that is broken as one that is *stretched*. In the case of credit expansion by the banks, loan losses end up showing the strain. The markets for financial securities also show divergent values from whatever may have been invested, and the mechanism to generate the prices of bonds and equities has even less of a relationship with production. Yet financial securities act both as a way of enforcing capitalist market dictates and as a means to extend the market power of the big owners of such securities. They also mean that the wealth and income of millions of people is linked to these securities, which will colour their political outlook and judgement about what is the 'good' or 'economic' to do.

The capitalist laws of the market are only modified, not abolished, by the financial system. This can lead to bigger booms, and bigger busts, than might have happened otherwise. The key point for now is that the extra power in the world economy that the financial system provides is made available mostly to those with privileged access to finance: the corporations and states of the richer, more powerful countries. This is an important means by which the major powers maintain their economic privileges: they can use financial markets to control world resources and siphon off the value created elsewhere. In doing so they need not necessarily depend upon military force, or upon direct political pressure. The mechanism of global finance appears to be a natural consequence of a natural capitalist market system: a perfect invisibility cloak for the process of value extraction.

5.

The World Hierarchy

Who runs the world? Surely, it is the United States. America has the biggest economy, many of the largest companies, and the world's most powerful military machine with bases in more than sixty countries. Nevertheless, there are other factors to consider. Firstly, although the US has exercised hegemony for decades, the balance of power in the world nevertheless changes over time. For example, the US did not have the same dominance before the First World War, and even between the wars its economic power was constrained by the political power of the British Empire. Furthermore, despite its ability and willingness to engage in mass destruction, it was fought to a standstill by China in Korea in 1953 and it lost the Vietnam War in 1975. History shows that the hegemonic power does not always prevail and the role of other countries must also be taken into account. Secondly, the question 'Who runs the world?' implicitly assumes that the capitalist global economy is managed in an orderly way, rather than being an anarchic system in which rival countries vie for position. A dominant state such as the US is indeed more able to influence events in its favour. But as the shambles in the Middle East and North Africa shows, that is not the same thing as managing the world.

This raises the question of how to gauge a country's economic and political status. I have chosen five measures to do this: the size of a country's economy, its ownership of foreign assets, the international prominence of its banking sector, the status of its currency in foreign exchange trading, and its level of military spending. Power is not expressed in one dimension only, and these measures capture its different aspects, presenting a plausible and striking picture.[1] The chapter begins by looking at the positions of different countries in the world hierarchy and goes on to explain how the five measures are related, drawing out the links between national states, the major corporations, and the financial system in the global economy.

The premier league

Few of the 200 or so countries in the world count for anything in terms of having much power or influence outside their own borders. The ones who do count for something, around twenty or so, play an important role in world trade and finance and are home to the world's largest companies. Some of them also send their warships, bombers, missiles, drones, soldiers, 'advisors', military aid and private mercenaries to threaten or kill people in other countries, so this sort of power is far from being only economy-related.

The first measure used to gauge economic and political power is nominal GDP, taken from IMF data for 2014.[2] GDP, or Gross Domestic Product, measures economic output, but it has some drawbacks. For example, it counts the value attributed to a particular country, but this is not the same as the value created *in* that country.[3] For example, if the GDP measure is 100, then it might be that only 95 is produced within the country's boundaries and five comes from outside, but is mistakenly included in the 100. Yet the degree to which the GDP measure is boosted by value appropriated from elsewhere, or is reduced by value lost to other countries, means that it is even more useful as an index of power. Global economic power implies a privileged position, and weak countries often service strong ones by providing them with cheap imports based on minuscule wage costs.[4] Of course, countries with a big GDP are not necessarily rich – they might have a large population with a low average income, such as India or China. Nevertheless, a high GDP ranking indicates that the country has weight, and potentially some influence, in the world economy.[5]

In 2014, the top ten countries according to their GDP rankings were: the US, China (including Hong Kong), Japan, Germany, the UK, France, Brazil, Italy, India and Russia. China's GDP was 61 per cent of that of the US, although China's population was more than four times bigger. Japan's GDP was a little over a quarter of that for the US, Germany's a little under a quarter. The UK and France have a similar sized GDP. Italy's is around 25 per cent below France's, while India, especially, as well as Brazil and Russia, have still lower GDPs despite their much larger population sizes.

For the second measure, I use figures for the stock of outward foreign direct investment (FDI) owned by each country at the end of 2013.[6] FDI usually means an investment in a foreign company (but it also includes property assets) amounting to more than 10 per cent of the total. This will not fully reflect a country's international economic power, but the FDI data can also be used as a simple index of one way in which companies in one country exploit workers in others, and it is difficult to find usable measures for the other more indirect, commercial relationships, or for portfolio investment and banking relationships. For example, FDI figures exclude the privileges and benefits arising from a country's commercial and trading relation-ships that may have little to do with actually *owning* companies and property in other countries. Neither do the FDI numbers reflect the power, influence and revenues associated with owning foreign port-folio assets (equities and bonds) or being in a position to extend or deny credit to foreign companies and countries. However, taking just the FDI figures alone, the US is clearly in pole position. At the end of 2013, it had FDI assets worth $6.3 trillion, compared to a much lower $1.9 trillion for the UK in second place, with $1.7 trillion for Germany and $1.6 trillion for France in third and fourth places, respectively.

Unfortunately, FDI figures for China are difficult to interpret. If the data for China is added to that for Hong Kong, this would give a number in excess of the UK's, but only due to the amount of invest-ment occurring *between* China and Hong Kong, so not really outside Chinese territory. Given that Hong Kong is part of China, it would make sense to count FDI from mainland China going outside Hong Kong and that from Hong Kong going outside mainland China, but data are not readily available to do this. Reports suggest that the bulk of Hong Kong FDI is into China, while only some of China's FDI is likely to be into Hong Kong. I have only included mainland China's

FDI figures in the China index measure, which is probably closer to the underlying figure for external investment, but will understate it.

The next two measures focus on global financial relationships. The more a country is involved in financial mechanisms, the more this will usually reflect its importance in how the world economy works. In particular, the more a country is involved in lending to or borrowing funds from others, or the more its currency is used for international trade and finance, the more prominent a role it will tend to play in world affairs.

For the third measure of international status, I use data from the Bank for International Settlements for the relative size of the international assets *and* the liabilities of banks *operating in* particular countries.[7] International assets are what banks in one country have lent to other countries; liabilities are what they have borrowed from others. Both can reflect economic power and influence. Being able to lend funds puts a country in an important creditor position, but being able to borrow on a large scale usually also reflects a country's world status and the degree to which it is accepted by other lenders. It does not necessarily mean that the country is vulnerable as a debtor to foreign banks or institutions, although that can also happen.

Taking data for the end of 2014, the top five countries on the international banking index are: the UK, the US, France, Japan and Germany. This is the one measure of power where the UK exceeds the US, and the only one in which the US is not in first position. Admittedly, this (slightly) exaggerates the UK position, since not all UK-based banks are UK-owned or controlled. However, this does not detract from the fact that the UK is the main centre of international banking, and a separate BIS measure of assets and liabilities by bank national *ownership* also shows that UK-owned banks have a scale of international business that is not far behind that of US-owned banks.

The fourth measure is the importance of a country's currency in global foreign exchange trading. This reflects how far a country's currency is used beyond its own borders, whether by foreign central banks, financial investors, companies involved in international trade, or ordinary people. Overwhelmingly, the US dollar is the major currency in this regard: in 2013 it was on one side of 87 per cent of all currency trading, with the euro at just 33 per cent.[8] However, while the US dollar is the national currency of one country, the euro is not. There is also an unresolved political divergence within the euro currency bloc, where richer parts of the supposed union baulk at funding its poorer parts. So it makes sense to divide the euro's foreign exchange importance between the nineteen member countries. This is done according to their relative GDPs, since the distribution of political power in the euro area is roughly related to GDP, as is the share of each country in the capital of the European Central Bank.

As a result, the top five currencies in 2013 were those of the following countries: the US, Japan, the UK, Germany and Australia. The UK's sterling took a share of 14 per cent versus Japan's 26 per cent. China would come tenth if its currency, the renminbi, were added to the Hong Kong dollar. Since 2010, global trading in the mainland China currency has been increasing dramatically.

These two latter measures of international financial power nevertheless miss out some important factors that are less easy to quantify or put in an index. A country may be able to use the financial system to appropriate value from the global economy even when this does not depend on banks operating in its territory, or from the rest of the world's use of its currency.[9] Nevertheless, the top countries in these measures also rank highly in these other forms of financial power.

The fifth and final measure is the size of military spending by each country in 2014.[10] The military spending might be for internal repression rather than for external power projection, but the six biggest military spenders in the world include five who are also the *permanent* members of the UN Security Council with a power of veto over UN decisions. As one might expect, the US is the biggest spender by far, at $610bn in 2014, followed by China at $216bn and Russia at $84bn. Saudi Arabia, surprisingly, comes next with $81bn. This figure largely reflects Saudi Arabia's extravagant payments to western powers, mainly the US, France and the UK, in deals for their military hardware in return for political support. Nevertheless, the Saudis do use the weapons. In recent years Saudi Arabia has actively been involved in regional repression, from crushing popular dissent in Bahrain in 2011 to its intervention in Yemen in 2015. France and the UK are in fifth and sixth place on the military spending list, with similar amounts of $62bn and $60bn, respectively. At the other end of the spectrum, 120 of the 143 countries in SIPRI's database spent less than $10bn on the military. Perhaps with the exception of Saudi Arabia, this looks like a good measure to use as one indicator of world power.[11]

Chart 5.1 brings together all the above information for twenty countries.[12] In line with the other measures discussed in this book, the results for this index of power show a small number of countries towering over the others. If the chart also showed the remaining 135 countries in the database, most of their index bars would be barely distinguishable from the horizontal axis of the graph! There are 118 countries out of the total 155 included whose index value is less than 1.0. By comparison, the index value for the US is 96, and 34 for the UK.

The US stands out as the top power on four of the five measures, but it falls behind the UK as a centre for international banking. In total, the UK remains a distant second behind the US, but it may be surprising that it is ahead of Germany, the dominant power in Europe. This is due to Britain's high scores for banks and foreign direct investment assets. Each of the longstanding members of the G7 group of countries is in the top eleven.

China (ISO code CN) is in third place, well ahead of the other members of the so-called BRICS – Brazil, Russia, India and South Africa (ISO codes BR, RU, IN, ZA, respectively). China's index value is only partly helped by the inclusion of Hong Kong in the data, as previously explained. In all index categories, from GDP to foreign exchange to military spending, China is likely to rise further in the power rankings in future years. This would be the culmination of the biggest shake up of the 'western' dominated world power structure since the end of the Second World War.[13]

The global position of a country can only properly be understood by assessing its relationships with others. Nevertheless, these index values provide a useful summary of the distribution of economic and political power. The chapter began with the question 'Who runs the world?' The index helps answer that question by highlighting the key role of the US – confirming not only that it is 'big', but also that there

Chart 5.1 The global pecking order, 2013–14

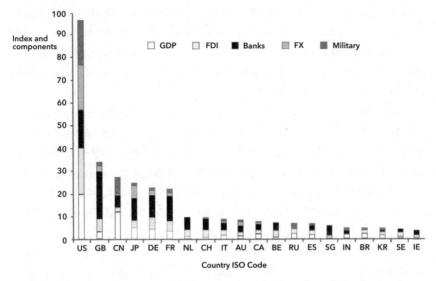

Note: The height of each bar is given by the country's total index value, which is broken down into the five components, with equal weights. Two-letter ISO codes identify countries. Note that CN is China, CH is Switzerland and DE is Germany.

Sources: Details are given in this chapter

are particular ways in which it is big. In turn, it shows that a small number of other countries also have important positions. In some respects, other key countries are not so far behind the US.

However, what the index cannot do is to reveal how the different dimensions of influence work, and the way they can interact with each other to reinforce a country's power. To get to grips with this means understanding how capitalism, while being an international system, is also bound up with the nation-state. This is especially true when it comes to financial relationships.

Capitalism and the state

The relationship of capitalist companies to particular nation-states can be tricky to unravel. Take the case of BP plc, a major world energy company. Formerly called British Petroleum, it developed out of the Anglo-Persian Oil Company, with operations based upon the discovery of oil in Iran. In 1913, the British government took control of just over 50 per cent of the company's shares, as part of a strategy to move the British navy's fuel supply from coal to oil. By the end of the 1980s, the government's stake had been sold and BP now has operations in some eighty countries. UK residents own only 40 per cent of its shares, so is it really 'British'?

This kind of question comes up all the time for big corporations, because of the international expansion of capital. The answer is not determined simply by looking at who owns the company, although the evidence does suggest that British-based capitalists and investment funds still own an important block of BP shares, with other key owners being US-based investment funds and the Kuwait Investment Office. The 'nationality' of BP can also be gauged by the fact that its headquarters is in the UK and the main location for the trading of its shares is the London Stock Exchange. Just as important to note is the close cooperation between BP plc and the British government. For example, John Browne, chief executive of the company from 1995 to 2007, used the political influence of Prime Minister Tony Blair to facilitate his corporate plans to control energy resources in Russia.[14] So, yes, BP is 'British', given its business and political connections, even if its top managers are not always Brits.

Big capitalist companies usually have significant international business operations, but they also depend upon maintaining a relationship with the national state. 'International' companies are usually national companies that have expanded beyond their original structure through mergers, takeovers and foreign investment. But while this can sometimes change the nationality of a company, it normally becomes clear that the change is from, for example, German to British, or British to American, etc., not from British or American to 'international'.

The evolution of a particular company might involve close cooperation between more than one country's capitalists – as with Royal-Dutch Shell and Unilever, which are based both in the UK and the Netherlands. But such fifty-fifty arrangements are unusual and probably only manageable when the states in question have compatible views. It is also interesting that a major capitalist might decide to *change nationality* if the bulk of his or her business interests ends up outside their country of origin and support from another state is important. For example, Rupert Murdoch, Chairman of News Corporation, changed his citizenship from Australian to American in 1985. Murdoch's business strategy was to move into television, and his purchase of the American Fox Broadcasting Company required that he become a US citizen.

A corporation may also decide to list its shares on a foreign stock exchange in order to secure greater access to funds in a larger market, or a more prominent global ranking for the company's corporate assets. In the past two decades, it has been common for all major stock exchanges to encourage listings and share offerings by companies seeking large volumes of funds from international sources. For this reason, London's FTSE 100 equity index does not represent the *domestic* British economy or even consist only of British companies. It includes companies that operate worldwide and that are also owned by a wide range of foreign capitalists. However, by the end of 2013, it was still the case that UK residents – individuals, financial institutions and others – held almost half of the value of shares quoted on the London Stock Exchange, one of the world's biggest.[15]

If the issue of a company's 'nationality' is not straightforward, there is nevertheless still a national core of companies, and a nation-state will tend to back those corporations that are viewed as its 'own'. This may not be guaranteed in every case, since one company's deals may conflict with those of others, or its demands may be seen as incompatible with the 'national interest'. However, capitalist companies can depend more consistently upon their nation-states to back them up in foreign business relationships – a natural reflex – than they can rely upon the foreign recipients of bribes, or other inducements, to be able to do the same. This does not mean that capitalist companies are patriotic or sentimental about 'home'; they will invariably make hard-headed business calculations. And sometimes these will conflict with the 'national interest', as with transactions made with countries that are considered enemies of national policy. Examples are many. Recent instances include European banks dealing with Iran in defiance of the sanctions policy agreed by EU member states, or European companies

doing deals with Russia that evade the EU sanctions imposed following the conflict in Ukraine. In earlier years, companies like Shell and
BP dealt with Rhodesia (now Zimbabwe) when trade was officially
restricted by UK sanctions.[16]

Even the growth of international trade and investment – 'globalisation' – does not mean that corporations can avoid their dependence
on the nation-state to which they nominally belong. As one conservative US columnist put it:

> the next time [US corporation] IBM China gets in trouble in China,
> call Jiang Zemin [then President of China] for help. And the next time
> Congress closes another military base in Asia, call Microsoft's navy to
> secure the sea-lanes of the Pacific. And the next time Congress wants to
> close more consulates and embassies, call Amazon.com to order a new
> passport.[17]

He could have added: 'the next time US corporations complain about
infringement of intellectual property rights, call on McDonald's to
refuse to sell Big Macs to the country concerned'. The capitalist corporation clearly depends on the power of the nation-state, even if it
is also inclined for good business reasons to do things its government might not like. It is a bitter political irony, making a mockery
of Marx's call for the 'workers of the world' to unite, that a common
theme in trade union criticism of big business is that it is unpatriotic.

The more powerful capitalist states can also be key players in the
world economy, setting the terms of business both for international
trade and for cross-border investment flows. While a company will
set the price of the product or service it provides, that price may be
subject to an import tariff and local taxation, or the product may not
even be saleable in another country if there are government standards
it fails to meet. Or a company wanting to invest in another country
may face restrictions on which parts of the economy are open to
foreign investment. These are limitations on the operation of the
market set by state policy. Such policies can be negotiated between
different governments, but this also gives room for one state to put
pressure on another.

Corporations headquartered in particular countries will tend to be the main ones benefiting from the actions of their respective governments, also making it easier for them to consolidate their position in the world economy. In turn, they will contribute to the country's economic income and employment, and will generate tax revenues for the government. While companies do not necessarily look upon their *national* economy as the main source of their profits, the national government will be concerned with the viability of the domestic economy. The state will mediate in this process and attempt to find policies that facilitate *both* a profitable expansion of its capitalists into the world market *and* the growth of domestic business. This is why states implement policies to attract inward capital investment and at the same time support an outflow of capital.

There is then a two-way process: the more resources are available to the national state, the more powerful it becomes, to the potential benefit of all 'national' capitalists and often also to the national population at large. There is an important symbiotic relationship between the nation-state and corporate power, one that can back up, or undermine, the power of some countries at the expense of others in the world market. For example, if a state is under economic pressure, it may have to scale back its military spending if it cannot be afforded, a situation that British policy-makers had to accept in the strategic decision to withdraw militarily from 'East of Suez' in the late 1960s.[18]

The state and finance

The state plays a key role for capitalist business in setting the framework for the national monetary system and in managing monetary institutions, especially banks. What is the 'legal tender', the currency acceptable for paying wages or taxes, or buying goods and services within national boundaries? How can the banking and credit system to be organised in a way that does not disrupt business calculations and transactions? Such issues are determined by the state. State regulation of the money and credit system is important for all capitalist economies, and this can also extend the power of the state, and its corporations, beyond the national sphere.

Historically, state regulation of national money occurred before central banks were established. But central banks eventually emerged everywhere as the main state tool for managing the monetary system. The oldest central banks were initially set up as private companies with government backing, for example, Sveriges Riksbank of Sweden and the Bank of England, in the late seventeenth century. Central banks were a means for the state both to issue currency and to raise the money to fund state spending, especially for wars. The instability of a system consisting of purely private banks also led to central banks taking on the role of 'lender of last resort' to banks in trouble, although in the case of the US Federal Reserve System this was introduced only in 1913. Whatever the fantasies of 'libertarian' pundits in the US, no major capitalist company wants to operate in an economy where every bank issues its own currency, or where the paper currency issued has to be fully backed by gold to prevent 'corruption' by the government.

Private capitalist banks also gain a special status vis-à-vis other capitalist companies in this kind of system. They normally have unique access to central bank credit, although they must usually also meet official criteria to get a licence before they can begin operations, in particular if they intend to take deposits from the public. In the UK, for example, money *lending* is lightly regulated, but it is far more difficult to get a *deposit taking* licence from the Bank of England. The debtor need not worry if the creditor goes bust (the money has been already lent and the terms of a loan are usually fixed), but the depositor has much more reason to worry if the bank holding his or her deposits is under threat. One bank's failure will also raise the risk of others failing and could cause trouble in the national (or international) payments system. This can even be true for a smaller bank, as with the UK's Northern Rock in 2007. The UK government had to guarantee bank deposits and the Bank of England extended massive loans to Northern Rock and others.[19]

The links between capitalist companies and the nation-state help explain the different status of countries within the world economy.

This also gives an *economic* definition of the term 'imperialism'. My argument is that imperialism is *not* the same thing as colonial rule, and should not be understood only in terms of some countries dominating others through military or political pressure. A country does not have to rule politically over another for it to be imperialist, and imperialism did not die out with the end (almost) of colonialism.[20] Today, imperialism is characterised by economic privileges in the world economy, reinforced by monopolistic control of industry, commerce and finance, and backed up by powerful states, directly or indirectly. The stark reality of a global hierarchy of power represented in Chart 5.1 is a useful counter to news media euphemisms about the 'international community'.

Monopoly and imperialism

Capitalists in dominant countries have a variety of methods for exploiting other countries. For example, a powerful state can undermine industries in weaker nations, making them dependent on the major country's exports, as with Britain's moves against India's textile industry in the eighteenth and nineteenth centuries. Stronger countries may also restrict the ability of weaker ones to export to them, especially with subsidies on their own agricultural products, as in the US and the European Union today. Powerful countries can try to undermine 'unfriendly' governments elsewhere, or bring about what nowadays is called 'regime change', both to protect the interests of their capitalists or to force through new avenues of profitable investment. Such cases are important, but they are examples of *political* power and fall outside the more distinct *economic mechanism* for ensuring imperialist gains. Force, extortion or robbery may bring a high return, and they are important features of imperialism.[21] But they are not the *modus operandi* of an economic system any more than piracy can be seen as a mode of production.

To see what is special about imperialism as an economic system, it is worth noting Lenin's characterisation in his famous pamphlet *Imperialism*, written during the First World War. For Lenin, the factor underlying the economics of imperialism was monopoly: 'If it were necessary to give the briefest possible definition of imperialism we should have to say that imperialism is the monopoly stage of capitalism.'[22] But he is careful to relate this concept to the capitalist system as a whole, not simply to monopolies on a national stage. The tendency towards monopoly is a natural result of competition and capital accumulation and, at first sight, this may appear to have little to do with any separate stage of capitalism. Instead, the process by which large corporations come to dominate different areas of production, commerce and finance could be seen simply as a later phase of capitalist development with no clear dividing line from an earlier stage. However, the important distinction comes from looking at developments in the *world* market.

Imperialism involves the control of the global economy by groups of monopolistic companies. These can exert power over the operation of markets, whether by price fixing, by cutting prices to drive out competitors or by other means. For example, one clue to the nature of the world economy today is that the number of mobile phones sold worldwide in 2014 was 1.9 billion, but 41 per cent of these were made by just *three* companies: Samsung (South Korea), Apple and Microsoft (both US). Add just another eight companies and the total market share of this still small group rises to two-thirds.[23] This despite the many changes in mobile phone technology over the last three decades, which might have been thought to work against such monopolistic developments.

Before the 1980s, major countries invested in the rest of the world directly, where they owned a significant stake in foreign companies, plantations or property, or in portfolio investments, where they owned foreign equities and bonds, or perhaps just in terms of foreign loans. But a key feature of the world economy in recent decades has been the formation of 'global value chains'.[24] These occur when international companies employ foreign suppliers to deliver goods and services that they then use in their final production. The big corporations may not fully own the foreign suppliers, or even have any ownership stake in them at all. But the suppliers, especially those in low-wage countries, will be tied into the production cycle of the major corporations from the rich countries. The most infamous example is Apple's use of Foxconn's factories in China for the assembly of most of its iPhones and iPods. Similar connections exist for other big corporations, to the extent that some will manufacture almost nothing and provide only brand design and marketing for the end product.[25]

My key point is that the economics of imperialism is distinguished by the monopolistic features of the *global* economic system. Furthermore, the role of the state is critical here. Economically developed countries will tend to have more productive companies that are larger and stronger in the world market, and their states will have more resources than other less developed nations. Where the critical business interests of corporations based in a particular state are threatened, this also threatens the economic viability of that state. In such a case, one would not expect the state to 'go gentle into that good night' as its capitalists lose out in competition, especially if the latter is deemed to be 'unfair' or aggressive, but instead to 'rage, rage against the dying of the light'. Nevertheless, the interests of monopolists are not identical to the more general interests of 'their' state.

Monopoly power may be good for the monopolist, but it will be less so for the national economy in which it operates. This is why there is usually a state policy against local monopolies and cartels, complete with legislation or regulatory bodies to limit any abuse of market power that could lead to a few companies maintaining a stranglehold over the supply of key commodities and services in the domestic economy.[26] Probably the earliest significant example of this was the Sherman Antitrust Act of 1890 in the US, although it took further state measures to limit the power of Rockefeller's Standard Oil. Rockefeller's company refined 80 per cent of the national US oil output and overwhelmingly dominated the production, transport and markets for a wide range of other oil and energy products.[27]

In the past century, further 'anti-monopoly' policies have been implemented in the US, and other countries have also set up agencies to regulate the corporate domination of markets. One such is the UK's euphemistically titled Competition Commission, a successor to the Monopolies Commission, whose more explicit title may have offended the wrong people. Yet these policies and agencies have done little to prevent the fairly steady drift towards an increase in monopoly power. A fascinating book on the subject, published over four decades ago, and based on evidence from US Senate sub-committee hearings dating back to 1957–62, uncovered widespread market manipulation in US domestic industries as diverse as auto, steel, pharmaceuticals, bakeries and defence.[28] There has been no similar work in relation to the UK, apart from some low-key reports from the Office of Fair Trading. One of the most extreme examples of monopoly today can be found in South Korea, dubbed by local people 'the Republic of Samsung'. Samsung's conglomerate structure covers road construction, oil rigs, hotels, insurance and smartphones, and accounts for a fifth of national output.[29]

In many countries, state-backed rescues of companies in crisis, from shipyards to banks, have also involved promoting mergers and takeovers. Despite what may be a formal anti-monopoly stance in state policy, capital accumulation generates yet more monopolies. Even where the 'privatisation' of formerly state-owned industries and services has occurred – which capitalist governments claim will promote competition and efficiency – the result has been that the state has sold most of the shares to, or given the contract to, one of a very small number of major private corporations. One of these, the UK's G4S, the world's largest security company, operating in 125 countries, has distinguished itself both through the abuse and death of prisoners in its custody, and by screwing up operations at the UK 2012 Olympics so badly that the police and the army had to step in.

Any concern a particular state might have about market domination in the domestic sphere obviously does not extend to the operations of its own companies in the international market. On the contrary, large companies get significant backing from their states for expanding their foreign business. Any exercise of monopoly power abroad is another country's burden, one that might even favour the home country through the higher profitability of the domestically based company's foreign operations benefiting domestic investors.

Perhaps the only exception to this relaxed international policy is the EU, where member states have adopted an anti-monopoly policy *within the EU area* as a means to regulate the large single market. This has led to some limited measures against price fixing in the EU, as detailed in a study of some twenty cartels.[30] These cases were the most egregious examples, and hence the ones uncovered by official investigators. The likelihood is that there are still many others operating under the official radar.

Monopoly today

Worldwide production of most of the key commodities of modern capitalism, and the provision of most of its key services, is today dominated by a small number of companies. Fewer than ten companies often control the bulk of *global* activity in particular products and services.

Nearly one-third of global automobile production in 2011 was attributable to just three companies: General Motors (US), Volkswagen (Germany) and Toyota (Japan). Thirteen companies accounted for three-quarters of output.[31] Two US companies, Lear Corporation and Johnson Controls, account for the bulk of the supply of automotive interiors, following a string of acquisitions in Europe and Asia. In China, Johnson Controls was reported to have supplied 44 per cent of car seats in 2012.[32] In the case of beer, so to speak, the output of *five* companies provided just over half of the world's consumption in 2013: Anheuser Busch InBev (Belgium-Brazil), SABMiller (UK), Heineken (Netherlands), Carlsberg (Denmark) and China Resources Snow Breweries.[33] For elevators and escalators, just four companies controlled some 65 per cent of the market in 2012, one American and three European.[34] Otis Elevator, the largest, is itself owned by United Technologies, the huge US military contractor and engineering corporation.

As mentioned earlier, a similar domination of the market occurs even for relatively new products such as mobile phones. The mobile phone market is worth noting as an example of how, while the monopoly names might change, the outcome is much the same. In 2012, just two companies, Samsung (South Korea) and Nokia (Finland), accounted for 41 per cent of worldwide sales of mobile phones. Apple was in third place with 7.5 per cent of the total.[35] But the development of smartphones has changed the picture dramatically. Nokia, previously the dominant player, decided it could not compete, and moved to focus on its other business in telecom networks and equipment, selling its mobile phone operations to Microsoft in 2014. In that year, Samsung took 24.7 per cent and Apple 15.4 per cent of smartphone sales. Yet they were clearly beginning to lose ground to other players, even though Nokia was out of the game and Microsoft had not made much of a success of its purchase. Chinese companies, especially, were building significant minority positions in the smartphone market, helped by their purchases of foreign patents and takeovers of, or deals with, foreign companies. One Chinese company, Lenovo, bought Motorola's mobile handset business via its link to Google, as well as patents from Japan's NEC, helping it to build a third-placed 6.5 per cent share of the smartphone market in 2014. Other Chinese companies – Huawei, Xiaomi, TCL and ZTE – had done similar deals, and like Lenovo had invested vast sums in research. Together, these latter four likely had around 15 per cent of the smartphone market in 2014. These Chinese companies, like others in different sectors of the economy, are not yet registering in the global tables simply due to the huge size of the domestic market in which they are based. But they are also expanding their international presence.

Large corporations dominate not only the industrial markets. For example, ahead of its takeover of Xstrata in May 2013, Glencore, the biggest Swiss company and a constituent of the FTSE 100 equity market index, 'controlled more than half the international tradable market in zinc and copper and about a third of the world's seaborne coal; was one of the world's largest grain exporters, with about nine per cent of the global market; and handled three per cent of daily global oil consumption'.[36] It is worth making a brief aside here to note the power of the individuals running these organisations. In 1983, Glencore's founder, Marc Rich, was indicted in the US for tax evasion and for making oil deals with Iran, which was then subject to US sanctions. He fled from the US to Switzerland just before being arrested and, by a literally incredible 'stroke of luck', was later pardoned by US president Bill Clinton on his last day in office on 20 January 2001.[37]

In the financial sphere, one indirect measure of monopoly can be gleaned from the bank asset data for major countries. In 2011, the share of total bank assets of the *top three* banks in the US, the UK and Germany was, respectively, 40 per cent, nearly 80 per cent and nearly 70 per cent.[38] A more direct measure of global monopoly is available for the foreign exchange market: ten banks accounted for nearly 80 per cent of business in 2012. Four were from the US, three from the UK, two from Switzerland and one from Germany.[39]

Although the leading companies may lose their market domination, this tends to take many years, and the end result is usually that the key monopolistic corporations still belong to the major powers. A United Nations report showed that in 2013, of the top 100 international non-financial corporations, ranked by total foreign assets, seventy-five had a 'home' in just six: the US, UK, France, Germany, Japan and Switzerland.[40]

The monopoly plot thickens when allowance is made for the links between companies. Here, the position of a company is not measured by the share it has of, for example, vehicle production, but by the ownership it has of *other companies*. One study used a network analysis of the ownership links between some 43,000 international corporations based in 116 countries in 2007.[41] Assuming that owning 50 per cent or more of a company's equity directly or indirectly (through subsidiaries, etc.) implied control, it found that *less than 0.5 per cent* of these companies – principally financial companies, but also non-financial ones – controlled an astonishing 40 per cent of the world's international corporations, measured by their stock market value. Table 5.1 lists the top corporations at the centre of this global ownership network, compiled in order of the implied controlling share, with the respective controlling companies noted according to their 'home' country.

The ranking for 2007 by the home countries of the top companies generates a list similar to those seen before, and a similar pecking order. Of the top fifty, not all of which are shown in the table here, twenty-four were US companies, eight were from the UK, five from France, four from Japan, two each from Switzerland, Germany and the Netherlands, and one each from Canada, China and Italy.

Table 5.1 Corporate control by controlling company, 2007

Rank	Company name	Country	Cumulative % network control
1	Barclays PLC	GB	4.1
2	Capital Group Companies Inc	US	6.7
3	FMR Corp	US	8.9
4	Axa	FR	11.2
5	State Street Corp	US	13.0
6	JP Morgan Chase & Co	US	14.6
7	Legal & General Group PLC	GB	16.0
8	Vanguard Group Inc	US	17.3
9	UBS AG	CH	18.5
10	Merrill Lynch & Co	US	19.5
11	Wellington Management Co LLP	US	20.3
12	Deutsche Bank AG	DE	21.2
13	Franklin Resources Inc	US	22.0
14	Credit Suisse Group	CH	22.8
15	Walton Enterprises LLC	US	23.6
16	Bank of New York Mellon Corp	US	24.3
17	Natixis	FR	25.0
18	Goldman Sachs Group Inc	US	25.6
19	T Rowe Price Group Inc	US	26.3
20	Legg Mason Inc	US	26.9
21	Morgan Stanley	US	27.6
22	Mitsubishi UFJ Financial Group Inc	JP	28.2
23	Northern Trust Corp	US	28.7
24	Société Générale	FR	29.3
25	Bank of America Corp	US	29.8
26	Lloyds TSB Group PLC	GB	30.3
27	Invesco PLC	GB	30.8

Note: Countries are indicated by a two-letter ISO code (CH is Switzerland, DE is Germany).
*Source: S. Vitali, J. B. Glattfelder and S. Battiston, 'The Network of Global Corporate Control',
2011, at plosone.org.*

In 2007, Britain's Barclays plc was in top position, with just over 4 per cent of total network control, the largest share for an individual company. In 2008, Barclays bought parts of the North American business Lehman Brothers (ranked at number thirty-four) when the latter went bankrupt. However, Barclays' position will likely be lower in the ranking today, following its 2009 sale of Barclays Global Investors to BlackRock of the US, the world's largest asset manager. When the 2007 data were compiled for the table, BlackRock was half-owned by Merrill Lynch, ranked at number ten. In 2008, Merrill Lynch was taken over by Bank of America (ranked at number twenty-five), but Bank of America later sold its stake in BlackRock.

Incidentally, the 2008 Barclays-Lehman deal is an interesting example of imperial negotiations. On the weekend of 13–14 September, when it became clear that Lehman Brothers was going to go bust, Hank Paulson, the US Treasury Secretary, tried to get the British government to support a takeover of Lehman by the UK's Barclays. Paulson claimed that Bank of America was also interested in buying Lehman, but this was stretching the truth somewhat, since Bank of America had already decided that same weekend to buy Merrill Lynch. Alistair Darling, the UK Chancellor of the Exchequer, smelt a rat and told Paulson that the British government could not give support to the takeover, essentially by guaranteeing any risks that Barclays would take on when it bought Lehman's (likely toxic) assets. Barclays would not go ahead without a UK government guarantee. 'The British screwed us', Paulson declared to an emergency meeting of bankers in New York when he received the news.[42] Lehman filed for bankruptcy late on Sunday, 14 September, helping to exacerbate the financial crisis, and Barclays subsequently got what it wanted from the collapsed Lehman at a much lower price than in the earlier proposed deal.[43]

Table 5.1 summarises an important feature of the world economy today, namely the degree to which a small number of giant companies from a small number of countries have a huge influence over the world's production of goods and services. What it does not show is the mechanism by which this came about. How was it possible for these corporations to reach such a position? This will be explained in

Chapter 6, which discusses the role of financial securities in contemporary capitalism.

World projection of power

The means by which states support their 'own' large corporations in the world market can range from protecting 'intellectual property rights', usually patents owned by domestic companies, to key politicians fronting trade delegations to get into foreign markets. This is a defining feature of an imperialist world economy and is part of the economics of imperialism. The trend towards monopoly results from the accumulation of capital, and is the normal result of capitalist business development. When projected onto the world stage, a critical part of a monopoly's power derives from the state to which it formally belongs, even if the owners of the corporation include capitalists from many countries, and even if most of the corporation's business revenues accrue from other countries. State power in the world market is a key element supporting the monopolist's position, and vice versa, strong companies support the economic position of the national state.

What distinguishes an imperialist *company* is not its size or competitive success, or even its global importance as a major producer of goods or provider of services, although it will often be a big company given the advantages it enjoys. What distinguishes it is the backing it receives from a powerful nation-state in the world economy, and any advantages it gets because it is located in and identified with that imperialist state. Likewise, what in economic terms distinguishes an imperialist *state* is its ability to exert power in the world economy on behalf of its 'national' capitalist companies. This can include, but goes well beyond, military power. In this sense, the term 'imperialist' can apply to companies as well as to states, given a company's relationship to the imperialist state.

Monopolistic tendencies are endemic to capitalism, as can be seen in diverse parts of the economy. When the results are viewed from the perspective of the world economy, this also becomes the domination of one group of countries over the rest, as illustrated by the index of power presented at the start of this chapter. In purely economic terms, leaving aside military and political power, the methods of domination are not necessarily any different from what a monopolistic company might try to do within the national sphere. But they are projected *worldwide* with the support of that company's state. The financial dimensions of this domination are discussed more fully in the following chapters.

6.

Profit and Finance

Profitability is critical for capitalist production, as it is for everything else in the capitalist system. Commercial buying and selling, money dealing and other aspects of finance depend for their revenues on the profits made in the productive sector. Simply buying or selling commodities, lending money, or exchanging titles of ownership to property or financial securities do not by themselves create new value for the economy as a whole. In a similar way, state expenditures on education, health and welfare, on the police and the military, or on subsidies to the arts, industry and agriculture are financed by taxation, but essentially these taxes are also taken from the profits of the productive sector.[1] Company profits are not all derived from capitalist production within a particular country, but are sourced from all over the world, especially through trade and financial operations. Financial markets can also appear to generate new types of wealth, separate from the actual production of value, in the creation of bank deposits and in the prices of financial securities, as shown in Chapter 4. This chapter looks more closely at the relationship between profitability and finance.

Return on equity and leverage

The owners of capitalist companies usually advance some of their own money to start up their business. But they will normally also borrow investment funds via the financial system. While owners worry about the returns they may get on the *total* capital invested, including the borrowed funds, they focus especially on the profits they receive from *their ownership stake.* This point is best explained by way of a common measure of profitability used by all large corporations quoted on the stock exchange: the *return on equity* (RoE). The RoE measure takes the *net* profit received after paying interest on borrowings and divides this by the capital advanced *only by the owners*, in other words, by the company's equity capital.[2]

If the interest rate on borrowing is less than the rate of profit on its new investment, then it makes sense for the company to borrow funds from banks or to issue bonds to get finance that way. Then, the borrowed funds will cost less than the extra profit gained from the investment, and the returns on the owners' investment will be increased. For example, if a UK company's rate of profit is 10 per cent, it will make £10 in profit for every £100 invested. Let's assume that it pays 5 per cent interest on any funds borrowed. If the company then borrows an extra £200 for investment on top of its own £100, it will now receive £30 in profit (10 per cent of the 300). The profit due to the owners is then £30 minus the 5 per cent it has to pay as interest on the 200 borrowed, or £30 minus £10. The owners of the company count this net profit of £20 against what they have personally invested in the company's equity, which remains the original £100. So as a result of the extra borrowing the rate of profit on their equity investment has now risen from 10 to 20 per cent. Of course, this happy result depends on the rate of profit on the total investment remaining at 10 per cent and being higher than the rate of interest.

Company owners obviously face a risk when they borrow: the interest and principal repayments on bank loans, or on the bonds they issue, must be made even if the company's investments turn out badly. Otherwise, the company is declared bankrupt. So, while industrial and commercial companies invariably borrow funds, they will tend to limit the amount. Stock market investors will also be wary of companies that have borrowed too much. This tends to put a ceiling on the amount of borrowing a company makes compared to the equity capital invested in it. The ratio of a company's borrowing to its equity capital is called its 'leverage'.[3]

Data for the leverage of US manufacturing companies show that on average borrowing was less than the value of the company's equity capital in each year from 2001 to 2010. The average leverage ratio was therefore *less than 1*.[4] This was also true for mining and wholesale trading companies, and it contrasted with the sharp rise in borrowing elsewhere in the US economy during this period, among consumers buying real estate (property) or taking on credit card debt, as well as among financial companies.

Higher leverage for an investor usually means that the returns on their investment may be much higher or much lower than usual; in other words, there is a higher volatility of returns. If profits from the investment are high, a low cost of borrowed funds relative to the investment returns will magnify the return on equity. Then there is a higher profit with little or no extra investment cost financed by the owners, so this 'accentuates the positive', as in the example given earlier. But if the investment goes wrong, the return on equity becomes a big negative, incorporating not only the losses from the operating business but also the extra drain on profits from the interest and debt repayments that still have to be made. As one might expect, particular calculations have been developed for this kind of economy to make an adjustment for this risk. In portfolio investment theory, or the mathematics of financial parasitism, investment returns are divided by the volatility of the returns when calculating a 'Sharpe ratio' on investment performance.[5]

Not surprisingly, financial companies have much higher leverage ratios than non-financial ones. Banks, especially, are in a good position to manage this because they can *create* loans and deposits very much larger than the equity capital that has been invested in bank operations. This process increases leverage. For banks, leverage is measured in terms of total *assets* compared to equity capital, because the focus is on the risk of investment losses on these assets.

It is considered normal in major capitalist countries for banks to have a leverage ratio of around *twenty times the size of their equity*.[6] Non-bank financial companies, like hedge funds, can increase their leverage too, but usually by borrowing from banks or by banks allowing them to invest 'on margin'. This means that they do not pay in full for the assets they own but only a fraction of the total to cover the potential losses from the assets held. It also means that financial companies will tend to have a lower *return on assets* than non-financial ones when all their financial investment assets in the form of loans, bonds, equity investments, etc., are taken into account. However, their *return on equity* might still be high, which would keep these companies favoured on the stock market because they would then show strong returns for their investors.

The leverage ratios of banks reveal an important dimension of what happened in the run up to the 2007–8 crash. From the 1990s onwards, bank profitability had been coming under pressure from narrower interest rate margins – the gaps between their borrowing and lending rates. These had tended to fall in line with the trend towards lower money-market interest rates. For example, if market interest rates for borrowing between banks are close to 10 per cent, then a bank might offer its customers deposit rates of 7 per cent, but only lend to companies or individuals at 12 per cent, giving it a premium of five percentage points that then contributes to its revenues. However, if the level of market interest rates drops to 4 per cent, then it becomes more difficult for the bank to charge a five percentage point margin, for example by making its rates to depositors 2 per cent and its rate for borrowers 7 per cent. There is not necessarily a consistent theory behind this, just a calculation by banks of what they can get away with. Lower levels of interest rates can also reflect weaker business conditions or lower inflation rates, which reduce the ability of the bank to charge such high margins.

In the case of US banks, net interest margins fell from around 4.0–4.5 per cent in the 1990s to below 3.5 per cent by 2006.[7] This meant that their net revenues had fallen to less than $35 million for every $1 billion lent out, rather than being at $40–45 million, a drop of some 20 per cent. This encouraged banks to step up their lending operations in order to boost profits with a higher volume of assets. By increasing the latter, the total volume of profit they received was higher, even if the profit they got on each billion dollars of assets was lower. The result was much higher bank leverage. At the same time, the banks also boosted the volume of their trading in foreign exchange, financial securities and derivatives, helped both by the boom in financial markets and by what has been euphemistically called 'financial

Chart 6.1 Leverage ratios of major international banks, 2007–11

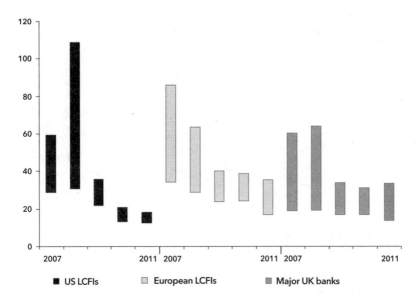

Note: Leverage is measured by total assets divided by bank capital. The high–low range
for banks in the survey is given for each year. The LCFI stands for 'large complex financial
institution'. UK banks are not included in the European LCFI columns. In 2007 and 2008, the
weighted average numbers for leverage ratios were about two-thirds down the relevant bars.
Source: Adapted from Bank of England, Financial Stability Report, June 2012, Chart 1.19, p. 14

innovation'. This refers to the invention by banks of complex deals to
gain more revenues from their customers, while minimising their tax
liabilities and allocation of capital. In general, such deals increased
both bank interest income *and* their trading income from dealing
spreads and commissions.

In the early 2000s, a relatively stable rate of economic growth in
the major capitalist countries made the higher leverage among banks
seem less risky. Ahead of the crisis, leverage ratios for some major
institutions hit levels in excess of 100 in the US and more than 80
in Europe, four or five times 'normal' levels, as shown in Chart 6.1.
This development led to a huge amount of bank lending, helping to
fuel credit-based demand in the major economies, adding to what
seemed like rosy economic prospects for capitalist companies and
providing governments with extra tax revenues to support more state
spending. But the credit-fuelled bubble burst, most directly due to the

Chart 6.2 Leverage ratios of major UK banks, 1960–2010

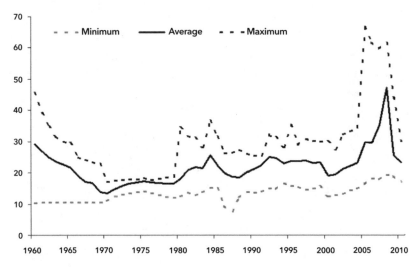

Source: Bank of England, Financial Stability Report, *June 2011, Excel file 3: 'Resilience in the financial system', Tab Box 3, Chart A*

over-extended level of debt in the economy compared to the income that was meant to finance it. This meant that any slowdown in the growth of income became a big problem, and it gave a particular 'financial' form to the crisis that broke in 2007–8. Even if banks lost 'only' 2 per cent of their assets in loans that could not be repaid, then, with a leverage ratio of 50 they would lose an amount equivalent to *all* of their equity capital. This led to potential bankruptcy, state-supervised mergers, and government bailouts in the UK and a number of other European countries as well as in the US.

Data on bank leverage is not available for all major countries over a longer time period, but the leverage data for major UK banks since 1960 supports the view that the 2000s were exceptional. Chart 6.2 shows that the leverage ratio fell steadily through the 1960s, but was then on a modest upward trend from 1970 to 2000. After settling around the long-term average of close to 20 in 2000, the average leverage ratio for major UK banks jumped to new historical highs in the period leading up to 2007–8. It then fell back down towards the long-term average as bank assets dropped with the fall in lending, while official regulators demanded that bank capital had to be increased.

The financial system can develop a destructive dynamic in the search for extra profit. This is one consequence of the fact that banks can expand their assets by credit creation. Banks also have a clear incentive to boost the volume of their financial *transactions*. While the financial system grows alongside and is intertwined with the accumulation of capital, weak economic growth and lower profitability prompts the accelerated growth of different types of financial business, especially if there is also a decline in returns on *financial* investments in an environment of low interest rates.

It was these lower returns that prompted the extra leverage and the explosive growth of derivatives markets in the 2000s. Financial institutions could not maintain the returns they needed from their loans or from bond and equity investments. For example, many pension funds needed annual yields on their investments of around 7 per cent if they were to meet their promises to pensioners of an attractive income in retirement. But government bond yields were only around 4 to 6 per cent in the early 2000s, and returns from investing in equity markets were also relatively weak. So pension funds switched some of their investments into commodity derivatives – betting on the price of oil, wheat, copper, etc. – and other 'alternative assets', like property or forests, and some even put their money into hedge fund investments.[8]

The relationship of financial returns to the underlying rate of profit of productive capital investment is a complex one. However, the lower the rate of profit, the more likely it is that returns will also fall, and that what ends up taking the form of a 'financial' crisis has its roots in weak profitability. In turn, the lower the capitalist system's underlying rate of profit, the greater the economic damage wreaked by what appears to be 'only' a financial crisis.

The ability to expand assets is a key driver of profitability for the banking system, and the search for acceptable yields on financial investments helps spur financial market 'innovation' and all kinds of madcap speculation that, sooner or later, turns investment geniuses into morons. A famous example from 2012 was that of the 'London Whale'. The big mammal in question was a trader for US bank JP Morgan Chase in London named Bruno Iksil.[9] After successfully betting on credit derivatives in 2011 and making hundreds of millions of dollars, things started to go wrong for him the following year. In time-honoured fashion, he began doubling up on his positions to recover his losses. This was much worse than betting $200 on red in roulette after losing the previous $100 bet. A roulette wheel will continue to give you the same odds of just less than half that red will come up next time. But the credit derivatives market is very small, and other traders had an idea of who was doing what because a gigantic whale-like position could not be hidden in such a small pond. Other market traders saw Iksil's vulnerability to a move in prices and bet against him. His trading strategy ended up losing JP Morgan Chase more than $6 billion.

Comparing profits

For many decades, Marxist analysts have not paid much attention to financial markets, and one would have to look back more than 100 years for a comprehensive, systematic view. Rudolf Hilferding's analysis from 1910 is probably the most developed. He argued that 'banking is a sphere of investment like any other, and it [capital] will only flow into this sphere if it can find the same opportunities for realising profit as in industry or commerce; otherwise it will be withdrawn'.[10] This formed part of his analysis of bank profit, according to which the 'total revenue, calculated on the basis of the bank's own capital, must equal the average rate of profit'.[11] Like Marx, he does not analyse the impact of banking capital and bank operations on the rate of profit. But whereas Marx does not comment on a rate of profit for banks, Hilferding implies that banking capital will tend to earn the *same* rate of profit as other capitalist companies.[12]

Not only is there no empirical evidence to support this, there is also a more theoretical argument against the idea that an equalisation of profit rates tends to occur. While banks play a role in allocating capital across different sections of industry and commerce, there is a 'structural separation between control of money capital and control of productive capital'.[13] Banks are the 'general managers of money capital', and bank lending operations, plus the stock market and the credit system generally, assist the equalisation of profit rates between different sections of industry and commerce. However, there is no mechanism for equalising the returns of banking and financial operations with those of the *other* capitalists.

This point can be illustrated by taking into account the different kinds of investment involved.[14] The advance of capital for buildings, technology and hiring a labour force is *not* the principal basis on which companies with largely financial operations generate their returns. Banks can *create their own revenue-earning assets*, and other financial companies are also in the business of attracting external funds for financial investment. This marks them out from non-financial companies whose main activities are in industry and commerce, and it also raises the question of how their 'capital investments' can be compared with the investments of industrial and commercial capitalists.

Comparing profits against a company's *fixed assets* is one method,[15] but this ignores the role of *financial assets* as the principal lever for financial sector profits. The revenues of banks are not based upon their imposing buildings, dealing screens and slick communications software. Any version of 'fixed and circulating capital' advanced by the bank will have little relationship to the bank's ability to generate a return. This is a structural difference between the two sets of capitalists, based upon the special position of the banks in the monetary system. There is no mechanism for equalising the rate of profit between the two sectors *because* there is no sensible basis on which to compare the rate of profit of a steel producer or a retail company with that of a bank.

A manufacturing company's operations, for example, involve advancing capital for the plant, machinery, raw materials, IT systems and workforce with which it produces commodities. The profit it makes from the sale of those commodities might be reduced by payments of interest on its borrowings, licence fees, etc. Its net profits will also be affected by all kinds of financial transactions in which it may be involved, from hedging its exchange rate and interest rate risk to investing in financial securities. But in so far as the company can be called a manufacturer, most of its business will be focused on performing that function, and the profits it can make will depend principally on its advance of capital for that purpose.

Things are quite different for a bank, as for other forms of financial company. Banks can create their own assets in the form of loans from which they generate a return; in other words, this is *not a new advance of capital by the banks' owners*. When the loans they make have a higher interest rate than that on their deposit liabilities or other borrowings, they then have a reason to expand their assets as much as they can, to boost their net interest income. Except for the function of credit creation, the situation is similar for other financial companies that attract money from investors, invest in securities and other assets, and take a fee based on the volume of assets. The result is that their recorded profits will have no clear relationship to the capital they have invested in buildings, technology, software or a workforce.

UK statistics reflect this point. While there are published data on the rate of profit for the industrial, manufacturing and services sectors on the basis of 'capital employed', there is no such thing for the financial sector.[16] In discussion with the UK Office for National Statistics on getting access to profit and investment data on the same basis for both financial and non-financial companies, an official told me that: 'Other than Gross Operating Surplus, comparable data for financial companies are not available.'[17]

My argument is not that bank profits, or some version of a rate of return for banks, cannot be calculated, only that there is no basis on which any measure of a 'rate of return' or 'rate of profit' for financial companies can sensibly be *compared* with that for other capitalist enterprises. The difference between companies involved in the production and merchandising of commodities as compared to those whose relationship to commodity production is advancing money-capital suggests that any empirical results would only measure the accidental coincidence, or otherwise, of rates of return. Even for what would appear to be a comparable rate of return between the different sectors, such as the return on equity measure, there would be a material difference of outcome based upon whatever happened to be the leverage ratios of the different sectors. While industrial and commercial companies would be likely, on average, to keep their leverage ratios close to 1, in the case of banks, leverage can change dramatically over time. For example, between 1970 and 2010, major UK banks had an *average* leverage ratio that moved from a low of around 15 to a peak of just below 50 (see Chart 6.2).

One other factor will also have an influence on the discrepancy in profit rates, however they are measured, between banks and other capitalist companies. Normally, a bank can only set up as a deposit taker if it gets a licence from the central bank. This helps banks maintain a monopoly position in the money markets. There is also usually a licensing process for investment banks (although they do not take deposits from the general public), and this helps them maintain a privileged position in the securities market. In the UK, despite the apparently excess profitability of the banking sector in recent decades, there have been remarkably few new banks set up. Metro Bank, established in 2010, was the first new High Street bank for 100 years, and it took eighteen months for it to be granted a licence to take deposits.[18]

Financial assets and derivatives

A bank's financial assets include its loans to industrial and commercial companies for investment purposes, its consumer loans, and its own purchases of securities. But bank loans often have little to do with financing productive or commercial investment. For example, banks provide finance for 'private equity' funds or hedge funds that then buy equities, bonds or other financial securities. This is just allocating credit to these funds for their purchase of *existing* securities or to make other forms of financial investment. In general, it is wrong to think of bank assets (even their loans) as financing much investment in the economy, although this does tend to be somewhat larger in continental Europe than in the UK or the US.

Large corporations, especially, do not rely upon bank loans or even upon bond issues to fund their investments. Selling extra shares on the stock market is usually more important than bond issues, but a lot of corporate investment is financed from retained profits. The growth of a bank's financial assets mainly arises from their short-term lending, including to the rest of the financial sector, and from their purchases of financial securities. It does not result from them funding productive investment. Although the securities may have claims on the surplus value arising from the productive sector, in the form of interest or dividend payments, the purchases are of existing securities traded in the market, so they do not represent any *new* investment in industry or commerce, or even any new investment in the financial sector's own business operations.

Financial companies can also accumulate financial assets by issuing new securities themselves. In this case, they raise funds to advance further loan capital or to buy other financial securities. One striking example of the accumulation of financial assets, mentioned briefly in Chapter 4, was the boom in the issuance of Collateralised Debt Obligations (CDOs) by banks from the late 1980s, especially in the US. These securities were largely based on the payments received by the banks from mortgage loans they had already granted. Banks could sell the mortgage-backed securities to investors, turning the original loans into new cash which could then be used as fresh capital to fund a new round of mortgage business. CDOs are issued as securities that are claims on a bank's *existing loan assets* and were a means by which banks tried to boost their profitability by receiving a dealing margin and by not having to wait until the mortgages were fully repaid to get the funds back. From an estimated $68bn in 2000, annual global CDO issuance increased nearly eightfold to a peak of $521bn in 2006.[19] Alongside this, profits reported by the US financial sector, the source of most CDO issuance, more than doubled over the same period – before the collapse that occurred shortly afterwards when mortgage defaults soared in the US. The banks' sale of mortgage securities played a major role in the expansion of mortgage debt to more and more borrowers, including in the end to those who were in no position to pay that debt back.

Banks also create other kinds of security, known as derivatives, for hedging and speculative purposes. These include interest rate swaps, and futures and options on interest rates and currency values. They appear on a bank's balance sheet as an asset or a liability, and the banks also earn dealing margins and other fees when they buy or sell derivatives. While derivatives are part of a bank's business dealings, they are *not* capital invested in a bank's or any other company's operations. A derivative 'asset' is simply a derivative recorded on a bank's balance sheet whose market value is positive, i.e. when it is worth more than was paid for it, or, in the case of selling a derivative, when its market price falls *below* the price at which it was previously sold. If the derivative's market value drops into negative territory, it becomes a 'liability'.[20] While this procedure makes sense from an accounting perspective, it also shows how derivatives can confuse the understanding of what is normally considered to be an asset or a liability. It is strange for the value of an asset to fall below zero and become a liability; normally it just becomes worthless. It is equally odd in common sense terms that a liability might become an asset.

I have personally created both derivative assets and liabilities for banks as the market values of the derivatives in which I traded moved from positive (asset) to negative (liability) and *vice versa*. For example, when dealing in money-market derivatives, my position was registering a loss just ahead of the release of some important US economic data. The loss got worse as the seconds ticked down to 1.30 p.m. London time (8.30 a.m. New York time, when the US data were released). Suspecting that some banks in the market were trying to push prices to levels that would make others capitulate, I held on, thinking that the price move did not make sense, given my understanding of market conditions. After the data were published, a dramatic move in prices left me with a profit on my position, as much by luck as by judgement. The gods – Mammon, at least – had shown mercy to one unfaithful to the creed, and the bank now had an asset on its books. On other occasions, I created new assets or liabilities for the bank I worked for simply by doing a deal with another bank on the interbank communications system, or with the broker on the futures exchange who was employed by the bank I worked for. Creating assets with a telephone call is how the magic of the financial markets can make you 'productive'!

Table 6.1 gives an example of UK bank financial assets and liabilities to illustrate these points. These figures exclude the *fixed* assets of banks (the value of buildings, etc.), which are not shown separately in UK data. But the total of fixed assets for *all* financial companies was only £142bn at the end of 2011, compared to the huge volume of financial assets shown. The totals of both financial assets *and* liabilities nearly doubled in value in the six years after 2005, helped especially by a big jump in the figures for derivatives.

At the end of 2011, derivative assets and liabilities accounted for more than a third of the totals. A bank's creation of and dealing in derivatives results in massive volumes of assets *and* liabilities, in most cases with the transactions offsetting each other in terms of a bank's risk exposure. This is shown by the fact that the net derivatives position was usually less than 1 per cent of the gross derivatives figures. This happens as follows. If a dealer buys a derivative that will increase in value if interest rates go down, then, if that turns out to happen, the derivative will rise in price and register a profit. But it may not be so easy to sell that particular derivative and realise the profit, so the dealer may decide to do another deal in the opposite direction, buying a derivative that will gain in value if the interest rate goes back up. If interest rates continue to fall, any extra gain on the first position will be cancelled by the loss on the second. Or, if the interest rate does go up, the gain on the second position will offset the drop in value of the first. The net risk of the dealer's position is hedged, with little or no further change in the net profit on the positions held. But the bank now has two positions, an asset *and* a liability, on its derivatives book. This kind of thing happens all the time, and it escalates the size of recorded assets and liabilities in tandem. These data do not indicate any 'capital investment' or investment asset as normally understood.

Nor are a bank's loans necessarily any form of capital investment. The loan may simply be a mortgage or a loan for consumption purposes. Even if the money were used for capital investment, then that would be counted separately in official GDP statistics. So, counting both the loan *and* the economic data for investment would involve a double counting: once as the investment recorded by companies in GDP data and again as a bank asset. Including a bank's financial assets as a factor in total capital investment would be a mistake.[21]

Table 6.1 UK monetary financial institutions' (MFIs) financial balance sheet

(£ billion, end-year)	2005	2007	2009	2011
Financial assets				
Currency and deposits	2210	2565	2934	3150
Loans	2510	3373	3434	3443
Shares and other equity	261	328	255	295
Short-term money market instruments	154	149	120	87
Medium & long-term bonds	570	785	1106	1204
Financial derivatives	*1407*	*2368*	*4080*	*5413*
Total financial assets	**7114**	**9570**	**11929**	**13591**
Financial liabilities				
Currency and deposits	4721	5946	6488	6752
Loans	3	3	3	3
Shares and other equity	136	139	159	172
Short-term money market instruments	292	348	360	181
Medium & long-term bonds	314	394	660	652
Financial derivatives	*1407*	*2357*	*4027*	*5388*
Other	6	8	25	27
Total financial liabilities	**6878**	**9195**	**11723**	**13174**
Net MFI financial assets	**236**	**375**	**206**	**417**
Net financial derivatives position	*1*	*11*	*53*	*25*

Source: *UK Office for National Statistics 'United Kingdom National Accounts – The Blue Book, 2012', 15 August 2012, Table 4.2.9, pp. 178–9, at ons.gov.uk, and author's calculations*

The relationship of bank financial assets to productive investment can be illustrated by examining the asset numbers for 2011 in Table 6.1. The currency and deposits item of £3,150bn is simply cash that banks have placed with other banks. The loans item of £3,443bn is principally made up of business lending, but Bank of England data suggest that less than 15 per cent of total loans are to *non-financial* businesses.[22] In addition, two-thirds are short-term loans, most of which are not likely to be for business investment, but for cash-flow purposes. Some 30 per cent of total bank loans are also secured on dwellings, largely representing residential mortgages. Of the £295bn of equity investment, only a small proportion is likely to be the banks' purchases of newly issued securities. Secondary market purchases of existing bonds or equities do not advance any new funds to the companies concerned. The £87bn of short-term money-market instrument assets is the banks' ownership of money-market securities, not an advance of investment funds. One-third of the MFIs' bond assets of £1,204bn are investments in UK government bonds; much less than half is likely to be in private sector bonds bought in the primary market. Financial derivative assets, a massive £5,413bn, can be excluded as forms of capital investment, for the reasons previously noted.

In summary, the large volume of assets recorded by financial companies, especially by banks, will mainly reflect their loans to each other, as well as their holdings of financial securities, derivatives and other such items. Banks obviously play a key role in handling the transfers of payments in the economy and providing cash flow for businesses and individuals. The longer-term funds they provide for businesses are also important. But only a very small proportion of their assets represents an investment in productive activity. Instead, the assets on their balance sheets reflect the pervasive role of finance in the capitalist economy.

Financial revenues, surplus value and securities

Finance neither produces new value nor even transfers any value from its operations to commodities. All of its profits, as well as its costs, are a deduction from the total surplus value produced elsewhere.[23] Even when financial sector revenues flow directly from workers' wages, as in the case of interest payments on loans or mortgages, the ultimate source of these payments is from surplus value arising from the productive sector of the economy. The regular wage paid by employers would need to be adjusted to make an allowance for such deductions, if they were widespread and persistent. They would then become part of the 'cost of living'. But financial sector revenues involve more than a redistribution of the *existing* surplus value produced in the rest of the national economy (or even from other countries). This can be seen by examining the links between surplus value and the price of financial securities (fictitious capital), going beyond what was covered in Chapter 4.

The price of a financial security is essentially made up from the discounted value of the expected future cash flows – dividends for equities, and coupon and principal repayments for bonds – and also how attractive the security might be to other potential buyers. The security's price does not represent existing value, although there is a minimum price that reflects the creditworthiness of the state or the value of a company's net assets. Instead, the price is largely driven by interest rates in the market, influencing the rate at which future revenues are discounted, and also, in the case of equities, expectations about future company profits. Therefore, the security's price does not have a direct relationship to the surplus value currently being exploited from the productive workforce. The price can rise sharply if interest rates fall or if expectations about future coupons, dividends or repayments improve, or it could slump in the opposite case. The divergence between surplus value production *now* and movements in fictitious capital values means that while the underlying conditions for capital accumulation might worsen (implying a lower rate of profit), the price of securities could still *rise*. For example, most world stock market indices and bond prices rose dramatically from the lows seen in early 2009, in the immediate wake of the crisis, up to the end of 2014, as the major central banks pushed official interest rates towards zero levels. But that was hardly a sign that the world's economic problems had come to an end. Changes in the prices of financial securities, nevertheless, clearly have a big impact on capitalists' wealth and the monetary value it represents for them.

There are some other oddities. It is common to think of transactions in these securities as being a 'zero sum game': a gain for one party in the deal must be a loss for the other. But consider what happens when a company sells its shares on the stock market at a price of 100. If the market price then rises to 120, one might assume that the company has 'lost', because it could have waited and issued shares at 120, while the investors have gained. However, although the influx of money-capital to the company is less than it might have been, the company's stock market value has still risen, based on the higher price of its shares. This gives the company's owners more financial power, and it also raises the likely price for further share issues. So, it can appear that 'everybody wins', both the company and the holders of the equity, when equity prices are rising. Similarly, 'everybody loses' when they fall. That is why the reporters and talking heads on TV news can look genuinely happy, or suitably downcast, when reporting on big moves in stock market indices.

The situation for bonds is similar to that for equities in this respect. A higher bond price implies a lower yield, because more is being paid now for the future coupon payments received, and *vice versa*. Higher prices will also tend to lower the company's future interest rate for bond-market borrowing, while the investors still have the original coupon payments and a capital gain on the security they purchased. Rising prices for bonds will, though, reduce the yield that *new* purchasers of bonds can get.[24]

Trading revenues

Another important dimension is the revenue that derives from *trading* in financial securities, which is separate from capital gains or losses. The dealing revenues of banks are usually derived from the spread between buying (bid) and selling (offer) prices. But the revenue from these spreads depends on the size of the deals done, so the effect is similar to the gap in interest rates applied to amounts of money-capital borrowed or loaned out.[25] The dealing revenues do not depend upon security prices going up or down, as with capital gains and losses. Instead they are based upon taking a cut from the underlying price of each transaction (hence, the bid-offer spread) and the volume of transactions in both buying and selling.[26] Nevertheless, rising security prices usually encourage a higher volume of deals because they attract more funds into the market, while collapsing prices scare financial investors away. Trading revenues boost the profits of financial companies, from banks to brokers to securities and futures exchanges, so where do *these* revenues come from?

The answer can be seen by looking again at the price of financial securities. Security prices are mainly based on market calculations of *future* financial flows discounted by market interest rates, profit expectations, and so forth. This appears to make the future *a present reality*, but obviously the future has not yet happened! The value has not yet been created from which the dealing revenues can be deducted.[27] Here we find a fundamental contradiction in the capitalist financial system, one that also puts the previous issue of security price changes in a different light.

Financial trading revenues are real enough if they are received as money. *Then* they are a claim on society's resources, even if no extra resources have been created. The same is true of the value represented by the price of financial securities, if those securities can potentially be turned into money. A sum of fictitious capital – consisting of bonds, equities, etc. – can be valued on a company's balance sheet, or as assets owned by individuals, and these might also represent a large amount of wealth at current market prices. There is no problem as long as there is little doubt in the market that the recorded prices represent what the wealth is 'really worth'. If security prices are steady or rising, then the 'wisdom of the market' judges that, yes, you really are a millionaire or a billionaire. But this assessment is made on the basis that other holders of financial securities will not attempt to transform their assets into money at the same time, and that there is no series of unfortunate events that will lead the market to question its previous wisdom. Pricing fictitious assets at their 'future value' persists until a crisis shatters what is called 'market confidence': then prices collapse, and what was thought to be real wealth disappears as the red digits flash across the dealing screens.

The rate of profit and capital's limits

Financial crises often look as if they are the result of stupid levels of debt or excessive speculation. In some cases, this may be true: borrowing money to bet on the markets can sometimes look like a quicker route to riches than working for a living. But this only becomes a bigger, *social* phenomenon, and leads to an economic crisis, when many people, especially many companies, do the same thing. The explanation then needs to go beyond the mistakes, greed or idiocy of individuals.

Even when the financial system appears to be the cause of a crisis, a closer look at the background would reveal how its origins lie in the trouble capitalism has generating enough profits. This is not to deny that financial troubles can disrupt the economy. But all major upsets are closely linked to the problems that capitalist businesses face when trying to secure a return on their investments, even if there are many links in the chain between cause and outcome. This raises another question: what if capitalism has a systemic problem with generating sufficient profits? Such a problem does tend to emerge, and this is the driving force behind major capitalist crises.

Marx argues that there is a 'progressive tendency of the general rate of profit to fall' and this is 'just *an expression peculiar to the capitalist mode of production* of the progressive development of the social productivity of labour.'[28] Elsewhere, Marx states that this is 'in every respect the most important law of modern political economy, and the most essential for understanding the most difficult relations.'[29] As such, it is worth spending a little time on this subject.

Competition between companies forces them to cut costs. They may try different ways of doing this, including cutting pay, or moving production to low-wage areas, but these manoeuvres can only go so far. In the end, they have to raise productivity. Raising productivity means that more commodities are produced per worker in a given time, thereby increasing the mass of the means of production – raw materials, machinery and technology – compared to the number of workers employed and the labour time they work. This is what Marx called a rise in the 'technical composition' of capital. Alongside this, the *value* of the means of production will also tend to increase relative to the money that capitalists have to advance to pay wages. For example, even the infamous Foxconn, with its vast assembly plants in China employing very low-paid workers, had to increase the number of robots a *hundredfold* in order to lower its unit production costs further.[30]

Marx's concept of the rising 'organic composition' of capital is used to refer to the process of capital accumulation where *both* the technical and the value compositions rise *together*. This combined 'organic' concept of the composition of capital is critical for understanding what happens to capitalist profitability. While the number of hours of surplus labour determines the *amount* of capitalist profit, the *rate* of profit is measured by the amount of profit divided by the value of the total capital invested. The implications for the rate of profit can be seen by taking a typical worker in a productive capitalist enterprise as an example.

Productivity increases will usually mean that the value represented by the worker's wage will fall, because the socially necessary labour time contained in the commodities the worker needs to buy also falls. But even if it costs nothing to hire the worker, he or she must still work for less than twenty-four hours a day. So there is a limit to how much surplus value a worker can produce for the capitalist. But there is no definite limit to the mass of raw materials and machinery that he or she can work with. Over time, the mass of profit created by the worker will tend not to rise as much as the value of the capital invested in the means of production rises. This results in a tendency for the rate of profit per worker to fall, and so too throughout the whole capitalist economy.

This tendency is modified in practice by many factors. Improved productivity often means that a given portion of the means of production, such as computers or raw materials, will cost less than before. But usually a revamp of the productive system is needed for significant productivity increases. In this case, companies do not work with the same amount of machinery, etc., that now costs less; they must work with *a new, expanded system of machinery*. Each item may cost less, but there are more of them used per worker. Unless the productivity gains are dramatic, the socially necessary labour time embodied in the expanded system of machinery and raw materials per worker will tend to increase. There are of course examples of dramatic productivity improvements that do significantly cut costs for capitalist businesses: more efficient transport systems such as container ships; better telecommunications; new or improved computer technologies; and the use of cheaper synthetic materials. These can certainly have the effect of boosting the rate of profit. But this effect will also wear off, and the cost of investing in research for the next innovation also has to be taken into account. It is obvious that the volume of machinery and raw materials per worker will rise inexorably; it is only the cost of this greater volume that might sometimes be lower, or rise very little.

Over time, perhaps many years, the rate of profit will thus tend to fall. As it does so, the capitalist system becomes more prone to crises. Companies may earn more or less than the average rate of profit, but, as the average drops, more of them come closer to making a loss. Even if their *rate* of profit is still positive, the *amount* of profit they make might be insufficient to provide them with the funds necessary to invest in the new technology they need to stay competitive.

Outcomes

There are two consequences of this long-term trend to lower profitability. One is that profit becomes a *specifically capitalist* barrier to improving productivity, or even to producing anything at all. What is produced is not determined by what society decides democratically or by what science is capable of engineering. It is only a question of whether an investment will make a profit, not a question of delivering what society needs with the resources it has available. This Marxist indictment of capitalism is more fundamental than those criticisms that focus on monopolistic barriers to production or on how the struggle for ownership and control of the world's resources can lead to war.

The second consequence is that, as it becomes more difficult to generate a profit via capitalist production, 'making money' via finance begins to look like the easier option, particularly for those countries in a privileged position to take it. This was the context for the huge explosion of financial dealing from the 1980s, the seeds of which were sown in the 1970s as the world capitalist economy came under serious strain. The financial illusion of creating value out of nothing, particularly by extending credit, can work for a while. But when there is insufficient new value produced on which the illusion can feed, the world is then confronted with an increased burden of debts that cannot be repaid.

It is this problem of capitalist debt repayment that plagues the world today, seen most evidently in the collapse of the Greek economy as European creditors desperately search for ways of getting their money back. Some form of debt write-off for Greece has seemed inevitable since its crisis first broke in 2010, but that would then create a huge problem for the creditors. They find it difficult to recognise as a reality, because they are already faced with massive financial liabilities of their own. Collapsed property bubbles in some countries have left many banks with dubious mortgage loan 'assets'; in others, governments have struggled to maintain a semblance of financial viability as their spending on pensions, welfare payments and social services runs beyond what their stricken economies can afford. A 'debt crisis' is not really a crisis of debt, but more a sign that the economy's production of value can no longer support the previous illusion of wealth. The chronic nature of the current crisis, with persistently low rates of growth compared to earlier decades, is another sign that the game is up.

Rather than being the result of terrible, avoidable mistakes, as government policy advisers like to claim when advocating their 'solutions', economic crises play an important role in the capitalist market system. They are both the culmination of previous economic trends and a means by which the rate of profit might be increased back to levels that will allow investment and growth to resume. This can happen in several ways. If capital values are destroyed through a collapse in asset and commodity prices, those capitalists left standing will be able to buy means of production more cheaply and so secure a higher rate of return on their investments. This was what happened after the Second World War. But, at least in the rich countries today, governments have been reluctant to allow the mechanism of crisis to get into full swing, fearing social turmoil. Instead, huge levels of debt, which in earlier crisis resolutions would have been either written off or devalued, still remain in place. As a result, one of the classic mechanisms for resolving a crisis, the destruction of capital values, has not, at the time of writing (mid-2015), yet come into play. The major central banks have done their best to prevent this outcome with successive 'quantitative easing' policies and historically low interest rates; weaker countries have more directly borne the brunt of the economic damage.

Another key way of trying to restore profitability is to increase the exploitation of the workforce, by cutting real wages and imposing onerous new conditions. So far in the rich countries, this has only been attempted in a piecemeal fashion. For example, between 2010 and 2014, the number of people in the UK on 'zero hour' contracts, with no guaranteed working hours, quadrupled to some 700,000, or 2.3 per cent of all employees.[31] More drastic measures have been taken in poorer countries.

Related to this is a third policy driven by the exigencies of the crisis: the elimination of 'waste'. This involves expenditures that capital can do without, those that do not look like directly contributing to profitability, either now or in the near future. Why bother paying to educate workers with public funds when there are plenty of skilled and educated workers available already? Why bother providing more than the absolute minimum of health and welfare services? This is the reality behind so-called austerity policies today, to the extent that even the privileges of the middle-class professions, traditional bastions of support for established political parties in all countries, are coming under attack.

Profits, financial and global developments

Measuring the rate of profit on capitalist investment is complicated by many factors, not just companies hiding or boosting their profits with creative accounting tricks. Above all, it is difficult to pinpoint the location of the investment that generated the profit when giant corporations supply their own global networks with their own transfer prices, or when they get cheap inputs from other companies in low-wage countries. In addition, a key distinction in Marxist value theory, between operations that are productive and those that are unproductive, cannot easily be determined when using economic data. Many companies have both kinds of operation that are not distinguished in the statistics. Furthermore, a company might be able to register a large profit or a loss on its financial investments, which may have little connection to any production at all.

From the data available, I do not think it possible to come up with an accurate measure for the rate of profit on capitalist production, as this was understood by Marx. Many valiant attempts have been made, mostly using US economic data and making adjustments to it as the writer sees necessary.[32] My main disagreement with the approach of these authors is that they do not pay enough attention to how the operation of the global economy – and the US role within it – affects the figures for US profitability. With no definitive empirical data solution available, my approach to measuring the profit pulse of the capitalist system is to see what a simple calculation of profitability might imply, and then judge if other evidence, including global developments, would suggest a different perspective. As the previous analysis has shown, the world is dominated by a small number of powerful countries and a given country's position in the hierarchy will have an important impact on its economy, not least when allowance is made for international trade and finance. So these things have to be taken into account, as well as the raw data.

Almost all measures of the rate of profit for the major countries show a trend decline from the 1950s into the early 1970s.[33] As a result, there is little dispute about falling profitability being the underlying cause of the 1970s economic and financial turmoil, at least among those who base their views on some version of Marxist theory.[34] For the period since the 1970s, however, that consensus breaks down. Take the example of the US, for which we have the most comprehensive, detailed and easily available data. Chart 6.3 shows the US corporate rate of profit, in which there is a clear downtrend in both pre-tax and

Chart 6.3 US corporate rate of profit, 1948–2013

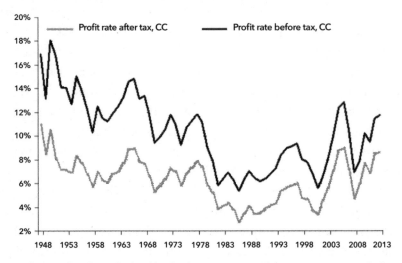

Note: The rate of profit is calculated by dividing current year domestic corporate profits by an average of the domestic fixed assets for the current end-year and the previous end-year. CC means that the 'current cost' measure of fixed assets is used.

Source: US Bureau of Economic Analysis, Fixed Asset Report, *Table 6.1, line 2;* NIPA Report, *Table 6.17, line 2, Table 6.19, line 2, at bea.gov*

post-tax measures from the late 1940s into the early 1980s. Pre-tax profits are obviously higher than post-tax profits, because, despite their best efforts, US governments have never managed to make the overall corporate tax rate zero or negative.

For the subsequent period, from the 1980s into the mid-2000s, most analysts argue that the rate of profit was on a *rising* trend, at least for US capitalists. There is, however, far from universal agreement on this, since a number of reasonable adjustments to the data would undermine that claim, at least to some extent. But the plain data do show an uptrend from the mid-1980s to 2007, although one severely punctured by the slump in the late 1990s that witnessed crises centred on Russia and a number of Asian countries. There was then a sharp drop in the rate of profit with the 2007–8 market seizure, followed by a recovery. On the basis of this data, many have argued that the crisis starting in 2007 in the rich countries was a result of *financial excess*, rather than having any relationship to a capitalist profitability crisis. The financial form of the latest crisis – the massive build up of debts, speculation, fraudulent deals, etc. – has encouraged this view.

If the evidence shows that the rate of profit in the years before the crisis was relatively high, that would appear to support a 'blame the bankers' position, and the US data do indeed show that profit rates were rising in the years to 2007. But the data do not need to be accepted uncritically. Four important factors put the calculations of a rising trend of profitability from the 1980s in a very different light.

The first factor behind a recovery of profitability, noted by a number of writers, was the attack on working-class living standards by the US government and business, in particular through the use of migrant labour and the marginalisation of labour unions. A signal event was the Reagan administration's destruction of the air traffic control-lers' union, PATCO, after it declared a strike in 1981 – a destruction intended *pour encourager les autres*. These measures would have boosted profitability to some extent, although by how much is diffi-cult to judge, but it was likely to have had only a one-time influence in the 1980s. Most measures of US rates of profit show lower rates from the mid-1990s onwards.

A second factor has arguably been more important, but does not directly appear in *any* US data and is far less remarked upon for its impact on profits: the low-cost products available to US capital through trading relationships with low-wage countries, particularly China. US data do show the profits from foreign investment (although these are not included in Chart 6.3, covering *domestic* profitability), but there is no accounting for how the low cost of *imported* cheap labour products boosted the recorded profits of US corporations. If the goods are supplied cheaply, that is judged to be what they are worth, and the huge profit margins made on the sale of these goods to final consumers are then supposedly due to 'value added' in the US after they are unloaded at the port.[35] The domestic profits of US companies (such as Wal-Mart and Apple) appear to come from their domestic operations, but in reality part will depend upon these prod-ucts of foreign, super-exploited labour. This would help explain the paradox that while US domestic corporate profits might look high, domestic US investment remains weak.

Fans of the imperial system applauded this development – labelled the 'Great Moderation' in the US – where a lower cost of living for most US workers coincided with cheap inputs for business, resulting in reasonably steady growth and lower inflation. They did not look into the stratification of global production between rich and poor countries on which the development was based. Immigration controls in rich countries, along with the strong popular support for these, have also been important factors preventing an equalisation of rates of exploitation globally.

This point is also relevant beyond the US. In the UK, for example, it was one factor supporting an unprecedented period of uninterrupted quarter-on-quarter GDP growth from late 1991 until early 2008. Optimism about the outlook for the capitalist economy became entrenched: things could only get better! It led ordinary people, businesses and most economists to dismiss the possibility of a serious setback, which in turn encouraged higher levels of borrowing.

Cheap foreign labour did deliver a significant boost to *global* profitability, principally in all the richer countries, but its incremental impact is now likely to be much reduced. It is becoming more difficult for major corporations to find the extra tens of millions of ultra-cheap, productive workers, and wages have begun to rise in China, India, Bangladesh and elsewhere.

The third, related factor boosting US corporate profitability for industrial and commercial capitalists was progressively lower nominal and inflation-adjusted interest rates. This was based on a reduction of the previous very high interest rates that followed the tightening of US monetary policy by Fed Chairman Paul Volcker in the early 1980s, on the success of capital in attacking the US working class, on the low cost of imports, and on Asian countries accumulating huge foreign exchange reserves (buying US securities and so reducing their yields) as an insurance against financial trouble after the crisis of 1997–98. The end result was a sharp rise in US consumer borrowing that generated more credit-fuelled demand for the products of industry and commerce, plus a rise in the price of securities and the volume of financial trading, which helped boost profitability in the financial sector too. These influences reinforced

Chart 6.4 US Federal Reserve holdings of Treasury and mortgage securities

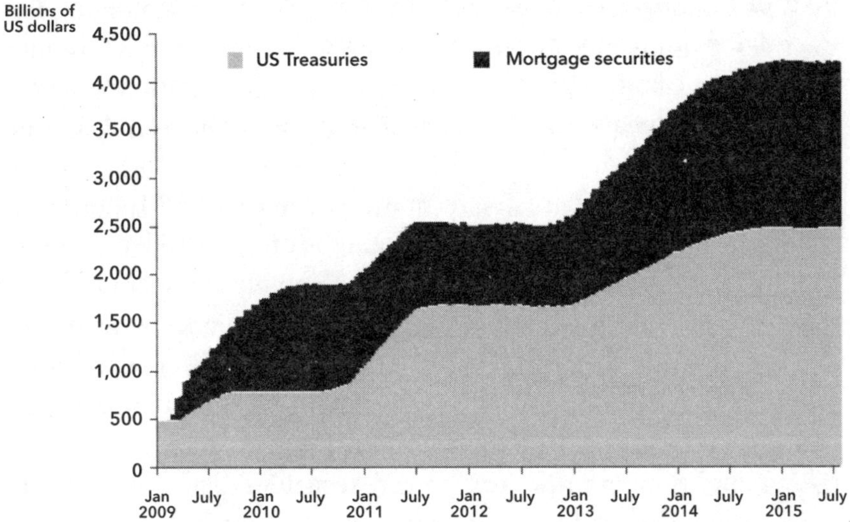

Note: These are the biggest assets on the US Federal Reserve's balance sheet, making up 95% of the total. The increase after 2008 reflects the impact of the successive 'quantitative easing' programmes, which ended in October 2014.

Source: Federal Reserve Bank of St Louis, FRED Economic Database, 2015, mortgage securities data at research.stlouisfed.org

each other to raise the recorded rate of profit in the years leading up to 2007.

But, of course, that credit bubble burst, the pinprick provided by rising mortgage loan defaults. These not only damaged the profitability of banks and crashed the price of securities based on the mortgage payments, they also justifiably raised broader worries about bad loans and over-extended credit in the whole economy, leading to the money markets seizing up as banks stepped back even from lending to each other. Many banks went bust or relied on government support to survive.

Lower interest rates, especially since the 1990s, helped fuel the financial boom and bust. Still lower interest rates – heading towards zero or even into negative territory for official levels of borrowing costs – followed after the 2008 collapse. The world's major central banks tried to revive their economies with such policies, but the main areas of 'growth' have been in levels of debt and some recovery of stock market prices. Economic growth has been weak, much weaker than in the normal bounce back from a recession, suggesting that underlying problems persist. With interest rates more or less as low as they can go already, there appears to be no more room for this measure to have any further material effect, at least in boosting economic growth.

The fourth element missing from the data in Chart 6.3 is the financial rescue mounted by the US Federal Reserve from 2007. What is one to think about buoyant private sector profitability shown in the data that has been sustained only by aggressive action, otherwise known as a bailout, from the central bank? After 2008, the Fed bought many *hundreds of billions* of dollars' worth of both US Treasury securities and private mortgage-backed securities from banks in its 'quantitative easing' programmes. This forced securities' prices higher and yields lower, and, at the same time, gave the owners cash for their securities. The stated rationale was to boost spending, by encouraging consumption and investment as interest rates on borrowing fell and there was more room for banks to lend out funds. Little recovery followed. Instead, the main effects were to benefit owners of financial securities and to stabilise the financial system.

The result is shown in Chart 6.4. As of 1 July 2015, the Fed had $2,461bn of Treasuries and $1,732bn of mortgage securities on its books, roughly 25 per cent of US GDP. Buying Treasuries pushed all borrowing rates lower in the US economy, despite banks still being unwilling to lend to projects deemed to be risky. The buying up of mortgage-backed securities also took unsaleable 'assets' off the books of crisis-hit US financial companies. Many American citizens making payments on their mortgages might be surprised to learn that the recipient is actually the US government! Still, you can't keep an innovative capitalist system down. When the US Treasury pays interest on its bonds and notes to the US Fed, the Fed ends up giving the Treasury most of that money back. The miracles of imperial finance know few bounds.

In 2007–8, during the initial phase of the crisis, the Fed also dramatically boosted its lending to financial companies and undertook a series of rescue operations. These were later reversed as what remained of the US financial system was put back on its feet by ultra-low funding rates and mergers. What has not been reversed, at least up to mid-2015, are the Fed's huge purchases of US Treasuries and mortgage securities, even though the US administration has long declared the crisis to be over.

The Fed was not alone in taking such measures. Other central banks have done similar things. Starting even earlier, in 2001, the Bank of Japan began a series of purchases of government bonds, asset-backed securities, and even exchange-traded funds, as it attempted to ward off deflation and economic stagnation. This programme was stepped up further in 2013, and the Japanese central bank's balance sheet rose from around 20 per cent of GDP in 2008 to some 60 per cent in 2014. In its own 'quantitative easing' programme up to 2013, the Bank of England purchased £375bn of UK government bonds, roughly 20 per cent of UK GDP, though it had only a small, tempo-rary holding of private sector bonds. In January 2015, the European Central Bank announced a new programme of buying government bonds and asset-backed securities of €60bn per month, likely up to September 2016, but possibly beyond, which could lead to the buying of more than 1 trillion euros of securities, or more than 10 per cent of euro area GDP. This would add to its previous large purchases of government and other supposedly 'high quality' securities in its own crisis-stricken, anti-crisis measures.

This is the real world backdrop to the US data on profitability. International economic and financial developments have a complex relationship to the data on the rate of profit. But one should not look upon any US figures showing credit-fuelled profit rates for the period up to 2007, still less the more recent figures, as a sign that there is, or was, no problem with profitability and that, instead, the capitalist economy was held back only by mistaken government policies and irresponsible financiers.

Moribund capitalism

The operations of finance include using leverage as a means to boost profitability and pricing financial assets on the basis of value that has not yet been created, and may never be created. Such operations can give capitalist investors economic power, but are part of the same system that now sees the world mired in an intractable crisis. Attempts by the governments of the major powers to ameliorate the many problems caused by the wreck of their system have had little effect. Extraordinary measures are taken that completely contradict the former axioms of what they once declared to be 'sound' economic policy, in particular the central bank schemes to buy government debt and even private sector debt and equity securities. Emergency stopgaps remain in place more or less indefinitely.

This is a socialisation of capitalism's chronic liabilities by the capitalist state – a means of trying to rescue private capitalism, and pretending that a failed system can overcome its problems to the benefit of all. Such policies have produced only mediocre results at best, and still leave hundreds of millions of people's lives destroyed. This evokes Lenin's description of imperialism as 'moribund capitalism'. The financial system is an expression of contemporary imperialism shot through with many contradictions.

7.

The Imperial Web

In 2009, *Rolling Stone* magazine's Matt Taibbi described Goldman Sachs, the US investment bank, as a 'great vampire squid wrapped around the face of humanity, relentlessly jamming its blood funnel into anything that smells like money'.[1] The striking image was detailed with examples of Goldman's relationship to the US economy, although Taibbi also noted that its many alumni had secured powerful jobs in government or central banks worldwide to help it feed off 'blood', or value created, all over the world. But the financial mechanism is more pervasive than the operations of a single company, or even of all financial companies combined. Finance is a core feature of the world economy, holding *all* corporations and all states in its web, because it is an inevitable outgrowth of the capitalist system of production. More than this, the financial system is also a means by which powerful companies, and their states, can increase their domination in the world economy, by extracting value from the labour of other countries.

A country's financial position in the world economy, from how far its currency is used internationally to the status of its equity markets, affects the ability of its capitalists to extend their control over economic resources. These things often lie outside the perspective of those who are otherwise critical of capitalism. Financial operations and assets can expand not only well beyond what the production of value might imply – the financial sector of a particular country can also draw upon the surplus value produced in the *global* system.

Not many countries are in a position to establish a major *international* banking and financial operation. The possibilities are limited to those that have an extensive international trade and investment business. Successful countries have a powerful position in the world hierarchy, or they have strong financial links to countries that do. This is the basis upon which that business can expand. Today, global finance is dominated by the US and the UK, but there is also a division of labour that gives a role to regional centres such as Tokyo, Hong Kong and Singapore in Asia, and the fund management businesses of Switzerland and Luxembourg in Europe.

Currency, trade and seigniorage

Within a country's boundaries, a single national currency is normally used by all businesses. For international deals, more than one currency can be chosen. Which one is used to put a price on purchases and sales, to repay a loan or to complete a transaction? Overwhelmingly, it is the US dollar. As noted earlier, even in 2013, more than a decade after the birth of the euro, the dollar was on one side of 87 per cent of all global currency deals, far beyond the US share of international business and more than twice the 33 per cent share of the euro.[2]

It is simpler, and potentially less costly or risky, for a company to use its own national currency when doing a foreign deal. Even multinational companies with a wide range of foreign operations almost always use only one currency as the basis for their accounts, and that is usually the domestic currency of the corporation's headquarters.[3] If a company can use its 'own' currency for pricing its exports and imports, it will be subject to a much lower commercial risk when exchange rates are volatile. Even when it is possible to insure against such risks, for example through currency forward transactions, this will often come at a price or at least involve dealing costs. The European Commission claimed that avoiding such costs – estimated at 0.3–0.4 per cent of European Union GDP per year – was a key economic factor favouring the euro's introduction.[4] As more countries joined the euro, these costs would be reduced further, it argued, and further still if non-member countries also used the euro in their international transactions.

The US dollar is used as the invoicing currency for close to 100 per cent of US exports and over 90 per cent of imports.[5] By comparison, in 2013 the euro was used as an invoicing currency for two-thirds of exports to outside the euro area and for just half of imports.[6] The dollar made up most of the remaining currency share for euro country external trade. In the case of the UK and Japan, over half of their trade is priced in currencies other than their national currency, so they do not benefit in this way as much as the other two currency blocs.

The US gains most here because international commodities, from oil to metals, agricultural products, pharmaceuticals, plastics, aerospace and defence equipment, are priced in US dollars. This means that when US companies compete with foreign companies in international markets, the exchange rate risk falls principally on the others. While this can cut both ways – if the dollar's exchange rate goes up, then other countries might be more competitive in winning a contract – it is still a risk that dollar-based companies are under far less pressure to manage. Many contracts will run for more than one year, so even if the initial exchange rate works for a non-dollar company to secure a deal, that may not be true in later years as currency values change. This is an important reduction of commercial costs and risks for US international businesses.

Paper money notes cost a few cents each to produce but have a much higher nominal face value of $10, $20 or $100, etc. Governments that issue their own national currency can therefore gain from printing these notes, something called 'seigniorage', as long as it does not destabilise the monetary system. For powerful countries, seigniorage is also international. This occurs when the national currency is circulated in other countries and held as a cash balance, so is not exchanged for the goods and services of the issuing country.

If US dollars enter circulation in another country through a cash payment for its exports, then the US has exchanged its bits of green paper for the other country's resources. The non-US company involved in the transaction has still been paid for the goods or services it supplied, and it may use the dollar notes in a further purchase. However, unless the dollars end up being exchanged for US goods and services at some point in the chain of transactions, a share of US imports is paid for with US paper currency only. In aggregate, the US economy does not exchange its own resources for a portion of its imports and this means that it can appropriate value produced elsewhere.

Companies and individuals may hold onto the currency of another country, especially when their own is unstable. The foreign currency may be seen as a better 'store of value', for example when it is less likely to depreciate because of inflation. The US has an *imperial* advantage in this respect because the dollar is the most widely accepted currency in other countries as a means of payment. In 2012, the IMF listed forty-three countries that had the dollar as a currency anchor, from Ecuador, which since 2001 has used the US dollar as the sole legal tender for notes, to others whose currencies are managed in relation to the dollar through a currency board exchange rate peg or some other method.[7] The euro was used by twenty-seven non-member countries, and in a similar variety of ways. In Kosovo and Montenegro, the euro has replaced the national currency, while Bulgaria has a euro-linked currency board. Fourteen countries in Central and West Africa, twelve of which are former French colonies, use the CFA franc, which is pegged to the euro.

It is difficult to measure the value of international seigniorage to the US economy. The New York Federal Reserve estimated that in December 2007 the total stock of notes in circulation was $829bn, and 'the majority is held outside the United States' – a proportion believed to be close to 60 per cent. It also said that the amount of dollar cash in circulation had 'risen rapidly in recent decades and much of the increase has been caused by demand from abroad'.[8] In other words, a stock of some $500bn of US currency is circulating overseas, close to 3 per cent of US GDP. Part of this stock of foreign dollars will be cash taken out of the country by US citizens; part will be money used in drug deals and other illegal activities.

At bottom, this is a transfer of value produced elsewhere to the US. Some foreign suppliers have delivered the commodities and held onto the bits of paper. One risk to the dollar's role here, which also affects other currencies, is that it becomes dependent on the strength of its exchange rate against other major currency alternatives. For example, as the US dollar continued to fall in 2007, Brazil's Gisele Bündchen declared that she wanted to be paid for her services in any major currency except dollars.[9]

International seigniorage gains are much smaller for other states than for the US. While the numbers are not insignificant for the euro, they accrue to all euro members, not just to one country. Before the euro's introduction in 1999, Germany's Deutsche mark was the most important currency of the most powerful European economy, although France's CFA franc zone in Africa also carried some weight. After 1999, Germany's external trade partners now held euros, not Deutsche marks. But euro area financial markets expanded to a level well beyond what would likely have been possible for Germany acting alone, and despite the financial turmoil in the late 2000s the scale of euro seigniorage has risen sharply. The European Central Bank estimated the value of euro banknotes held outside the euro area countries at €36.4 billion in mid-2003, and the figure had jumped to €143 billion by the end of 2013.[10] The latter was about 30 to 40 per cent of the respective US figure and roughly 1.5 per cent of euro country GDP.

There has been speculation about how far the foreign circulation of euro banknotes is also due to criminal activity. In 2010, British banks withdrew the high-value 500 euro note from circulation after the Serious Organised Crime Agency estimated that 90 per cent of them were not being used legitimately.[11] When crossing borders, it is possible to stash a serious sum of euros undetected in your clothes: €20,000 in €500 notes would take up less space than a thin bar of chocolate – much less than a similarly valued pile of $100 bills, the highest denomination note currently issued by the US.[12]

I have found no estimates of foreign seigniorage for the UK, Japan or Switzerland, the other countries of relevance. The UK's figures will have declined with the dissolution of the Sterling Area in the early 1970s, and since sterling has a very much smaller role in foreign payments than the US dollar, the seigniorage amounts are probably negligible in relation to UK GDP.[13] This is not contradicted by the UK's major financial role in the world, since that is not really based upon sterling. Possibly the foreign circulation of Swiss francs and Japanese yen are more important in relation to their respective GDPs than in the UK's case. The longer-term trend of appreciation in the value of the latter currencies, and their low interest rates, makes holding cash in the form of notes relatively attractive.[14]

Nevertheless, seigniorage is only a very narrow measure of the potential economic gains to be had from a currency with an international role. The stocks of currency circulating abroad may be large absolute sums, but they remain only small shares of GDP. Even in the case of the euro, a newer currency than the other majors and one that was liable to have a faster rate of growth in holdings, the incremental amounts each year are not significant. There are far more important dimensions of financial privilege.

'Exorbitant privilege'

The global role of the dollar and the linked economic advantages have been described in terms of the US having an 'exorbitant privilege' in the world.[15] This can refer either to the privilege the US has in being able to fund its external deficits by borrowing at low cost in its own currency, its original meaning, or to its ability to earn an 'excess return' on net foreign assets.[16] These privileges accrue only to a select few powers, and are available to both their national governments and their national companies.

Most users of another country's currency for international trade, investment or finance do not hold the physical cash. Instead, they hold a bank account or securities denominated in that currency. With these, the holders may receive interest or dividend payments, so the company or country receiving funds does not get them for free, as with seigniorage. But a key benefit the US gains from the global role of the dollar is its ability (usually) to get cheap, low risk finance. This comes about in two ways.

Firstly, the US can draw upon the financial resources of the world economy and has much easier access to funds than do other countries. One important aspect of this is the dollar's high share – around two-thirds – of official foreign exchange reserves. As mentioned earlier, after the Asian financial crisis of 1997–98, many countries in the region – and elsewhere – built up their currency reserves as an insurance policy: if there were another flight of capital in a crisis, they could try to offset the impact by selling these reserves. The US dollar was the reserve currency of choice not only because it was the principal means of payment for trade and finance, but also because many countries had currencies linked to the dollar. During the 2000s, a growing US current account deficit was funded in this way by huge inflows of finance, especially from Asian central banks that bought US Treasury securities and other US dollar-denominated assets.[17]

From 2000 to 2007, the US current account deficit totalled a massive $4.7 trillion, with the annual deficit peaking at 6 per cent of US GDP in 2006. Over the same period, China's foreign exchange reserves, excluding gold, grew by $1.4 trillion. Assuming that three-quarters of these reserves were held in US dollars, this implies that China's official reserve accumulation of dollars was *by itself* enough to fund roughly one-fifth of the US current account deficit over that period.[18] The currency composition of China's FX reserves is not reported, but, when I discussed the issue with a Japanese finance ministry official in 2005, he told me that 80 per cent or more of China's reserves were held in US dollars in the early part of that decade. The dollar proportion was reduced in later years and is probably around 60 per cent now. Despite that, the further accumulation of China's FX reserves, from $1.5 trillion at the end of 2007 to $3.9 trillion by the end of 2014, showed continued support for US deficits from external finance, although that particular source of support had reversed a little in 2015, with China selling some reserves to prevent its currency depreciating too far.

It was not only the *easy* funding of US deficits that stood out in the 2000s. The demand for dollars was so high that, despite the huge deficits needing financing, US yields *fell*. Many factors were responsible, but one study suggested that the impact of foreign purchases of securities reduced the borrowing costs of the US government by 80 basis points for ten-year debt – for example, a yield being lowered to 4.2 per cent rather than remaining at 5.0 per cent.[19] Since the foreign purchases of US securities were made not only by foreign central banks, and were not only of US Treasury securities – but also of equities, corporate bonds and 'agency' bonds (securities issued by semi-official US institutions, based on mortgages and student loans) – lower bond yields and higher security prices spread throughout the US financial markets.[20] This was an important factor in the ensuing crisis of 2007–8, but, ironically, it also reflected a structural feature of US financial privilege in the world economy. This shows that analyses of what some have called 'financialisation' must be set in the context of global developments, and that it would be a mistake to treat the issue only from the point of view of what happens in individual countries.[21]

Secondly, by issuing debt denominated in US dollars, the US state can avoid taking on foreign currency risk. In a US-centred crisis, the value of the dollar might fall against other major currencies, but the US state has little debt denominated in euros, Japanese yen or sterling, so it will face a negligible increase in its liabilities from this source. Countries that do not occupy such a privileged position in global finance – those that are not imperialist powers – face much bigger risks. Even if their levels of debt to income, etc., look good, financial markets give these countries a high risk premium, making their costs of borrowing higher because they have little ability to borrow long-term in their domestic currencies.[22] Often they borrow funds denominated in the major foreign currencies, especially the US dollar, and they also borrow at much higher dollar interest rates than the US government would pay.

US interest rates may not be the lowest in the world, and financial privilege does not necessarily mean *lower* bond yields than elsewhere. These things will also depend upon credit ratings, domestic inflation and central bank monetary policy. For example, yields on German and Japanese government bonds have usually been below those on US Treasury securities. In July 2015, as German/euro and Japanese central bank policy was locked into zero rates, while financial markets believed the US Fed might raise interest rates later in the year or in 2016, the pattern of ten-year government bond yields was as follows: Japan 0.40 per cent, Germany 0.64 per cent, and the US 2.20 per cent.

However, the dollar portion of the credit market is the biggest in the world and the easier access to this for the US government and US companies, together with the absence of any exchange rate risk on borrowing, remain important financial advantages. The funds borrowed can finance extra imports for US consumers, or they can offset outflows on the financial accounts for investments in foreign assets such as direct or portfolio investments.

A key point is that the interest costs on US foreign borrowing have been far less than the returns on US foreign investments. This has enabled the US to maintain a positive net investment income, despite the persistent, large net *deficit* on its foreign investment position. At the end of 2013, the US net foreign investment stock position was *minus* \$5,457bn, in other words, foreigners owned this much more of assets in the US compared to US ownership of foreign assets. However, in 2013, US net investment income was \$209bn.[23] US investment income was higher than its payments on foreign investments mainly due to its ability to pay very low interest rates on the large volume of US government debt owned by foreigners.

Perhaps unsurprisingly, most economists prefer to avoid imperial power relationships when examining this issue and resort instead to wild speculation. One duo asks a pertinent question: why do foreign investors accept lower returns on US assets, thus allowing the US to derive a positive income balance from a deficit investment position? But their solution is to assume away the existence of different rates of return and instead to invent *extra* US foreign assets that do not appear in the statistics. I would be the last to argue that US statistics capture every cent of reality, but this is to ignore an evident fact that the yields *are* different. The extra US assets are given the name 'dark matter' and, as one might expect, including this results in the US having a net *surplus* on its investment position.[24] This feat is achieved by 'redefining the stock of assets in a way that more explicitly shows the value of the underlying services'. This transforms US imperialism's economic and financial power, its ability to appropriate value from the world economy, into a payment the rest of the world makes to the US for the services rendered! Inhabitants of the Middle East, Africa, Latin America, Asia and elsewhere might very well ask what 'dark' services they are paying for.

Running the world banking system: US dollar power

Given the fact that most world trade and finance is denominated in dollars, the US can be seen as the provider of 'global money', able to decide which policies to pursue based upon its domestic interests and on what it deems viable for the global economic and monetary system.[25] However, the mechanism through which this power is exerted is usually discussed in purely *political* terms, for example by citing the inordinate influence of the US on the regulation of international finance and on the policies of the IMF. The *economic* mechanism is left to one side. Yet it is this that illustrates most clearly how the financial system is a means of exercising such power.

An exceptional, but realistic and practical example will illustrate the point. Consider what happens when a company in China needs to pay Venezuela for oil imports. At first sight, no US company, still less the US state, would appear to be involved in this transaction, and neither country has a friendly political relationship with the US. Nevertheless, a US-based company will normally be involved in the deal and US state acquiescence is necessary. This is because oil is priced in US dollars and the payment, for example $50m, will go through the US banking system. The Chinese company does not post dollar cash from Beijing to Caracas in a large envelope! The companies in each country will likely have a US dollar account with their local banks. However, these accounts will be *held* in the US monetary system, possibly via a US 'correspondent' bank with which they have dealings or the US branch of the relevant Chinese or Venezuelan bank, if it is allowed to operate in the US. The Chinese company will tell its bank to credit the Venezuelan company's dollar account with $50m, either by deducting the sum from its existing dollar account or by asking the bank to exchange the appropriate amount of its local currency into dollars. In either case, it is the US-based bank that will, on behalf of the Chinese company, transfer $50m to the account of the Venezuelan company at another US-based bank. The dollar transfer between banks is made via a payments system based in the US, either the Fedwire Funds Service, which is under the direct supervision of the US Federal Reserve or, more usually, the Clearing House Interbank

Payments System, a privately run international bank-owned system whose US membership is regulated by the US government.

If the Chinese and Venezuelan companies did not want to use the US banking system, they would have to agree on a separate, non-dollar-based means of transacting. This *could* be done, but it would mean agreeing on another currency basis for the deal, for example either Venezuela accepting China's renminbi (ISO dealing code CNY) in payment,[26] or China agreeing to pay in terms of Venezuela's bolivar (ISO code VEF). This would mean that the Venezuelan company would end up with CNY, which it may have little use for and which it might then need to exchange into VEF. Or, the Chinese company would have to buy VEF to deliver to the Venezuelan company. There is a relatively active foreign exchange market in USD versus CNY and in USD versus VEF, but the foreign exchange costs of dealing in CNY against VEF are relatively high, given that very few banks do this, and it may not be easy to do such a deal in terms of market liquidity, making it commercially unattractive. In any case, in existing financial market conditions, the CNY-VEF exchange rate transaction would probably be done via the US dollar as the intermediary currency (sell CNY and buy USD, then sell USD and buy VEF). But of course this would return the transaction to the US system! The consequence of all these aspects of currency dealing is that even the opponents of US imperialism tend to fall under its commercial rules.

Given the role of the dollar in world trade and finance, a company planning to make significant and repeated foreign deals will need a bank account in US dollars. Some countries have agreed barter deals to avoid such foreign exchange transactions, for example, exchanging barrels of oil for a quantity of other goods. But this is even more cumbersome: what is the exchange rate of a barrel of crude oil in terms of tractors, cement, sheet steel or televisions?

While there have been attempts by political opponents of the US to bypass the dollar with direct deals – as with plans initiated in 2009 by Russia and China – for some time to come this will leave the US government with an astonishing power to isolate opponents economically. This can happen without the US necessarily having to do anything extra in the political or military sphere, although such measures often

follow. All it need do is declare economic relationships with a particular country out of bounds and that country's economic links with the
rest of the world will be severely restricted, putting its economy under
drastic pressure. The impact does not depend on a country dealing
directly with the US, only with its banking system, even indirectly as
in the previous example. Furthermore, even if a country in political
conflict with the US plans to avoid dealing in dollars altogether, thus
avoiding these restrictions, the US government can still, in practice,
prevent *other* countries' banks from dealing with the targeted country.
As one legal adviser in Dubai, which has close business relationships
with Iran, noted in relation to US sanctions on the latter:

> The real tipping point was at the end of 2011, with the latest round of
> US banking sanctions, potentially exposing non-US banks to sanctions
> by the US … That was a real wake-up call for banks outside the US still
> dealing with Iran. They didn't want to run the risk of being cut off from
> the US banking system.[27]

Being cut off from the US banking system would severely damage a
major company's international business operations, so the real power
of this sanction is that it rarely has to be implemented. A number
of major international banks in Europe and Japan have escaped this
penalty after paying hundreds of millions of dollars in fines to the US
government, apologising profusely and promising not to do it again.[28]
The US has found it easy to threaten other countries in this way whenever it so wishes. The fact that there has been widespread compliance
with US policy, particularly in Europe, indicates that financial power
is a tool that can be used against other rich countries, not only those
that are evidently subordinate in the world hierarchy.

Another dimension of US financial power derives from the Federal
Reserve's provision of dollar liquidity to global financial markets. All
central banks influence the availability of funds, and the level of interest rates, in their *domestic* monetary system, but the international role
of the US dollar makes the US central bank critical for the functioning of the *global* system. In 'normal' times, the Fed need play no role,
and private banking relationships will service the liquidity needs of

the market. However, the financial crisis of recent years has put the Fed more obviously in a key position. It has provided extra funds, for a fee, to the European Central Bank, the Bank of England and other central banks to redistribute to their local banks and support financial market stability. The *New York Times* reported on why this move was also in US interests:

> In recent days some European banks have faced difficulties in borrowing dollars, whether from other banks or from money market funds in the United States. There was fear that if they could not borrow dollars, they would be forced to cut off loans to American companies or sell dollar-denominated assets, perhaps forcing prices down in already unsteady markets.[29]

The vulnerability of the European banks was a consequence of much of their business being conducted in US dollars, especially for international trade finance, so that it was (and is) critical for them to be able to access dollar funds. This illustrates once again how the US is arguably in an even more privileged position in the midst of a financial crisis, even if it did not necessarily profit much from these particular funding operations.

Financial services exports

'Exporting' a service simply means that a foreign buyer pays you for the service you perform for them; you may not have to travel to another country to do it. In the case of financial services, foreign buyers come to you via the telecommunications network, especially if the service you provide is exported from one of the world's financial hubs. The US is the world's largest exporter of financial services (if insurance is excluded); in other words, US-based companies derive the highest revenues from providing financial services to businesses in foreign countries. This is one way that the US appropriates surplus value from the world economy: in dealing revenues, fees and commissions, and the management costs charged by US financial companies to their overseas subsidiaries.[30] These revenues derive from the global status of US dollar finance, but are additional to the interest or dividend income on US ownership of foreign assets. They also include revenues earned by US financial intermediaries from foreign investment coming into the US to buy government bonds, corporate bonds and equities. So, in addition to the US having privileged access to foreign funding, US-based financial companies – and these are principally US-owned – can make money from *incoming* deals. Nevertheless, these foreign financial services revenues are relatively small compared to the size of the US economy. For example, the 2011 financial services receipts from abroad were $73bn, but this was barely 0.5 per cent of US GDP.[31] The total activities of the financial services and insurance sector were much higher, accounting for close to 8 per cent of US GDP.[32]

By comparison, the UK financial services export revenues in 2011 were some 2 to 3 per cent of GDP, five or six times higher than for the US, but the share of the financial services and insurance sector in the UK's GDP was similar, at 7.5 per cent in 2011.[33] This reflects the bigger *external* orientation of UK finance. British financial services export revenues derive largely from bank dealing spreads and commissions, plus the fees of banks and securities dealers.

Even more so than in many other areas of global business, financial services export revenues are very highly concentrated in a small number of countries. Table 7.1 shows that the top three countries – the US, the UK and Luxembourg – accounted for close to 60 per cent of the world total in 2013, while countries ranked below France, in ninth position, each had a share of less than 2 per cent. The potential for concentration in this particular realm of finance means that, especially for smaller countries, financial services can be a major component of national export earnings and GDP.

Luxembourg, a country with a population of barely half a million people, has a profitable niche in this area. It could aptly be named a 'paragon of parasitism', offering an extreme example of how a large financial sector unproductive of value can benefit a country if it can appropriate value from others. Luxembourg is an important private banking sector for wealthy individuals, helped by its low tax regime,

Table 7.1 Financial services export revenues, 2000–13 ($ billion)*

	2000	2005	2010	2013	% of 2013 Total
US	22.1	72.3	76.4	83.9	25.0%
UK	20.2	54.0	59.0	62.6	18.7%
Luxembourg	n/a	36.8	40.0	42.7	12.7%
Singapore	1.8	12.2	16.5	18.4	5.5%
Hong Kong & China**	4.4	13.1	13.7	15.8	4.7%
Switzerland	10.6	15.8	16.1	16.7	5.0%
Germany	3.5	12.8	14.3	15.3	4.6%
Ireland	2.1	8.4	9.1	9.9	3.0%
France	1.3	2.9	6.5	6.6	2.0%
Other	31.4	53.8	56.8	63.0	18.8%
Total	**97.6**	**282.1**	**308.5**	**334.9**	**100.0%**

Notes: *Financial services revenues exclude insurance. **Separate figures for Hong Kong and China have been added together.
Source: United Nations Conference on Trade & Development, Handbook of Statistics, 2014, Table 5.2, p. 260, at unctad.org

and it has also done many infamous tax deals with large international companies. In a curious twist of fate, Jean-Claude Juncker – the prime minister of Luxembourg for nearly nineteen years up to the end of 2013, and for many of those years also its Finance Minister, so officially endorsing such deals – distinguished himself by lecturing the Greek government in 2014–15 on its need to raise taxes and improve its tax collection system after he became President of the European Commission. But Luxembourg's principal claim to financial fame is that it is the biggest fund management centre in Europe. It accounted for more than a quarter of European assets under management in 2012, a share that was nearly double that of the next biggest country, France.[34] Luxembourg's financial services, including insurance, generated export revenues equivalent to an astonishing three-quarters of its GDP in 2011! These services also made up nearly a quarter of the country's GDP,[35] the highest share in Europe and probably in the world.

Switzerland is another relatively small country with a large financial services sector, accounting for 10.3 per cent of its GDP in 2011. This was made up by the banking sector (6.2 per cent) and the insurance sector (4.1 per cent). According to the Swiss Bankers' Association, the value attributed to these financial services amounted to CHF 59.4 billion in 2011 – or CHF 260,000 per employee (roughly $280,000 in 2011) – so that 'productivity is almost two times the Swiss average'.[36] This 'productivity' is a function of Switzerland's role as a tax haven. It can profit from small percentage cuts taken from the huge volume of financial business such a regime attracts from the rest of the world economy. The tiny lakeside Swiss canton of Zug is reputed to host 27,000 corporations – about one for every four inhabitants.[37] The Swiss entrepreneurial spirit is unlikely to be so strong that even a conservative backwater sprouts tens of thousands of companies. Evidently, it is the result of tax dodging by wealthy elites worldwide, from which the Swiss financial system and economy, among others, benefit.

Hong Kong was an important trading post of the British Empire. Britain seized the territory from China in several stages during the nineteenth century, most notably after China's defeat in two Opium Wars forced it to accept British terms, including buying British-trafficked narcotics from its colony in India.[38] Opium trading and maritime commerce were the foundations for Hong Kong's development into a financial centre, but its business in recent decades has grown on the back of mainland China's economic prowess. In 1997, Britain handed the colony back to China. Part of the territory had a lease that expired in 1997, and it would have been unwise for Britain to try to dispute this, and unsustainable for it to try and hold on to the remainder. Hong Kong then became a 'special administrative region' of China through which the Chinese state and Chinese companies practised dealing with world financial markets. As with Switzerland, the bulk of Hong Kong's financial services revenues come from banking. The Hong Kong financial sector made up 15 per cent of the area's GDP in 2010. It also registered a well above average GDP per person employed of HKD 1,194,000, roughly $154,000.[39]

Mainland China, by contrast, is still in a very early stage of development in this respect. China has grown dramatically in recent decades, producing a significant proportion of the goods consumed in rich countries, based upon low-cost labour-power exploited, directly and indirectly, by western companies. But in an effort to shield its domestic economy from the ravages of the international financial markets, China's government has refused to open up its financial system as quickly as the IMF (read: the US) has advocated. Instead, it has experimented with using Hong Kong as a base for such activity, with continued restrictions on deals between mainland financial companies and others. Nevertheless, in recent years there has been a rise in the number of financial deals between mainland China and the rest of the world. In terms of financial services, its exports rose from a minuscule $78m in 2000 to $3.2bn by 2013. Another sign of the rapid pace of development is the growth, albeit from a very low base, of global trading in the national Chinese currency. From a position of just $15bn per day in 2007, close to zero per cent of global foreign exchange dealing, by 2013 trading in the renminbi had jumped to $120bn per day and was 2 per cent of the global total.[40]

Singapore is also an ex-British colony. Its prominence in regional commercial and financial business developed under British rule, having been originally established as a trading post of the East India Company in the early nineteenth century. In 2012, the country's finance and insurance sector made up 11.9 per cent of GDP.[41] Most of Singapore's financial services export revenues derive from banking, including foreign exchange and derivatives turnover, but its official statistics give few details. A notable moment in Singapore's financial development occurred when its government set up 'sovereign wealth funds' to manage national financial resources: Temasek in 1974 and GIC in 1981. Temasek holds both Singapore-based and foreign investment assets, while GIC mainly manages Singapore's foreign exchange reserves and invests in foreign financial securities. They invest in property assets, industrial and commercial corporations' shares, bonds and currencies. GIC has also made many banks wary of its aggressive dealing strategy. I witnessed one occasion when GIC contacted a number of banks, asking for prices for a particular exchange rate, and then hit each of the banks simultaneously with large deals on which they would have made losses. One sales person in the dealing room likened it to a 'drive-by shooting'. Although a melodramatic turn of phrase, this reflected the damage that had been done to the banks' profitability. Together, these two Singapore investment funds have assets worth probably in excess of $500bn, and they each contribute to government revenues.

Ireland offers a sorrier tale, beginning its move into financial services in less auspicious circumstances. Having been partitioned in 1921, after several hundred years of British colonial rule, Ireland stagnated economically until it found a means of escape through the economic subsidies that flowed from its 1973 membership of the European Economic Community. Compared to Hong Kong and Singapore, it had no developed financial or commercial services expertise or status, but in the late 1980s the Irish government took a gamble by offering the country up as a low-tax venue for corporations interested in Europe, especially financial businesses. It built a new International Financial Services Centre, based in Dublin, which attracted traditional fund managers, hedge funds and the branches of some major global banks. I once visited an Italian asset manager based in Dublin and wondered why its European investment headquarters was located there. By 2007, Ireland's financial and insurance services accounted for nearly 11 per cent of GDP.[42] This was not directly linked to the Irish property bubble and bust that left the economy under a mountain of debt, but both were results of the same magical thinking that often accompanies the expansion of finance.[43]

The Irish economy depends heavily on foreign capital, and a large proportion of Ireland's GDP ends up being transmitted abroad in foreign investment income payments. For this reason, Ireland has possibly the biggest percentage gap between GDP (a measure of its national *output*) and Gross National *Income* (what is retained in the country) in the world. In 2011, the gap was equivalent to 19 per cent of GDP.[44] This meant that the value of nearly one day in five worked in the Irish Republic became revenue owed to foreign investors!

The Irish example clearly demonstrates that it would be wrong to think a country has financial strength or is prominent in the world economy just because it has a large financial sector, still less that it is an imperialist power. Smaller financial hubs, even more significant ones like Luxembourg and Switzerland, need to be understood in terms of the role they play in the global financial system.[45] The example of

Singapore illustrates that financial firepower can also develop outside the traditional centres. Data on financial services revenues are, in any case, useful for illustrating some of contemporary capitalism's parasitic features.

Equity markets, financial power and control

Although difficult to quantify, financial privilege and value appropriation also operate through the equity markets. In these markets, stakes in the ownership of companies are bought and sold, along with rights to receive dividend payments on the shares. Equity markets are usually represented by stock exchanges located in particular countries, although nowadays dealing is done electronically and across borders. They put a price on company securities and function as places where these securities can be exchanged for money. But two other related functions are just as important.

Firstly, equity markets operate as a way of allowing capitalist companies to issue new securities for sale to money-capitalists. This should not be exaggerated, however, since companies derive the bulk of their investment funds from retained profits, bank borrowing, or from issues of corporate bonds. For example, UK gross fixed capital formation in 2011 – buying machinery, vehicles, buildings, land, etc. – was £215 billion, compared to less than £23 billion raised on the UK stock exchange through new share issues, initial public offerings and further share issues in that year.[46]

The second, more significant, role the equity markets play is in corporate takeover and control. In this case, the valuation of equity capital indicates not only the sum of money a capitalist owner could have at his or her command, it can also act as a *means of payment* for another company's equity. This occurs in a common form of equity market transaction: the 'share swap' or 'stock swap'. Here the acquiring company offers a certain number of its shares in exchange for those of the takeover or merger target company, a ratio that depends on the relative prices of each company's share plus any incentive given to get the transaction accepted by the target company's shareholders.

This kind of deal can avoid cash payment altogether. Even when it does not, the main factor in the transaction will still be the relative attraction of each company's equity. The global size and status of the different equity markets is influential here, since the equity capital means of payment has to be sufficiently liquid.

Vodafone's 2000 takeover of the German mobile telecom company Mannesmann offered a striking example of how the stock market can be used in the competition between *imperialist* companies. Mannesmann had been an 'alliance partner' of Vodafone, but had then bought another UK mobile company, Orange, in October 1999. This had 'contravened a gentleman's agreement not to compete on each other's territory', according to the head of Vodafone, Chris Gent. Upset that its own monopolistic plans were under threat as the industry was in the middle of a merger boom, Vodafone launched a bid for Mannesmann in November 1999. The deal was at the time the world's biggest hostile (not mutually agreed) takeover. Mannesmann shareholders were given close to fifty-nine shares in Vodafone for each (higher priced) share they held in the German group.[47] The share swap involved no bank borrowing or cash transaction, except for payments to the companies' advisors. The combined company's value was estimated at £228bn on completion. Mannesmann could also have bid for Vodafone, but the greater prominence of the London Stock Exchange compared to Frankfurt, where Mannesmann was listed, and the strong links between British and US money-capitalists among Vodafone's shareholders, put the balance of power with the latter. Even if the takeover had gone the other way, this would still support the point that corporations based in the imperialist financial centres have the privilege of being able to use their own equity valuation as a means of payment.

It would be more difficult for a company to execute a takeover in this way if it were listed only on a small stock exchange and wanted to acquire a company listed on a big exchange. The shareholders of the takeover target might be reluctant to accept shares traded in a smaller market, especially if the share price quotation was given in a minor, less liquid currency, for example, the Norwegian krone or the Mexican peso. These minnows are not attractive to money-capitalists!

This gives an advantage to companies whose securities are priced in terms of one of the major global currencies, especially the US dollar, but also the euro, the Japanese yen and sterling. The latter three currencies trading against the US dollar accounted for half of total currency turnover in 2010.[48] Not surprisingly, even if they originate from smaller countries, major global corporations will also tend to list their equities in the bigger equity markets based in the major capitalist powers.

Carving up the market

Countries prominent in finance can punch further above their domestic economic weight by attracting foreign company listings on their equity markets. This kind of development means that the US equity market, in both the market value of companies listed (capitalisation) and the volume of trading in shares (turnover), is bigger compared to other centres than a relative GDP measure would suggest. The same is

Table 7.2 Equity market capitalisation and turnover, 2013 ($ billion)

Country	Exchanges	Capitalisation*	Turnover **
US	NYSE Euronext (US) plus NASDAQ	24,035	23,285
China	Shanghai plus Shenzhen plus Hong Kong Exchanges	7,050	9,665
Japan	Japan Exchange Group	4,543	6,516
UK	London Stock Exchange Group	4,429	2,315
Belgium, France, Netherlands, Portugal	NYSE Euronext (Europe)	3,584	1,722
Canada	TMX Group	2,114	1,333
Germany	Deutsche Börse	1,936	1,383

Notes: *Market capitalisation for end-2013. Data for Shenzhen estimated by the author.
**Electronic order book volume of trades for 2013. Data for Hong Kong estimated by the author.
Source: World Federation of Exchanges, 2013 WFE Market Highlights, 28 January 2014, at world-exchanges.org, and author's calculations

true for the UK. In stock exchange terms, the US is four or five times bigger than Japan and the UK roughly twice as big as Germany, as Table 7.2 details.

Stock exchange prices are the most widely reported aspect of the financial markets in the general news media, from regular television news bulletins to daily newspapers and internet sites. The attention paid to these indices reflects the importance of financial securities, and of financial wealth, in capitalist society today. The ups and downs of share prices affect the data, but the relative size of each country's stock market does not tend to change very much. The exception is China, which has risen to prominence in more recent years. Although the Shanghai exchange only opened in 1990 and the Shenzhen exchange in 1991, when their data is added to that for the Hong Kong exchange, which is more than 100 years old, then the total China-based equity market comes in second behind the US in terms of capitalisation and turnover.[49] The US markets are, however, head, shoulders and elbows above the others, assisted by the US economy's greater size and its ability to attract foreign company listings. The London Stock Exchange ranks behind Tokyo's, but is far bigger than the exchanges for other European countries, including the combined Euronext exchange figures for Belgium, France, the Netherlands and Portugal.

A company listed on a major equity market will have access to world funds and be able to raise new capital. More importantly, having such a listing gives the company extra business influence because its equity capital now acts as *real* money in the market for the ownership and control of other companies worldwide. These advantages apply to any major corporation that lists on a major exchange, from whichever country, so one might question whether there are really any specifically *imperialist* factors involved. For example, if Kazakhmys, a mining company based in Kazakhstan whose majority shareholders are Kazakh capitalists, had appeared in the UK's FTSE 100 index, then it might seem to be just a question of big corporations *anywhere* taking advantage of the best, not necessarily national, financial markets in which to deal. This would, however, overlook the fact that the principal monopolistic corporations are also based in the major imperialist powers, as noted in Chapter 5.

Corporate control is a direct consequence of the growth of cross-shareholdings, mergers and takeovers made possible by global equity markets. This is another sign that the equity markets do not simply offer a means of turning a 'long-term' investment in a company's assets into a form of tradable money-capital. They also show how a defining feature of the economics of imperialism is the control of financial securities. What Marx described as 'fictitious capital' is a very *real* form of capital when it comes to exercising economic power, empire building and appropriating value today.

The daily grind

To borrow a phrase from military pundits, the US is the closest to 'full spectrum dominance' in global finance today, given the key role of the dollar and the power of the US economy. Many privileges follow from this. Not all of them can be easily quantified, however, and those that can, such as export revenues from financial services, might appear to be an insignificant percentage of US GDP. Nonetheless, the privileges need to be looked at as a *full package*, not simply in terms of those resulting from the activities of banks and other financial institutions. They include other parts of the mechanism by which the US relates to the world economy, for example the easy funding of its current account deficit and the foreign investments of its corporations. Some of these privileges, and the related economic benefits, accrue to US-based companies or to the US government simply because those trading with the US, or using the dollar, have to accept the existing financial infrastructure. The privileges do not have to depend upon the US using force. Being at the centre of the world financial system, it is able to 'peacefully' penalise other countries that have to use that system. Financial power hits the headlines when there is a debt crisis. But it is also a key part of the regular, *daily* mechanisms of power in the world economy.

The US is not the only country to enjoy such advantages, which boil down to an ability to siphon off value created elsewhere. While there is a division of labour in finance, from bank lending, to asset management, to dealing in currencies, interest rates, bond and equity securities, etc., the main operations are centred in a small group of countries. US-based international financial operations are not necessarily the world's biggest in every area, and they are often more important for other economies than they are for the US, as in the case of Britain. Less significant powers, such as Switzerland and Luxembourg, have carved out their own niches, and other more subordinate countries may have even smaller niches to service the major powers or to play the role of tax havens. The different ways in which capitalist corporations and powerful countries relate to the financial system today illustrate the parasitic nature of the imperialist world economy.

8.

Inside the Machine

The City of London is the pre-eminent international financial centre for the world economy. At first sight, this looks implausible, because US Federal Reserve policy is obviously critical for the international financial markets, setting the interest rate for and determining the supply of the key international currency, the US dollar. The financial exchanges in New York and Chicago are also the biggest in the world for trading financial securities. But London is by far the largest hub for foreign exchange dealing, for 'over-the-counter' derivatives deals (those between banks and their customers), for international bank lending and borrowing, and for trading in international bonds.

UK-based finance also brings economic benefits for British capitalism. To talk of 'benefits' might seem perverse in the wake of a huge financial crisis, but these have not only been important for the British economy in the past; they remain so. The financial sector of the UK economy ('the City') plays three important and related roles. Firstly, the international revenues this sector provides help offset the UK's chronic deficit in its trade in goods with the rest of the world. Secondly, the City's operations provide a means by which any deficit on the balance of payments may be readily financed, often at relatively low cost. The ease with which the UK's foreign investments can be funded by borrowing also enables British capitalists to gain from the international revenues that come from those investments. Thirdly, the City's role as a key market for global finance gives British-based companies access to funds with which they can extend their influence and operations worldwide.

The City is part of a mechanism through which British capitalists both operate in and extract revenues from the rest of the world economy, something that defines Britain's status as an imperialist power. That is precisely why the huge City operations exist! Referring to British imperialism may conjure up images of a past era of Viceroys, Royal Navy gunboats, and Home and Colonial grocery stores in every British town. But the relationship between imperialism and finance is far from being only of historical interest. Examining the international trade, financial and investment flows between the UK and other countries will reveal how the system works today and allow us to identify developments that suggest future problems for Britain's financial machine.

Number crunching

Just over two million people work in finance and related jobs in the UK, constituting 7 per cent of all employment, with a little over one million directly employed in banking and insurance. These employees in turn create a demand for goods and services in the domestic UK economy, anything from Starbucks coffees to business suits, from telecom engineers to office cleaners, from taxis to marble cladding and questionable artwork. In 2011–12, UK financial services contributed £63bn of tax revenues, 12 per cent of the total.[1] Alistair Darling, Chancellor of the Exchequer in the Labour government from 2007 to 2010, acknowledged the importance of British finance in his comment on the booming 2000s: 'we mistakenly assumed that the revenue that rolled in from the financial services sector and from stamp duty would keep on coming. Our spending was based on that assumption and, when it came to an end, borrowing rose.'[2] Just how important the financial sector is to Britain's position in the world can be seen by examining the data for the UK's international payments – the money flowing between the UK and the rest of the world. While there are problems with all economic data – the numbers get revised and may not properly measure what they claim to take account of – the broad trend in the numbers, seen in the light of other evidence, gives a more solid picture.

In presenting these data, I focus on the *net* figures, those which show the balance of transactions and investment positions between the UK and other countries. For example, I look at the net trade balance of exports minus imports, rather than exports and imports separately. These net figures are the simplest way of expressing the position of the UK economy vis-à-vis the rest of the world. They also relate to an important concept: Britain's *privileged* appropriation of value from other countries. If inflows of financial revenues were £100bn, while outflows were £90bn, then the net figure of £10bn is a better measure of such a privilege than the £100bn number since it is a sign of the *relative* position of Britain in the world economy. The net figures will nevertheless tend to understate the importance of finance for the UK. If the British-based financial sector ceased to exist, this would not only eliminate the surplus on financial services payments. It would create a *deficit* because British-based companies would still require some of the services currently provided, which would have to be imported from other countries. There would then be net flows out of the UK to pay for these services provided elsewhere.

One other issue is worth noting. In accounting terminology, balance of payments data must always 'balance'. In other words, the sum of all transactions, in and out, plus and minus, across all accounts, is zero. For example, a country's imports might cost £200bn, but its exports might only be worth £120bn, giving a deficit of £80bn and not enough to match the money needed to pay for the goods imports. So there has to be an inflow of funds from elsewhere, from borrowing, investment inflows or other items to fill that £80bn gap. In a country's overall balance of payments, it is typically the banking transactions that fill this gap. They are the residual, intermediary flows that facilitate other deals, for example, by lending funds for imports. By contrast, the trade in goods and services, the international investment in bonds and equities, or the foreign direct investment deals are usually the driving or underlying flows of funds that the banking sector accommodates. This means that a country with a large international banking sector, like the UK, is in a stronger position to borrow when it needs to do so, whether that borrowing is on behalf of private companies or to raise funds for government spending.

The surplus from City dealing

One feature of the UK's balance of payments today, setting it apart from all other major powers, is that a large part of its chronic trade deficit in *goods* is offset by a surplus in *services* revenues and, sometimes, investment income. Britain's surplus in services and foreign investment income was even bigger in the nineteenth century, and it lasted on a huge scale until 1914, when the costs of the First World War and the consequent disruption to international business took their toll. Ironically, despite Britain often being considered the 'workshop of the world' in the nineteenth century, its annual trade deficit in goods was up to 6 per cent of GDP. Nevertheless, the UK had large current account *surpluses* in those years because the trade deficit was exceeded by revenues from shipping and insurance services sold to the rest of the world, and by the huge income from Britain's rapidly growing foreign investment assets.[3]

In more recent decades, UK current account surpluses have been rare, with the last one seen in 1983. But the deficit on goods has remained a chronic feature of British international trade, and it again reached an extraordinary 6 per cent of GDP in 2014. How is the UK's large trade gap financed today, when its commercial and financial supremacy in the world is much less than in the heyday of the British Empire? The answer is that a new version of the old pattern persists. Britain's overseas assets were greatly reduced as it borrowed to finance the costs of the two world wars, so it no longer enjoyed a very large net income from foreign investments. But the *services* income was less affected, especially once financial services income was boosted in the 1980s. The trade in financial services, with help from insurance services, covered more than half of the huge UK trade deficit between 2008 and 2014.

Table 8.1 gives the key numbers for the UK current account breakdown over the past quarter-century. The deficit on the trade in goods trended higher as a percentage of GDP even into 2008–14, despite the drop in domestic demand after 2007. That deficit was over £120bn in 2014, or a huge 6.8 per cent of GDP. On the plus side, net surplus revenues from financial services grew fairly steadily, supplemented by

Table 8.1 UK current account balance and net components, 1987–2014 *

	1987–89	1990–99	2000–07	2008–14	2014 (£bn)
Trade in goods	−3.8%	−2.1%	−4.7%	−6.3%	−121.2
Financial services	0.7%	1.0%	1.6%	2.2%	37.9
Insurance services **	n/a	0.6%	0.4%	1.0%	19.8
Investment income	−0.3%	−0.2%	1.3%	−0.1%	−43.9
Other items	0.2%	−0.5%	−0.7%	−0.3%	1.8
Current account	**−3.2%**	**−1.2%**	**−2.0%**	**−3.6%**	**−105.7**

Notes: *Figures are the average annual % of GDP, except in the last column.
**This row of data is for 'insurance and pension services', but the pension services numbers are minuscule.
Source: UK Office for National Statistics, 'Balance of Payments, Quarter 1 (Jan to Mar) 2015', 30 June 2015, at ons.gov.uk, and author's calculations

those from insurance. Net investment income moved from an average deficit between 1987 and 1999 to a surplus in the 2000s, although it had fallen back into a large deficit by 2014. Any positive investment income figure remains a surprise, nevertheless, given that the UK has a net *deficit* on its overseas investments (foreigners own more UK assets than UK investors own in other countries), a deficit that has grown since 1995. The 'other items' in Table 8.1 include other business services (a surplus, including accounting and law), tourism (a deficit, as Brits spend more going to sunnier climes than is spent by foreign tourists visiting the UK), net EU payments and net military grants (deficits).

One feature of Table 8.1 is that while the UK trade deficit grew sharply from the late 1980s, the current account gap did not widen by as much as a share of GDP. This shows that, in some respects, the policies of successive governments to back the expansion of the UK financial sector worked for British capitalism for about twenty-five years. UK-based industry failed to remain competitive in world markets, leading to bigger trade deficits. But revenues from the expanding financial services and insurance sector funded an important share of an otherwise disastrous trade deficit – with imports sustaining the living standards of the general population.

Net income from foreign investments also helped the British

Chart 8.1 Key components of the UK current account, 1987–2014

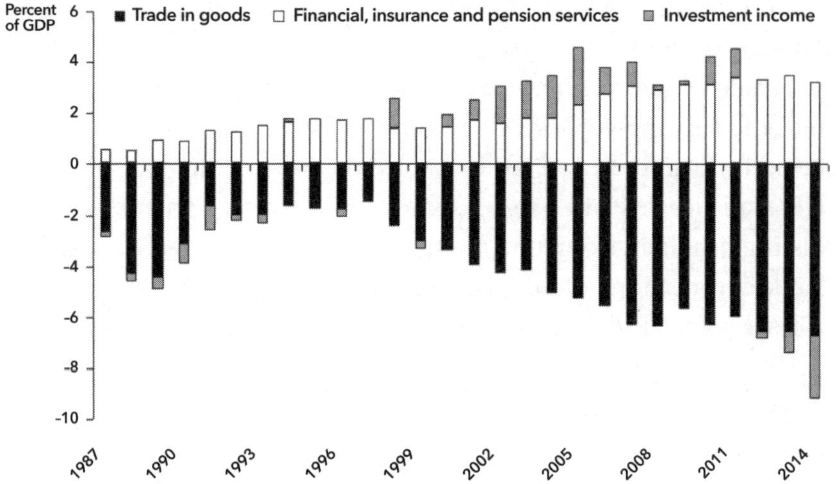

Source: UK Office for National Statistics, 'Balance of Payments, Quarter 1 (Jan to Mar) 2015',
30 June 2015, at ons.gov.uk

balance of payments in the 2000s. Although this net income turned sharply negative from 2012, this was largely due to BP plc paying compensation to the US for the Deepwater Horizon oil spill, and UK banks paying US fines for sanctions breaking, money laundering and rate fixing.[4] While there are some signs that the net income may not easily recover (see the discussion of direct investment below), overall one mark of the success of this financial policy was that the average sterling exchange rate in 2014 was very close to its level of twenty years earlier. Exchange rates are volatile, but this long-term stability indicates how Britain's financial power helped offset its weakness in producing goods that people want to buy.

Global capitalism's financial broker

The UK has the second biggest surplus on financial services in the world, just a bit smaller than that of the US. If insurance services are added to the reckoning, then the UK surplus is the highest, given that Britain has surplus net revenues on insurance while the US has a large deficit. Apart from highlighting the UK's role as the world's key centre for international banking and financial trading, these net revenues are a good measure of what it takes from the world economy by hosting these operations.

Financial services net revenues are usually around twice the size of those for insurance (see Table 8.1), and the financial operations that bring in the largest foreign revenues are those of the banks. Official UK statistics refer to banks as 'monetary financial institutions' and distinguish them from fund managers and securities dealers, although bank corporations often have separate divisions that take on these roles. Financial services are also listed separately from insurance and pension fund services in the official data, although many observers might put the latter under the same 'financial' heading, given that they also use their incoming funds to invest in securities.[5]

Banks get more revenues from *dealing spreads* – the difference between buying and selling prices – than they do from fees and commissions.[6] On the other hand, securities dealing operations, considered separately from banking, gain almost all of their income from commissions and fees, rather than from dealing margins. Fund managers based in the UK are usually less important in terms of total financial services revenues, as is the Baltic Exchange, the main international broker for dry cargo and tanker fixtures, including the sale and purchase of merchant vessels. Despite the UK no longer running merchant shipping, or producing many merchant ships, it has maintained its role as a centre for *trading* in this traffic.

The UK's earnings on financial services have not yet shown much sign of being affected by the post-2007 crisis. In the immediate pre-crisis years 2006 and 2007, total UK net earnings were close to £29bn and £36bn, respectively – significantly higher than previous years and boosted by higher volumes of dealing. In 2013 and 2014, the total net revenues from financial services averaged £38bn. Such figures indicate the continued importance of financial market trading for the British balance of payments.

Table 8.2 details the UK's international banking position compared to other countries. The totals in the table are for forty-four countries that report to the agency collating these figures, the Bank for International Settlements (BIS), based in Basel, Switzerland. Notably,

Table 8.2 External positions of banks, end-2014 ($ billion)

Country	Claims + Liabilities	Share of Total
UK	8,941	16.7%
US	7,326	13.7%
France	4,527	8.4%
Japan	4,246	7.9%
Germany	4,120	7.7%
Cayman Islands	2,866	5.3%
Hong Kong	2,280	4.2%
Netherlands	2,159	4.0%
Switzerland	1,720	3.2%
Singapore	1,479	2.8%
Belgium	1,240	2.3%
Luxembourg	1,184	2.2%
Australia	1,136	2.1%
Other *	10,441	19.5%
Total	**53,665**	**100.0%**

Note: *Each of the remaining 30 countries in the BIS survey has a share that is less than 2% of the total.

Source: Bank for International Settlements, Quarterly Review, June 2015, Table 2A, and author's calculations

the UK has by far the largest total of claims on (loans to) and liabilities to (deposits from) other countries. The data are for banks *located* in a particular country, including their 'international banking facilities' which, as in the case of the US and Japan, are located in their respective national territories, although they operate under a different set of financial rules. The UK had 17 per cent of the total outstanding global business at the end of 2014, while the US was in second place with a 14 per cent share. France and the other countries had less than 9 per cent.

UK-*owned* banks do not do all this UK-based business; foreign banks in the City conduct a large part of it. But a separate table compiled by the BIS on the business done by banks according to the nationality of the bank's head office still shows that British banks have a significant volume of international business compared to the banks of other countries. In December 2012, British-owned banks had the most international claims plus liabilities, at $9 trillion, while US-owned banks had the second biggest, at $8.4 trillion. By the end of 2014, however, the UK banks had fallen to third place behind those of the US and Japan.[7] All banks have cut back on their international loans and deposits to some extent, partly in response to tighter regulation and partly to focus on more profitable business, but UK-owned banks have cut back more than some others in the top group. Nevertheless, the common cliché that City business is like the Wimbledon tennis tournament – a UK location where foreign players overwhelmingly dominate proceedings – does not allow for the big international role of UK banks.

The figures for the UK in Table 8.2 include foreign banks based in the UK, but exclude the separate banking business of UK-linked tax havens outside the UK, including the Cayman Islands, the Bahamas, Bermuda, Jersey, Guernsey and the Isle of Man. While these islands are not technically part of UK territory – the Bahamas is a British Commonwealth member, while the others are either British Crown Dependencies or British Overseas territories – the UK authorities give them a special status. Obligingly, British officials do not talk about them very much. It would be *embarrassing* to point out that so many important people (or their family members) have bank accounts in these convenient havens! Despite some clamour in the British media about tax evasion, the UK government came up with only a weak proposal for a 'central register' of who owns the more than *two million* companies and partnerships registered in these havens, a proposal that was not expected to make much difference.[8] Taken together, the UK-linked tax havens would rank *sixth* in the table of international financial bankers, just below Germany, and would make up 7.4 per cent of international bank business at the end of 2014.[9]

Table 8.3 details another dimension of global finance: the foreign exchange markets. Banks in the UK (overwhelmingly, in London) have a clear and persistent lead in terms of market share, one that has grown over the past two decades. Foreign exchange dealing is not bank lending or borrowing, but exchanging one currency for another, and banks make money on these deals by taking a dealing margin. The margin can look very small – perhaps only one hundredth of

Table 8.3 Foreign exchange turnover, 1995–2013 (daily average, April, $bn)*

	1995	2001	2007	2013	% of 2013 Total
UK	479	542	1,483	2,726	40.9
% of total	29.3%	31.8%	34.6%	40.9%	–
US	266	273	745	1,263	18.9
Singapore	107	104	242	383	5.7
Japan	168	153	250	374	5.6
Hong Kong	91	68	181	275	4.1
Switzerland	88	76	254	216	3.2
France	62	50	127	190	2.8
Australia	41	54	176	182	2.7
Netherlands	27	31	25	112	1.7
Other	304	355	798	951	14.2
Total	**1,633**	**1,705**	**4,281**	**6,671**	**100.0**

Note: *These figures adjust for local double counting, but not cross-border double counting; if they did, the world total in 2013 would be lower at $5,345 billion.
Source: Bank for International Settlements, 'Triennial Central Bank Survey: Foreign Exchange Turnover in April 2013, Preliminary Global Results', September 2013, Table 6, and author's calculations

1 per cent of the value of the deal for widely traded currencies. But given the gigantic volume of global dealing – more than $5,000bn *daily* in 2013 – this can still add up to big earnings.

London has by far the biggest share in all segments of the global foreign exchange market, in spot, forward, swaps and options transactions. This might not seem surprising, given the City's historical lead in international commerce. However, Britain has more than twice the volume of currency dealing of the US – the top trading nation – despite being only in sixth position in world trade in goods and services. The size of London's foreign exchange market is the clearest indication of the City's role as the broker for global capitalism, taking a cut from deals that account for two-fifths of all foreign exchange transactions in the world economy. This was despite the UK's own currency, sterling, being involved in only 16 per cent of the total $2,726bn of deals done from the UK in 2013.[10]

London's dominant position in trading all world currencies has remained intact despite the advent of the euro and the earlier fears of UK authorities that Frankfurt or Paris might erode its market share. The boom in electronic trading has neither undermined the City nor led to a shift of business to cheaper, alternative locations. As noted in Chapter 2, the UK has a number of advantages that are difficult to replicate elsewhere – the dominant language for international business, a convenient time zone location between Asia and the Americas, a skilled workforce, commercial and employment legislation favourable to capital, and official regulation that is both strong in defence of capitalist property rights and also friendly to finance. These helped London's historical position at the centre of British Empire finance evolve into its key role in today's global financial business.

Table 8.4 shows London's even stronger dominance in the 'over-the-counter' (OTC) interest rate derivatives market – where trading is done directly between banks and their customers, not on a financial exchange. This global business, of which London has nearly half, began only in the 1980s, but it forms the biggest part of the derivatives market, principally made up from the trading of interest rate swaps. In these transactions, companies and dealers exchange with their counterparties one form of interest payment for another, usually an interest rate that is fixed over a number of years for a rate set according to market conditions every six months. Other trading of derivatives takes place on exchanges, and the US is home to the biggest of these, mainly based in Chicago. However, the volume of trading on exchanges is a small fraction of that in the OTC market. UK and US financial centres together account for 70 per cent of the world market in OTC interest rate derivatives, illustrating once more the extreme concentration of global trading. The US and the UK are also the leading issuers of international debt securities – to which a lot of this derivatives trading is linked – giving them easy access to investment funds from across the world.

There are other dimensions of global financial dealing in addition to those already noted, including commodities trading and pricing, fund management and insurance, but I will limit the torrent of data

Table 8.4 OTC interest rate derivatives turnover, April 2013 ($ billion)*

	FRAs	Swaps	Options	Other	Total	% World Total
UK	472.7	795.8	76.5	2.7	1347.7	48.9%
US	141.6	382.5	102.1	1.9	628.2	22.8%
France	56.6	141.7	3.9	–	202.2	7.3%
Germany	77.2	23.0	1.2	–	101.3	3.7%
Japan	2.7	55.9	8.6	–	67.1	2.4%
Australia	18.2	46.7	1.3	–	66.2	2.4%
Denmark	18.8	39.5	0.9	0.1	59.4	2.2%
Singapore	13.5	22.8	0.9	–	37.1	1.3%
Canada	6.8	25.2	2.0	–	34.0	1.2%
Switzerland	13.7	18.9	0.0	–	32.6	1.2%
Netherlands	13.6	14.9	0.2	–	28.7	1.0%
Hong Kong	2.0	23.7	2.0	0.1	27.9	1.0%
Other	45.2	75.3	5.5	0.1	126.1	4.6%
Total	**882.4**	**1,665.7**	**205.4**	**5.1**	**2,758.6**	**100.0%**

Note: *Single currency derivatives, daily average turnover. FRAs are 'forward-rate agreements' for money-market interest rates. Components may not add up exactly to totals due to rounding.
Source: *Bank for International Settlements, Triennial Central Bank Survey: Interest Rate Derivatives Market Turnover in 2013, December 2013, and author's calculations*

and simply note that the UK ranks at the top end of these global tables too, often second only to the US.

In summary, the UK plays a very big role in world financial markets, much larger than one would expect given the size of the British economy. This international role explains why UK banks have assets valued at five or six times the size of UK GDP. Although the UK is home to some of the world's largest corporations, such as BP, British American Tobacco, Vodafone and Rio Tinto, the striking development over the past two or three decades has been how UK-based international financial dealing has taken on such a large share of world business.

UK financial account: FDI, portfolio flows and bank funding

The 'financial account' of the balance of payments throws further light on the UK's financial dealing.[11] This account covers international banking and investment, and includes the most dramatic flows of money. For example, in the crisis year of 2008, as banks worldwide were going bust, UK banks *brought back* £147bn of their deposits abroad and £123bn of their short-term loans.[12] In addition, securities dealers in the UK reversed £338bn of their deposits with foreign banks. This amounted to a net reversal of some £607bn in previous outflows. In other words, UK-based banks and other dealers brought back funds equivalent to 40 per cent of the UK's GDP! Each of these flows was recorded in the 'other' category of the financial accounts; but they did not lead to a net *inflow* of 'other' funds into the UK because there were even larger disinvestments from the UK by foreign players. The usual trend of foreign loans *to* UK-based securities dealers turned into a reversal of £262bn, and deposits held by foreign residents in UK-based banks also fell by a massive £459bn. So, in the same year, UK-based banks sold an extraordinary £243bn of their foreign *portfolio assets* – including £161bn in bonds and £67bn in equities. The flows of funds were massive – a result of the rush to secure finance from any source as bank lending collapsed and market prices tumbled. It was no wonder that finance ministers, in the UK and elsewhere, were losing sleep. Never a dull moment on the financial account when there is a crisis!

The financial account is divided into five sections: flows of foreign direct investment, portfolio investment, financial derivatives investment, official reserves, and 'other'. When an investor owns more than 10 per cent of the equity capital of a company or a property asset, the investment is defined as a *direct* investment flow. Portfolio investment involves buying bonds (or money market and debt securities) and also equities below a 10 per cent share. Ownership of a larger share of equity capital in a company implies more control over the investment and less likelihood that it will be traded on the market. Reasons for not using the financial derivatives asset and liability data were discussed in Chapter 6, and the official foreign exchange reserves data are relatively small, change little and have no role to play in the analysis. The last item in the financial accounts – 'other' – may appear to be just the things that do not fit into the previous categories. But it is important because it is principally made up of banking flows.

Inflows and outflows in the financial account work very differently from how they do in the current account. In the current account, if a good is imported or exported, that same good will not generally be re-exported or re-imported in the same form.[13] By contrast, such additional buying and selling of the same thing is very common for transactions in financial contracts and titles. An asset manager in the UK might buy German or French government bonds or company equities, but might later decide to reduce these holdings of euro-based investments and switch in favour of US or UK assets. These transactions have an impact. On one occasion when I was working in a dealing room, one of the bank's asset manager clients sold billions of euros of German Bunds and bought UK gilts with the proceeds. Bund prices went down, along with the euro's exchange rate against sterling, and gilt prices went up. That particular move was the result of a considered change of investment policy. But, in times of crisis, market panic dominates. Then, rushing to get out of 'bad bets' and into what are seen as 'safe havens' is the rule of the day.

The different items in the financial accounts are often closely linked, and it would be a mistake to focus only upon one particular number. For example, if a domestic company buys a foreign company, this will normally result in an outflow of funds being recorded in the foreign direct investment category, increasing the foreign assets held by UK-based investors. Yet the company may not pay for the acquisition with its own cash, or with borrowed funds, but with its own equity capital in a so-called 'share swap'. Then, the owners of the foreign takeover target will be recorded as purchasing the equity of the domestic company and this will appear in the *portfolio* accounts component as an *inflow* of funds to buy UK equities, and an increase in UK liabilities to foreign investors. The two flows are clearly related, and here the driving element is the decision of the domestic company. If, on the other hand, the domestic company bought the foreign company with funds borrowed from foreign banks, then the financial

Table 8.5 UK financial account net annual flows, 1987–2014 (£ billion)*

	1987–89	1990–99	2000–07	2008–14	2014
Direct investment	−9.5	−15.9	−16.8	13.7	76.8
Portfolio investment	13.0	−1.7	51.1	25.7	99.9
Derivatives	n/a	0.9	−0.2	−5.7	14.0
Other investment	9.0	25.2	−11.1	19.9	−79.2
Official reserves	−3.1	0.1	−0.1	−5.0	−7.1
Financial account	**9.4**	**8.4**	**22.8**	**48.5**	**104.3**

Note: *All figures are average annual numbers. Positive means an inflow of finance into the UK, negative means an outflow from the UK.
Source: UK Office for National Statistics, 'Balance of Payments, Quarter 1 (Jan to Mar) 2015', 30 June 2015, at ons.gov.uk, and author's calculations

account statistics would record an inflow in the 'other account' division, an extra liability, and an outflow of these funds in the foreign direct investment category, as they bought an extra asset. In general, it is the banking flows that mainly facilitate other kinds of financial transaction, and this is important to bear in mind when interpreting the data.

In total, the UK financial account is almost always in surplus, offsetting the trend of current account deficits. Its components are volatile year-to-year, reflecting financial turmoil and crises as much as the whims behind the investment flows between countries. Nevertheless, there are still some distinctive features, and Table 8.5 gives annual average flows in order to highlight these. One trend was that from the late 1980s up to 2004, there was a net *outflow* of foreign direct investment from the UK. From 2005, the picture was erratic, but mostly showed net *inflows* of direct investment, partly reflecting a greater UK dependence on foreign capital to fund domestic investment projects. The earlier outflows of FDI were usually offset by a combination of net portfolio investment inflows into UK equities and bonds (positive numbers in the table) or by net inflows into the 'other' category. Taken together, these portfolio flows and the net inflows of funds through banks have more than accounted for the surplus numbers on the total financial account.

The overall picture for the UK balance of payments in recent decades can be summed up as follows: a chronic and large trade gap in goods was paid for by net financial services and insurance revenues, plus the portfolio and banking inflows. The latter provided surpluses that allowed the UK to maintain a steady net outflow of foreign direct investment, at least up to 2004, and for occasional years after. A particular company investing abroad did not necessarily have to borrow from foreign banks, or get the financing by selling bonds or equities to foreign investors. They may have had their own funds already. But this is how the international balances worked out *in aggregate*. The advantage for the UK of this pattern of flows becomes clear after examining the international investment assets and liabilities that result and the different returns on them. This also shows how the picture has been deteriorating in recent years.

UK assets, liabilities and returns

If a country runs a persistent current account deficit, this will eventually lead to a deficit on its net international investment position. Borrowing to pay for imports increases debts (liabilities), and these will tend to grow by more than the foreign assets owned. That is the general result, but there is no direct relationship. Data for investments owned abroad and the assets foreign investors own domestically are also influenced by exchange rates and by changes in the market prices of these investments. In the UK's case, its persistent current account deficit after 1983 meant that liabilities grew by more than assets. From 1995, UK liabilities were persistently greater than UK assets, resulting in a chronic deficit on the international investment position, a deficit that widened to more than £440bn by the end of 2014, roughly 25 per cent of GDP.[14] However, despite having had foreign liabilities greater than its assets since 1995, Britain nevertheless had a net investment *income* in every year from 2000 to 2011, with the annual average net income amounting to 1.1 per cent of GDP. Examining the trends in these figures shows both the privileges that Britain has enjoyed in international investment

Chart 8.2 UK net foreign investment stock position, 1987–2014

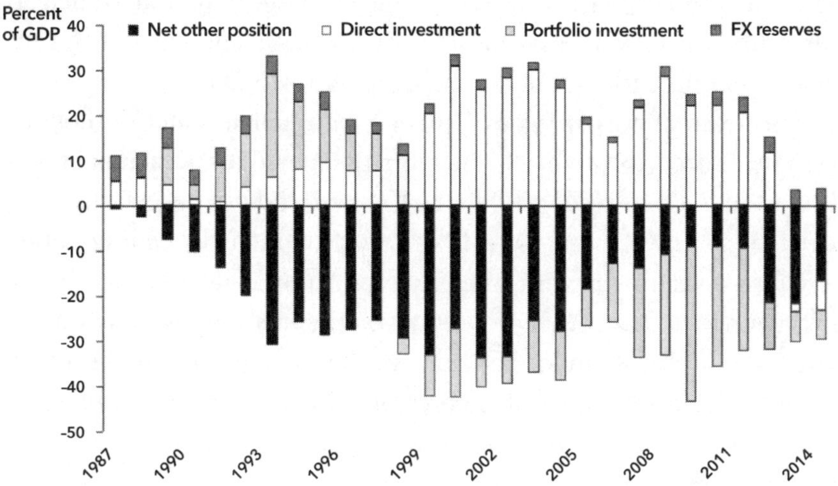

Source: UK Office for National Statistics, 'Balance of Payments, Quarter 1 (Jan to Mar) 2015',
30 June 2015, at ons.gov.uk

and finance and also the problems that the UK financial machine now faces.

Chart 8.2 shows the net stock of UK foreign investment, broken down into direct investment, portfolio investment, net 'other' positions that reflect international bank loans and borrowing, and the official foreign exchange reserves. In recent years, the foreign exchange reserves have been between £60bn and £70bn, receiving an income of about £700m per year from the ownership of foreign government securities, but these numbers are relatively small, change little and play a negligible part in the regular mechanism of British finance.

The solid black bars in Chart 8.2 are always negative, showing that over the whole period since 1987 the UK has been a net borrower of funds from international banks. In 2014, the net borrowing figure was 17 per cent of GDP, with British-based banks owing their foreign counterparts nearly £300bn more than foreign banks owed them. Another item on the deficit side from the late 1990s was on portfolio assets (the light-grey shaded bars). There was a massive deficit of £514bn in 2009, but UK investors then bought lots of foreign equities and bonds. Including revaluations, the negative balance was reduced to £120bn in 2014. These were the two main items, measured here as investment positions, that funded the UK's current account deficits and earlier net outflows of foreign direct investment.

This form of borrowing by British-based capital – via the banking system and/or through a deficit on the portfolio accounts – was important in two respects. Firstly, the main *deficits* tended to be in the types of investment with lower yields, while the *surpluses* were in those investments with higher yields. In other words, the cost of borrowing was lower than the return on the investments made. Until 2012, the UK investment position surplus was in direct investment, while its deficits were mainly in portfolio investments and bank loans. As Chart 8.3 shows, direct investment returns have been higher than on the other forms of investment.[15]

The rate of return on foreign *direct* investment has been significantly higher than that for portfolio investment or the interest on 'other' (bank loans) investment. This is clear from Chart 8.3, even though the returns on all types of investment have fallen since the early 1990s. To give a simpler picture, I have averaged the return made by UK investors abroad with that earned by foreign investors in the UK for each type of investment. However, this simplification hides some other differences. One is that the more detailed data show how UK direct investment abroad has consistently earned a higher rate of return than foreign direct investment in the UK, an average of 1.6 percentage points higher from 2000 to 2014, and even more in the 1990s. There are always concerns that the official data may not properly measure the profits capitalist companies are really getting. However, more detailed investigation of the data reveals a plausible story: the main source of above-average returns on UK foreign investments comes from investments in Asia, Africa (including the Middle East) and Latin America, particularly those in mining, oil and gas, which are dominated by monopolies from the major powers.[16]

The latest move into a *deficit* on the UK direct investment position in 2013–14 threatens British finances, since the historical data show that other forms of foreign investment have not given such high returns, nor returns that favour the UK. The overall rate of return

Chart 8.3 Returns on UK foreign investment assets and liabilities, 1990–2014

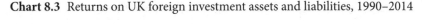
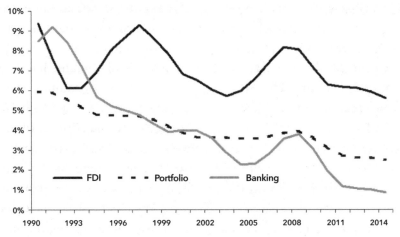

Note: Returns are calculated as the income in a particular year on one type of investment divided by the average stock of that type of investment at the end of the previous year and the current year. Returns are shown as an average over the latest three years. The lines show the average returns on liabilities and on assets for the three types of investment.

Source: UK Office for National Statistics, 'Balance of Payments, Quarter 1 (Jan to Mar) 2015', 30 June 2015, at ons.gov.uk, and author's calculations

(paid or received) on portfolio investments and bank loans has been lower than for direct investment, and the returns on bank loans/ deposits have also dropped much more than for direct investment since the late 1980s, especially following the moves of major central banks towards 'zero' interest rates in recent years. In the case of both portfolio investments and the returns on bank loans and deposits, the UK also tends to pay a higher percentage on its liabilities than on its assets.[17] A big problem for the UK's net investment income currently is that it no longer has a surplus position in the premium investment return item: direct investment. Since 2012, net investment income has been negative and falling sharply, reaching *minus* £43.9bn in 2014. Some of this was due to one-off factors, as noted above, but in recent years British capitalism has looked to be in a weaker position internationally, as shown both by the slipping of its banks in the global hierarchy and by the fact that, for the first time in modern history, foreign investors now own more direct investment assets in the UK than British capitalists own overseas.

Analysis of the pattern of returns shows that the boom in financial market activity since the late 1980s paid off for British capitalism for quite a while. But in many respects it is fading now. The extra revenues from financial and insurance services registered on the current account of the balance of payments helped plug the deficit on the trade in goods. There was also a much better investment income balance than might have been expected, given that since 1995 the UK has had foreign liabilities in excess of its foreign assets. This was based on developments in the UK financial sector that allowed easy funding of imports of goods, of outflows into the higher-yielding FDI, and also lower-cost inflows on the portfolio and banking accounts. Yet, while the City's financial operations are a key mechanism underpinning Britain's economic relationship with the rest of the world, they cannot fully compensate for the weaknesses showing up in the wider UK trade gap, the new deficit on direct investment assets, and the much worse investment income.

Maintaining access to higher yielding assets in foreign markets and having the ability to raise funds relatively cheaply is critical for British finance. Britain's status as an imperialist power, and the efforts it has made, together with the US, to open up foreign capital markets, help ensure that it can find destinations for its foreign investment. Yet, being able to borrow 'cheaply' is not under the control of any individual power, not even the US. It depends both on the position of a country in the world and on the general state of the global economy.

From the late 1980s, there was a general fall in the yields on bonds worldwide, and interest rates in money markets also fell back as central banks eased their policies in response to lower inflation. The reduction of the high interest rates on UK liabilities, including on government debt, was of major benefit for the UK's net investment returns. For example, in 2014 the UK was borrowing from foreign banks more than six times the amount it had done in 1990, but its total interest bill was actually *lower*, only a little more than half the previous amount. This initially reduced the UK's net investment income deficit and then for a while brought it into surplus. But with money-market interest rates close to zero in 2013–15 in most major financial markets, and with government bond yields already at historical lows, the potential for any further income benefits for the UK has been much reduced.

This sensitivity to the funding cost of debt makes the UK government worry about maintaining a high credit rating. This is not national pride; it is money! The UK's top credit rating of 'Triple A' was nevertheless lost in early 2013 when two of the three major ratings agencies, Moody's and then Fitch, cut the UK's sovereign rating by one notch.[18] Both agencies cited rising debt levels, although their focus was on domestic debt and the government's own liabilities. This reduction in credit status was not very significant and had no impact on interest rates, but it highlights a continuing vulnerability and one of the reasons behind the current UK's government's domestic austerity policies. If further credit downgrades or changes in interest rates pushed up UK borrowing rates by only 0.1 per cent – for example, from 0.9 to 1.0 per cent – the interest rate cost on just the UK's external bank borrowing would rise by nearly £4 billion per annum, based on the end-2014 numbers.

The City's network, tax havens and global finance

Because so many foreign banks and financial companies come to Britain to do business, UK financial companies have less need to go overseas. Only a quarter of total UK foreign direct investment was in financial services companies at the end of 2013; commercial and industrial investments are far more important. But it still makes sense for British financial operations to be established in other regional financial centres of the world economy, especially in the most important one, the US. These investments increase the power of UK-based financial companies because the UK head office can facilitate deals via foreign branches and also get easier access to foreign money-capital.

The largest single foreign location for UK-owned financial services assets is the US, accounting for 44 per cent of the total at the end of 2013. UK financial assets in Europe are mainly in the Netherlands (18 per cent of the world total), Ireland (12 per cent) and Luxembourg (6 per cent). Another European location is also important: the UK offshore centres: Jersey, Guernsey and the Isle of Man. These account for 7 per cent of total foreign financial services assets. Despite their strong political and economic links to the UK, they are just distant enough to allow the UK authorities to deny responsibility for the business conducted there.[19] Asia accounts for only a 13 per cent share of these UK assets, with Hong Kong at 5 per cent, Australia 4 per cent and Singapore 2 per cent.[20] These former British colonies are nevertheless important hubs for regional business.

A 2007 study of banking centres analysed the networks between banks in different countries and found that the UK's score was well ahead of all others on its five measures of 'network centrality'.[21] For example, banks in the UK took deposits from 382 other locations (counting bank and non-bank links separately), 90 per cent of the total, and the UK was the location for as many as 337 BIS-reporting banks. The City's status as a major dealing centre is solidly based on its connections with the rest of the world and its ability to act as an intermediary for global flows of money-capital and credit.

Major flows of finance in the form of deposits, loans, and the purchase and sale of securities between UK-based banks and the rest of the world are intermediated by banks outside the UK, but many of these are UK-linked. Data from the Bank of England enable these links to be examined in some detail, and they highlight a key role of the UK banking system, one that has not been analysed before. These data are shown in Table 8.6.[22] The figures are in US dollars, since this is the main currency used in the transactions, and they measure the *outstanding valuations* of bank assets and liabilities. But even if a liability of $100bn, for example, is unchanged from one year to the next, this does not mean there has been no underlying *flow* of funds. At least part of the borrowing through fixed-term loans or deposits, or the sale of securities to raise funds, may be renewed, especially when the terms of those loans, etc., are for less than one year. The outstanding amounts result from a wide range of underlying flows of lending or depositing abroad, and from investments in foreign assets, borrowing via bond markets, and so forth.

As is often the case, there are gaps in the official data. The geographical location of nearly 20 per cent of the UK's outstanding

Table 8.6 Net external position of UK MFIs by location (end-year, $ bn)*

		2000	2007	2013	2014
Total net position		−119	−808	−517	−343
Of which					
Offshore financial centres		−188	−526	−119	−101
Of which	**UK Offshore**	−138	−374	−247	−192
	Cayman Islands	−3	56	113	76
Developed countries – total		379	992	444	585
Of which	**Europe**	258	467	155	150
	US	82	413	73	245
	Japan	−6	−9	173	142
Developing countries – total		−77	−247	−15	−42
Of which	**Europe**	0	−40	59	56
	Africa & Middle East	−62	−181	−136	−107
	Saudi Arabia	−17	−79	−91	−71
	Asia & Pacific	−19	−33	34	−4
	Latin America	7	7	28	13
Addenda for UK MFI liabilities					
International issue of securities		−396	−396	−500	−469
Unallocated liabilities		−167	−709	−435	−436

Note: *MFI means 'monetary financial institution' or bank. Net figures are for UK-based MFI assets minus liabilities, including loans, deposits, bonds and money-market instruments. Negative numbers show net borrowing by UK MFIs. Positive numbers show their net lending. Some 18% of liabilities and 2% of assets are unallocated by country.
Source: Bank of England, Table C3.2 from Interactive Database, at bankofengland.co.uk, with author's calculations

liabilities (borrowings) is not identified. If it were known, then this might alter the relative importance of each area shown in Table 8.6. However, the unidentified lenders to the UK banks are likely to be mainly from richer countries, since this is where most of the world's wealth and income ends up. Given that the UK-based banks also *lend* vast sums to the same countries, this shows how the UK's international banking system acts as the financial go-between for the major capitalist powers. In other words, the City helps to fund the balance of payments of the rich countries, even if only by recycling funds back to them that were previously sent to the UK from other rich countries.

This can look like a pointless merry-go-round: companies or rich individuals in country A send funds to country B; country A is short of funds and then borrows from country B. Yet it does make (capitalist) sense when the motivations of the different players are taken into account. Not all investors and borrowers act in the same way when engaging in international deals, and the intermediary dealer is also happy to take a cut from the funds flowing in and out, or from the buying and selling.

The striking detail, however, is that UK-based banks are large-scale *net borrowers* from the rest of the world. This persistent deficit grew dramatically in the 2000s, peaking around 2007 at more than $800bn, before the onset of the latest financial crisis. As a comparison, consider that the GDP of Turkey, a country of some 75 million people, was close to $800bn in 2014. So UK banks had net borrowings more or less equal to the output of the Turkish economy in a year! UK net bank borrowing later fell following the financial squeeze, but it was still $343bn at the end of 2014, close to the GDP of Denmark or South Africa.

Within the total deficit, there is a continued net borrowing from developing countries and from offshore financial centres. The developing country total includes large net borrowing from Africa and the Middle East ($107bn at end-2014), especially from Saudi Arabia ($71bn). The latter depends both on Saudi oil revenues and on the continuing political and security links between the British state and the Saudi regime, which is why, to the bemusement of the blinkered British media, flags were flown at half-mast in Downing Street and at Buckingham Palace and Westminster Abbey on the death of Saudi King Abdullah in January 2015.

There are some other interesting details in the country location data. The largest proportion of financing comes from the UK 'offshore' centres. From 2011 to 2014, UK banks had lent roughly $100bn to these centres, but had borrowed more than $300bn. 'UK offshore' is an important source of funds helping finance the UK balance of payments. All offshore centres are closely linked to the interests of the major capitalist powers, and Britain has the closest links with the largest number. Many of these centres have Queen Elizabeth II as their monarch and sing 'God save the Queen' at official occasions – not because it is a catchy tune.[23]

My experience of working for London-based banks included several business trips to Jersey, and some contact with other centres. They are seen as a valuable, although small, line of City business. This explains why many UK-based banks have operations in the UK offshore havens, despite their extremely provincial and unfashionably retro ambience.[24] When it comes to hanging out as a member of the rich elite, Jersey has some way to go in competing with the offshore centres in the Caribbean and Central America. Nevertheless, the cost of obtaining funds from the tax havens is significantly less than from the 'onshore', more heavily taxed and regulated financial locations, and this is a key factor in the role they play for the major financial hubs, especially London. Compared to the UK offshore centres, other locations are much less important as net suppliers of funds to the UK-based financial system, although Hong Kong and Singapore also stood out in the 2000s and the Bahamas were important after 2006.

The Cayman Islands is an exception. As Table 8.6 shows, there has been a position of steady net *lending to* the Caymans from UK-based banks: it amounted to $76bn by the end of 2014. If providing cheap funds were the only function of tax havens for the UK, then that would not explain this relationship. The rationale for these particular flows is that the Caymans are a major centre for the legal home of international corporations, especially for those engaged in fund management and insurance, although their physical presence may amount to little more than a nameplate on a wall.

It might seem very odd for the UK banking system to be funding operations in the Cayman Islands, but the mystery is solved when other financial links are taken into account. The funds the UK sends to the Caymans are, in turn, routed into the US equity and bond markets. Evidence for this can be found in the US balance of payments data which indicate that investors registered in the Caymans hold very large volumes of US securities: at the end of 2011 these amounted to $128bn of US Treasury securities, $377bn of corporate and agency bonds, and $381bn of corporate equities.[25] Did the fewer than 60,000 Cayman Island inhabitants, man, woman and child, manage to accumulate US financial securities worth some $15 million each? No, the securities do not belong to them.

The UK banking system usually has a net lending of funds directly to the US. From 1991 to 2009 there was a persistent net position of UK-based lending to the US, and it reached a peak of more than $400bn in 2007. The figure reversed at the end of 2012, but went back to a large net lending of $245bn by end-2014. The volume of net UK lending to developed European countries has in the past been even higher. It exceeded $700bn during 2010 although it fell back to $150bn by end-2014. These data spell out the City's major role in global finance, not only in funding the UK balance of payments. By being the key intermediary for international flows of money and securities, the City also keeps the global financial system ticking over. And as the earlier figures for transaction revenues show, it takes a cut from all the deals passing through it.

Nice work, if you can get it

The UK's international payments and flows of finance highlight its position within the world economy. UK-based financial companies principally act as intermediaries using other people's money and also currencies other than sterling, but these operations bring large revenues into the UK economy and play a key role both for British and for global capitalism. This explains why a succession of British governments has backed the financial sector. Back in the heady, economic boom days of 2004, the UK chancellor, Gordon Brown, officially opened the new Lehman Brothers European headquarters in London with the following words:

> I would like to pay tribute to the contribution you and your company make to the prosperity of Britain. During its one hundred and fifty year history, Lehman Brothers has always been an innovator, financing new ideas and inventions before many others even began to realise their potential. And it is part of the greatness not just of Lehman Brothers but of the City of London, that as the world economy has opened up,

you have succeeded not by sheltering your share of a small protected national market but always by striving for a greater and greater share of the growing global market.[26]

Coming some four years before the collapse of Lehman in September 2008, this political perspective, while more vomit-inducing, is not so different from that of Prime Minister David Cameron's defence of City bonuses against threats of interference from the EU.[27] With more recent trends showing some of Britain's international balances worsening, the UK government is making renewed efforts to boost City business, as the next chapter discusses.

To sum up, the City of London's operations have funded, at relatively low cost, both the UK trade deficit in goods and the outflow of foreign direct investment. The yield on FDI assets has been persistently higher than that on the liabilities incurred to finance them, while financial services net export revenues – not to mention the related insurance, legal, accounting and other business service revenues – have reduced the UK's current account deficit. Furthermore, UK-based financial flows with the tax havens, especially with the 'UK offshore' centres, are part of the mechanism for financing Britain's balance of payments and for facilitating the flow of funds to other countries. Most writers on the offshore tax havens focus only on tax avoidance by the wealthy or by big companies, paying little attention to the relationships between the major powers. But the City's relationships with the tax havens are another means by which it facilitates international flows of finance – for example, by channelling funds into the US via the Cayman Islands – in addition to the City being the location for a large share of the international banking, foreign exchange and derivatives deals in the global system.

Simply to say that the City is responsible for a huge volume of international financial dealing and that it brings big revenues into the UK would ignore important characteristics of this business and of those revenues. The argument presented here is both that this business is based upon Britain's privileged status in the world economy and that, in a number of different ways, the City facilitates the transfer of revenues into the UK from what the rest of the world produces.

The City is also an important conduit for industrial and commercial corporations, pension funds, insurance companies, hedge funds and other asset managers to access foreign funds and securities issued or traded in foreign markets. This is a means by which ownership and control of the world's resources is concentrated among the major powers.

9.

Eternal Interests, Temporary Allies

> It is a narrow policy to suppose that this country or that is to be marked out as the eternal ally or the perpetual enemy of England. We have no eternal allies, and we have no perpetual enemies. Our interests are eternal and perpetual, and those interests it is our duty to follow.
>
> Lord Palmerston, British Foreign Secretary, 1 March 1848

A country's position in the global hierarchy is advanced or undermined by how it responds to changes in the world economy. Historians have described Britain in the nineteenth century as the 'workshop of the world', but it was also, if not more so, the world's banker and commercial centre. That position changed. After 1945, and especially from the 1980s, given its weaker economic status, it evolved into becoming the world's broker – deriving revenues from financial transactions, rather than providing new sources of capital. This concluding chapter examines developments that are further changing the patterns of global finance, and which will also influence British imperialism's future position.

'Open for business'

In a keynote speech, the Governor of the Bank of England, Mark Carney, gave his opinion on the future of British finance: 'Five simple words describe our approach: we are open for business.'[1] Carney's view is hardly surprising, although it is a more forthright expression of policy than is usually heard, one that could be termed 'constructive parasitism'. He noted that financial services directly accounted for a tenth of UK GDP, one million jobs and a large share of exports, and that being 'at the heart of the global financial system also broadens the investment opportunities for the institutions that look after British savings, and reinforces the ability of UK manufacturing and creative industries to compete globally'. In some neat sidestepping of the financial crisis, he also asserted: 'It is not for the Bank of England to decide how big the financial sector should be. Our job is to ensure that it is safe. The UK can host a large and expanding financial sector safely, if we implement a reform agenda that extends well beyond domestic banking.'[2]

That 'reform agenda' will be consistent with proposals discussed at the Bank for International Settlements in Basel to try to limit the scope for financial meltdown by increasing bank capital, if only because Carney is the chair of the Basel-based Financial Stability Board![3] The prospect of such reforms did not prevent him from suggesting that, by 2050, UK-based bank assets could grow much further to reach *nine* times GDP, assuming that the UK's share of global banking activity remained constant. These remarks, made at the *Financial Times* 125th anniversary celebration, were so much in favour of expanding finance – safely, of course – that even his hosts were taken aback. Martin Wolf, the veteran *Financial Times* columnist, wrote that Carney had placed a 'big bet on finance' and, while he admired his 'bravura', he doubted his 'wisdom'.[4]

Finance is such an integral part of the economics of British imperialism that it has been consistently promoted by a succession of UK governments that would otherwise claim to have different economic priorities. While Britain has slipped down the global rankings in many other areas of business, it has made a success of financial parasitism to boost its income, especially from financial transactions, with revenues coming from all over the world.

By contrast, in the wake of the crisis and financial turmoil of 2007–8, many European politicians, 'think tanks' and government agencies have recommended a tax on financial transactions or other means of limiting financial activity, for example via higher capital requirements for banks.[5] The proponents argue that these measures will limit both the size of the financial sector and the risk of further crises. It seems hardly necessary to point out that such policies are not motivated by anti-capitalist sentiment, but by a belief that curbing the more financial forms of capitalist excess will help to patch up the system. As a bonus, taxes on finance are often seen as easily available revenues to fund more government spending or worthy causes. For example, Oxfam believes that what it and others call a Robin Hood tax would 'raise billions to fight poverty and tackle climate change around the world'.[6] It seems that there is nothing a curb on finance could not achieve, while still keeping capitalism intact.

This is a delusion. If there were new taxes on equity, bond and derivatives transactions, or other measures to constrain financial trading, this would probably curb the growth of the financial sector in the countries to which the measures apply. But financial dealing has not caused the world's problems, and these measures barely address even the *symptoms* of the crisis that capitalism faces. They would be less effective in solving economic problems than homeopathic medicine is as a remedy for cancer or a brain tumour.

It is also unclear whether a ruling at the EU level would necessarily operate in countries that are against the new tax. By mid-2015, not even all of the euro member countries were in favour of it, with some arguing that only a *globally agreed* tax should be implemented. If the tax did go ahead, UK-based banks could get a boost as financial business migrated to the City, since *any* UK government is very likely to be opposed to it. However, in some versions of the proposed EU legislation, the tax would apply on a transaction if one of the parties involved were a bank based in a country that had agreed to the tax. In that case it would apply if Deutsche Bank, for example, did a deal in London and the German government had agreed to the new transactions tax. The UK government would then have to become the tax collector for Germany.[7] Even if the banks paid the levy directly, it would be passed on in extra transaction costs to their counterparties, including industrial companies. It should not be forgotten that the latter also perform these transactions.

Governments of all capitalist countries will do little to restrict the activities of their major corporations, banks and other financial institutions. The UK authorities are even less likely to sign up to international regulations that would disadvantage UK-based banks. Nevertheless, in June 2014, the Court of Justice of the European Union rejected the UK government's initial legal challenge to the tax, and it might still go ahead in some form.[8] Amendments to limit the impact of the tax will probably be made before any final, potential implementation, scheduled to occur in phases from 2016, and it has already been watered down from the initial proposals.

Financial scandals, such as those over the fixing of benchmarks for money-market interest rates (LIBOR) or exchange rates, are another possible problem for British finance. However, they are unlikely to have much lasting effect. For example, while the process for setting LIBOR interest rates has been changed and is now run by a New York–based company, NYSE Euronext, the actual market and the calculation both remain in London.[9]

The UK's international reach goes beyond financial transactions. Britain is a welcoming haven for foreign financial corporations and financiers, one where the financial dealings and other activities of 'non-domiciled' residents receive more favourable treatment from the British legal system than they might face in their home countries. UK courts are often called upon to rule whether a foreign billionaire is right or wrong in his case against another usurper of social wealth. No machine guns, bombs or even bribes are necessary, although substantial legal fees are due to our learned friends in the legal profession.

More loosely related to the UK's position as a welcoming centre for international finance are the purchases of UK commercial and residential property, football teams, newspapers and other trophy items by Russian and East European oligarchs, Middle Eastern plutocrats and others.[10] Economic analysts might find it interesting to work out the 'value' of the personal/political security enjoyed by the owner of a prominent UK football team, as well as the opportunities such ownership might give for money laundering. Notably, in the wake of Russia's incursion into Crimea at the end of February 2014, a UK government policy briefing made it clear that it would seek to exempt the City of London from any EU or US sanctions against Russia: Britain should *not* 'close London's financial centre to Russians'.[11] The value of the economic, political and social connections between the UK and foreign financiers was also indicated by the £7bn-plus crisis-related injection of capital into Barclays Bank from Abu Dhabi and Qatar's sovereign wealth funds in October 2008.[12]

Economics and domestic politics

Apart from possible taxes or similar curbs on financial activity, there are other economic and political developments that could undermine the economics of British imperialism. On the economic side there is the rising level of UK foreign indebtedness, driven mainly by its current account deficit, and the inability of British capital to finance many investment projects, so that it relies upon inflows of foreign money. Part of the growing UK current account deficit since 2012 is due to net outflows of investment income, because the inflows of funds on the financial account as direct investment, or foreign buying of UK equities and bonds, also imply that there will be extra outflows of interest and dividend payments. Part of the wider current account deficit may also be more short-lived, either due to one-off (although repeated) payments of fines by UK companies to the US, or to consumer demand for imports having recovered more quickly in the UK than in a depressed Europe. Nevertheless, the ability of British financial operations to plug the large trade gap has been diminishing.

Domestic political developments are also becoming problematic for Britain. There are two issues here: the relationship of the different parts of the UK to each other, and Britain's membership of the European Union.

Firstly, consider the 'British'. The British state has been the most secure political entity in Europe, if not the world, for centuries. The last major challenge to its territorial integrity came in the early twentieth century from a revolt in its next-door colony, Ireland. Britain neutralised that revolt by dividing Ireland: granting independence to one part, while retaining direct control over a 'loyalist' part of Ulster. In this context, the British government did not take the 2014 Scottish referendum on independence seriously until it was almost too late. It seemed fanciful that an English-Scottish political union that had lasted over 300 years could be broken. Scottish capitalists and their political elite had prospered from it, and the Scottish Nationalist Party was principally complaining about local powers and subsidies decided by a London-based government. However, although the referendum vote ended up with 55 per cent in favour of staying in the union, it was not a resounding majority. It was a blow to the previously unshaken belief in a fixed area of political rule and to the political image and status of the UK. Scotland is home to only around 8 per cent of the UK population, but its territory includes oil and gas resources, a nuclear base and a ready supply of military personnel. If the UK state cannot manage its own affairs, its ability to interfere in the business of other countries, an often exercised and arrogant reflex of imperialist power, is also called into question.

Another sign that economic turmoil can put political structures under strain is the possibility that Britain could leave the European Union, which it joined more than forty years ago. Britain has long had a 'mid-Atlantic' policy, being drawn to continental Europe for much of its business, but maintaining a wide range of non-European interests, including political, military and spying arrangements with the US. This meant that while the British state was happy to join the 'Common Market' in 1973 to secure easier access to an expanding economic area, it later resisted joining the euro, which would have limited its financial options and forced it into a political body in which it would have to share power, probably to its detriment.

The last thing the UK's large corporations would want to do is leave the EU, with the risk that trade and investment relationships might be affected, and with a knock-on effect for the City's business. But while that would normally be enough to justify a confident prediction that a referendum on the issue would result in the UK remaining in the EU, a disgruntled electorate could easily find solace in a policy that, ironically, harks back to the Labour left's views in 1975. The position of many at the 1975 Labour Party conference and of most trade unions, although shared by only a minority of the Labour Party leadership, was to oppose what it called the 'capitalist EEC' in favour of backing Britain's Commonwealth links (capitalist, but *British* capitalist, hence perfectly acceptable). At the time of writing, a UK referendum on EU membership is due to be held in 2016 or 2017. While a decision to exit the EU looks unlikely, the outcome is far from being certain. Support for an exit comes from many quarters, including the near four million UK Independence Party voters, one-in-eight of those who voted in the 2015 General Election. There is also support for an exit from some who would claim to have a more radical stance. Being opposed to EU austerity policies while also believing in an alternative, non-austerity capitalist system, they draw the conclusion that making concessions to British nationalism is the more progressive option.[13] This is a familiar and reactionary trajectory.

The world is becoming a more difficult place in which to realise the Governor of the Bank of England's dream of expanding UK finance. Yet, even in the continuing, debilitating crisis, the world economy has not stood still. There are other avenues of parasitism to pursue, and these also raise interesting questions about the future of the Anglo-American financial system within which the City plays such a major role. In the remainder of this concluding chapter, I will examine some of the questions arising from so-called 'Islamic finance' and the more prominent role of China in the world economy.

Islamic finance and the City

To some extent, Islamic finance is a contradiction in terms. Islam still today prohibits the payment of interest, an anti-usurer policy that dates from the birth of the religion in the commercial societies of the Middle East and North Africa in the early medieval period, a time when the Christian church also frowned upon usury, or the charging of high rates of interest. However, especially following the accumulation of huge oil and gas revenues in many Muslim countries, Islamic finance has become a bigger deal for global financial markets. Helpful Islamic scholars have advised financiers on ways around awkward religious opinions on interest rates. What is really a financial investment may nominally be turned into a 'shared risk', or else the resulting payments can be seen as being based on a service provided, perhaps formally accounted for as a rent, rather than being registered as an interest payment. Financiers had previously paid little attention to this sector of the market, but it has garnered a lot of 'interest' in more recent years.

British imperialism has strong links with Islamic countries, having established or supported many regimes in the Middle East and elsewhere since the late nineteenth century. Today these links are shown in the large inflows of funds to the UK from Saudi Arabia, the multi-billion-dollar arms deals made with the Saudis, and the many big property investments in London and elsewhere in the UK by Qatar. Another striking example is Brunei, where the Sultan pays for 1,000 British army Gurkhas to back up his 'security' and the interests of Royal Dutch Shell plc. In happier times, the wife of Syria's President Assad used to shop at Harrods and a member of Libya's Gaddafi family maintained a residence in Hampstead, London.

It might nevertheless seem odd for the UK, which has invaded a number of Muslim countries over the past decade or so, to warm to the idea of Islamic finance. But this is not so much a sign of *chutzpah* as proof that the contradiction between Britain's foreign policy and its financial policy is more apparent than real. Despite the invasions of Afghanistan and Iraq, and the bombing of Libya, not to mention other more covert interventions, the British state is not anti-Islam or anti-Muslim. It just wants to see its economic interests protected and advanced, as Lord Palmerston advocated. For example, it has no problem backing jihadist rebels, as it has done recently in Syria, if doing so will serve that policy. Similarly, it supported the Muslim Brotherhood in Egypt against the nationalist threat to British interests from President Nasser in the late 1950s.

Nevertheless, even taking this *realpolitik* into account, it was a surprise, in October 2013, to hear the UK prime minister David Cameron declare that: 'I don't just want London to be a great capital of Islamic finance in the Western world, I want London to stand alongside Dubai as one of the great capitals of Islamic finance anywhere in the world.'[14] He was addressing a conference of the World Islamic Economic Forum in London, the first time the event had been held outside a Muslim state. His presentation outlined a plan for the UK Treasury to launch an 'Islamic bond' which would meet the requirements of Sharia law. The £200m bond was eventually issued in June 2014, and was believed to be the first Islamic bond issued outside the Muslim world. Demand for it was ten times the amount on offer.[15]

The reason for all this attention is that 'global Islamic finance assets' – i.e. those that are 'Sharia compliant' – amount to some $1.5 trillion and are growing fast, with $139bn of bonds issued in 2012, two-thirds higher than in the previous year.[16] The existing economic, political and social links between the UK and Islamic countries had already created a business for twenty-two Islamic banks in the UK (six of them fully Sharia-compliant), more than in all other western countries combined, and there had already been $34bn of sukuk (Islamic bonds) listed on the London Stock Exchange. In response, the UK government decided to set up an Islamic Finance Task Force, although this particular force is not weaponised. The only downside to these initiatives is that with oil and gas prices having dropped from their extravagant peaks in 2014, the main sources of the funds supporting the growth of Islamic finance could well begin to fade.

Cameron's Sharia bond is of course minuscule in terms of UK government finance, but it is a sign that the government and the City is willing to do whatever is necessary to attract more business. Above all, Britain's financial policies make it easy for rich foreign investors to put their money in and take it out at will, with little fear of (UK) political moves against them, compared to the less predictable US. And 'Islamic finance' may still boost British financial revenues as UK-based institutions take their cut.

China, BRICS and the Anglo-American system

In 2013, trade with China accounted for more than 80 per cent of the US current account deficit of $400bn, but the US also received more than $200bn of portfolio investment from China, which helped plug the gap.[17] China's rapid economic growth in recent decades is a more ambiguous development for British imperialism, but one that is very important for global finance. Most rich countries depend on China not only to supply cheap manufactured goods, but also to buy their exports and invest in their enterprises. Canada and Australia, countries closely bound up with the Anglo-American financial system, have also found the values of their currencies being affected by changes in China's demand for their commodity exports, such as mineral ores, wood, coal, oil and gas. Beyond these bilateral links, China has emerged as a challenge to the established powers. It provides an alternative source of funds for countries not favoured by the World Bank and the IMF and, more recently, it has played a key role in setting up a 'New Development Bank' (NDB), with Brazil, Russia, India and South Africa, in July 2014.

This grouping of countries was prompted as much by the publicity arising from an article published in 2001, by an analyst from Goldman Sachs, as by their economic or political ties. He predicted that Brazil, Russia, India and China (South Africa, 'S', was added later to make BRICS) would likely play such a big role in the future world economy that they should be added to the structures of global decision-making, rather than being sidelined as unimportant countries compared to the established G7. This appealed to their national pride, and was also a means by which Goldman could tout for more business, particularly in China. Goldman had already been the lead underwriter of the new share issues for China Mobile (1997) and PetroChina (2000), making large fees from these deals.[18] In a neat irony of history, what the Goldman analyst did not anticipate at the time was that these countries might not simply want to be included in the *existing* structures, but that they would also want to set up and run their *own* organisations, over which they would have more control.

The BRICS are diverse countries, with different links into the world political economy. However, they all want a larger status in the world and that objective has been hindered by the established powers. After much negotiation, and scepticism in the western media that any deal could be finalised, it was agreed that the NDB's headquarters would be located in Shanghai, China. This reflects the relevant economic power distribution, with China in first position as it will be providing 40 per cent of the new bank's money. The bank's first president is from India; after his five-year term, the second will be a Brazilian.

Formally launched in Shanghai on 21 July 2015, the NDB represents one of the most important economic challenges to the position of the major powers since 1945, in particular to the US and its domination of IMF and World Bank policy. Reports suggest that the new bank will have $100bn of starting capital, plus a 'contingency reserves arrangement' of the same size, that might be operated separately from the NDB itself. These numbers are not particularly big, but could be increased. The reserves arrangement fund will also help developing nations avoid 'short-term liquidity pressures, promote further BRICS cooperation, strengthen the global financial safety net and complement existing international arrangements'.[19] The NDB will offer many trade and investment contracts that are outside the orbit of the Anglo-American system, in particular contracts that do not depend upon using the US currency and which might also bypass the City of London. An early indication of this occurred in May 2014, when Russia and China agreed a deal whereby Russia will supply China with oil and gas over many years. The deal was worth hundreds of billions of dollars, but was reported as *not* being settled in the US currency. This was a bilateral deal outside the framework of the NBD, but it suggests how alternatives to the established economic and financial mechanisms are being put in place.

China is far from being able to offer an alternative to the US dollar in the world financial system today, but it has certainly challenged the status quo on investment policy with regard to who receives funds, how much, and on what conditions. Of course, this is all being done in China's interests, so that it can secure access to raw materials and markets. The evidence suggests that the outcome has been no worse for developing countries compared to the previous western-dominated regime. That is not saying much, but it at least shows that these countries now have an alternative to the existing financial structures.

Equally, although they do have some shared interests, the BRICS countries do not act consistently as a group of alternative powers. The US, for example, has used India as a counterweight to China in the Asian region, and has supported India's nuclear policy, taking advantage of the border disputes between the two countries. Cooperation among the BRICS countries will nevertheless still likely facilitate China's evolution as a key world player.

The levels of 2013 nominal GDP and population give a simple guide to the potential status of these countries. China and India had the world's largest populations, at similar sizes of 1.37 billion and 1.27 billion people, respectively. But China's GDP is much higher, at just over $9 trillion compared to roughly $2 trillion for India. By comparison, Brazil had 203 million people and a $2.2 trillion GDP, while Russia had 146 million people and a GDP of $2.1 trillion. Relatively speaking, South Africa is tiny: only 53 million people and a GDP of just $0.4 trillion.

China's GDP is the second largest in the world, but still only a little over half that of the US – and with a very much lower *per capita* number – after many years of extraordinary growth. Taking a 'purchasing power' measure would make China's GDP comparable to that of the US, but this kind of statistical construct ignores the fact that it is the *monetary* resources you have that give you purchasing power in the wider world. The Chinese economy has problems of bad debt, especially in the construction sector, whose 'assets' provide the collateral for a huge volume of bank loans. Yet, unlike most other countries, China has some flexibility in managing a domestic or international financial crisis, given its huge foreign exchange reserves of more than $3.5 trillion. While it would be foolish for anyone to think that China will escape undamaged from the chronic problems in the world economy, it is just as short-sighted to think that economic and political turmoil will quickly remove China from its position as a threat to the established imperial order.

Placing a bet on China is not like putting money on a 100-1 long shot, hoping for a lucky break. The British state and UK financial corporations have also judged that money can be made in new areas of business with China. The problem the British face is that China does not necessarily have to deal with them! Or at least, the decision on whether it will do so will be determined by China's own interests. China is not the usual supplicant at the imperial table of the kind the Americans and the British have dealt with before.

China's authorities have taken steps to build up the role of its currency internationally, and the share of Chinese exports priced in local currency has risen sharply in recent years, from close to zero to around 14 per cent by 2014. China's central bank has begun to establish FX swap arrangements with a score of central banks in Asia, South America, Africa and Europe, and with Canada. These moves reflect, and will boost further, China's growing business links and influence. From close to nowhere a few years ago, China's currency has risen to be the *fifth* most used in the SWIFT system that sends most of the messages for international interbank payments.[20] At the end of 2014, its 2 per cent share was well behind the 45 per cent for the US dollar, 28 per cent for the euro and 8 per cent for sterling, but it was only a little behind Japan and had jumped above that of Australia, Canada and Switzerland. The rise of China in world finance has been so clear that British capitalists have tried hard to build up their role in the offshore trading of China's currency and to get access to China's financial markets. British ownership of Hong Kong's largest bank, HSBC, and another of the major banks, Standard Chartered, has made this easier.

The City of London already manages some 60 per cent of offshore currency trading outside China and Hong Kong, with the US at just 15 per cent and France at 10 per cent. But it took a while before the People's Bank of China gave the Bank of England the currency swap line for renminbi (CNY) versus sterling that it wanted. This facility is needed to provide a financial backstop for banks trading and doing business in this currency. Even then, the swap line opened in June 2013 was only around half the figure that had been mooted, at CNY 200bn (roughly £20bn), the same size as the figure for Australia and less than the CNY 350bn with the European Central Bank.[21]

After an agreement with China in October 2013, the UK Treasury announced the opening up of direct trading of the renminbi with sterling and that the City's financial institutions now had a quota (relatively small at CNY 80bn, roughly £8bn) for buying domestic Chinese equities and bonds with their CNY funds.[22] Another dimension of the new CNY business for London is issuing so-called dim sum bonds, debt securities issued by non-Chinese companies in renminbi. Up to the end of 2013, London had lagged behind Luxembourg in this market and in some other areas of CNY finance. So the UK Treasury made it easier for Chinese banks to set up in London.[23] To round off

its efforts, in October 2014 the Treasury issued a CNY 3bn sovereign
bond (roughly £300m), being the first western country to do so. As
with the Sharia bond issue, the UK government's aim was to boost a
small but fast-growing market by providing liquidity and attracting
other participants. The UK government's website even had its press
release available in both Chinese and English, a sign that British diplomatic skills continue in some quarters.[24]

Britain's policy on China has annoyed the US. In March 2015,
the White House reprimanded the UK government for its 'constant
accommodation' of China, just after the UK was the first of the G7
countries to sign up as a member of the China-led Asian Infrastructure
Investment Bank (AIIB).[25] To America's embarrassment, Germany,
France and Italy also joined a few days later.[26] Australia, a strong
US ally in the Anglosphere, having come under pressure to resist
the same temptation, also reversed its earlier rejection of membership.[27] China is Australia's biggest export market, which also led the
two countries to sign a Free Trade Agreement in June 2015. Even
South Korea slipped from America's grip, saying its membership of
the AIIB 'could open new doors for the Korean companies with substantial experience in wide-ranging projects such as construction,
telecommunication, and transportation'.[28] The laughable thing about
US opposition to its allies' actions is that it is expressed in terms of
doubting whether there would be 'good governance' at the AIIB. In
other words, it suspected that China would be able to veto any of the
new bank's policies it did not like, just as the US has been able to veto
IMF policies since 1945.

These developments show how the changing balance of forces
affects political and economic calculations, turning a 'united front'
of western policy into a more studied view by each country of where
its own advantage might lie. In 'normal' times, not much happens to
upset the existing institutions and ways of doing things, but in the
wake of a debilitating crisis, all the major powers take a look at each
other and around the world to assess the new opportunities. Having
been a loyal member of the established club, an individual country is
now more likely to take different decisions, especially when the power
of the current leading nation, the US, is being called into question.

Britain obviously wants to boost its financial business with China, but the more interesting point is how these developments reveal China's strong position in determining the rules of the game outside the regular orbit of Anglo-American finance. Especially in Asia, this is a big concern for the US. As US president Obama put it in April 2015: 'If we don't write the rules, China will write the rules out in that region.'[29] This shows the changing balance of strength among the key powers in the world, a shift that will disrupt the established political-economic order.

Finance and the rule of capital

What is or is not acceptable under capitalism today, what looks possible or 'uneconomic', is judged by the availability of funds, and the prices and yields on the relevant equity and bond securities. These are the new 'laws of supply and demand': the financial system sets the rules for capitalism. And because we live in a world dominated by a small number of companies from a small number of major powers, the system also works in their favour. I have focused on the British case because analysing this reveals the more hidden aspects of the world financial mechanism. Many writers cover the US, the world's major power, but in doing so they often miss out important ways in which things work, especially the regular, daily mechanism of finance and the role of other players in it.

The financial systems of different countries can only be understood when placed in a global context, and this is especially true for the US and the UK. It is foolish to analyse 'finance' or 'financialisation' on a national basis. Similarly, it makes no sense to try and separate 'bad' banks and financiers from 'good' productive capitalists. Although each type of capitalist plays a different role, they all depend upon the exploitation of workers and the latter also express their economic power through the financial system.

Financial parasitism remains alive and well, as shown by the recent British policy initiatives. These follow from the UK having the status of an imperialist power in the world economy, building on its network of commercial and financial relationships. Political tensions within the UK itself, and with the rest of Europe, nevertheless make the outlook more problematic for a state that has promoted itself as a haven of stability, better able to hide its aggression and to be more flexible than the US, and one more reliable than either the Americans or the Europeans in securing the interests of foreign capitalists.

Marx described capital as being like a vampire that 'only lives by sucking living labour, and lives the more, the more labour it sucks'.[30] This image of exploitation captures a persistent reality. However, the nature of modern imperialism demands that the metaphor be taken further. It is no longer simply about the exploitation and distortion of the productive abilities of humanity, but about how capitalist economic and social relations have taken on a financial form – a form not just confined to financial companies but one that also involves industrial and commercial corporations, in particular those from the leading powers. These corporations and their states dominate other countries.

Like others at the top end of the hierarchy, but sometimes with a more diplomatically informed strategy, British imperialism has created a financial machine that functions as a vampire's blood bank for the surplus value produced worldwide, from every country and in every currency. The City takes a sip from every value that flows through it in the financial deals it makes as a global centre. More than this, the securities traded by the City and elsewhere have a market price that, in terms of economic value produced, is unborn rather than undead. These securities represent a claim on the *future* value produced in the world economy, but also reveal the *present* wealth and controlling power of their capitalist owners. In this respect, at least, they have the edge on Dracula. Only a stake in the heart of the capitalist system, not simply in some of its financial forms, will be enough to see an end to the power of the beast.

Notes

Preface

1 'Markets Bemused as President Displays Yen for a Gaffe', *Financial Times*, 19 February 2002.

1. Britain, Finance and the World Economy

1 John Kampfner, *Blair's Wars*, London: Free Press, 2003.
2 UNCTAD, *World Investment Report 2014, Investing in the SDGs: An Action Plan*, United Nations Conference on Trade & Development, June 2014, p. 209.
3 'FT Global 500 2011 by Country', *Financial Times*, 26 June 2011, at ft.com.
4 UNCTAD, *World Investment Report 2014*, Annex Table 28.
5 UNCTAD, *World Investment Report 2013, Global Value Chains: Investment and Trade for Development*, United Nations Conference on Trade & Development, June 2013, Annex Table 30.
6 I will use 'the City' as shorthand for the UK financial sector. This is not strictly accurate, since a large amount of dealing is based in the newer Canary Wharf area of London, not in the traditional City. Edinburgh and Glasgow in Scotland also house important financial companies.
7 IMF, *Global Financial Stability Report*, International Monetary Fund, October 2014, Table 1, p. 163.
8 Stephen Haseler's *Sidekick – Bulldog to Lapdog: British Global Strategy from Churchill to Blair*, London: Forumpress, 2007, best exemplifies the 'lapdog' analysis.
9 As in John Dumbrell, 'The US-UK "Special Relationship" in a World Twice Transformed', *Cambridge Review of International Affairs*, Vol. 17, No. 3, 2004; Robin Niblett, 'Choosing between America and Europe: A New

Context for British Foreign Policy', *International Affairs*, Vol. 83, No. 4, 2007; William Wallace and Christopher Phillips, 'Reassessing the Special Relationship', *International Affairs*, Vol. 85, No. 2, 2009.

10   Mark Curtis, *Web of Deceit: Britain's Real Role in the World*, London: Vintage, 2003; John Newsinger, *The Blood Never Dried: A People's History of the British Empire*, London: Bookmarks, 2006.

11   P. J. Cain and A. G. Hopkins, *British Imperialism, 1688–2000*, London: Longman, 2002 (1993). Similarly, although Alec Callinicos, in his book *Imperialism and Global Political Economy*, Cambridge: Polity Press, 2009, notes the 'recent reorientation of British capitalism around the City', which now rivals Wall Street as the world's most important financial centre' (p. 193), he does not go on to analyse this.

12   Jerry Coakley and Laurence Harris, *The City of Capital: London's Role as a Financial Centre*, Oxford: Basil Blackwell, 1983; Geoffrey Ingham, *Capitalism Divided? City and Industry in British Social Development*, London: Macmillan, 1984.

13   See, respectively, Ranald C. Michie, *The City of London: Continuity and Change, 1850–1990*, London: Macmillan, 1992, and Leila Simona Talani, *Globalization, Hegemony and the Future of the City of London*, Hampshire: Palgrave Macmillan, 2012.

14   US data are taken from the Bureau of Economic Analysis (BEA), 'US International Transactions, 1960–Present', 2014, Table 1.1, lines 6 and 14, at bea.gov. The comparative GDP data are available on Wikipedia.

15   Benn Steil, *The Battle of Bretton Woods: John Maynard Keynes, Harry Dexter White, and the Making of a New World Order*, Council on Foreign Relations Books, New Jersey: Princeton University Press, 2013.

16   Michael Hudson, *Super Imperialism: The Origin and Fundamentals of US World Dominance*, London: Pluto Press, 2003; Barry Eichengreen, *Exorbitant Privilege: The Rise and Fall of the Dollar*, Oxford: Oxford University Press, 2011.

17   Peter Gowan, *The Global Gamble: Washington's Faustian Bid for World Dominance*, London and New York: Verso, 1999, pp. ix and 4.

18   Ibid., p. 127.

19   Ibid., p. 26.

20   Gowan gives some evidence for the view that US policies were directed against Japan's economic and political aims in Asia in the late 1990s (ibid., pp. 106–7), and that the US prompted high oil prices in the early 1970s as a tactic against European and Japanese competition (pp. 19–24). But he admits that he has only very circumstantial evidence, at best, of the US

government encouraging US hedge funds to disrupt various markets in US interests.

21 Sebastian Mallaby, *More Money Than God: Hedge Funds and the Making of a New Elite*, London: Bloomsbury, 2010, Chapter 9.

22 Eric Helleiner, *States and the Re-Emergence of Global Finance: From Bretton Woods to the 1990s*, New York: Cornell University Press, 1996, pp. 119–20.

23 Ibid., p. 144.

24 Ibid., p. 167.

25 This point is explained in Chapter 3 especially.

26 Leo Panitch and Sam Gindin, *The Making of Global Capitalism: The Political Economy of American Empire*, London and New York: Verso, 2012, p. 288.

27 Ibid., pp. 12, 117–18.

28 This will be discussed further in Chapter 8.

29 Panitch and Gindin, *The Making of Global Capitalism*, p. 312.

30 Martijn Konings, 'American Finance and Empire in Historical Perspective', in Leo Panitch and Martijn Konings (eds), *American Empire and the Political Economy of Global Finance*, Hampshire: Palgrave Macmillan, 2009, 2nd Edition, p. 51.

31 Chapter 2 explains the peculiar form of the US interbank money market.

32 Francis Fukuyama, *The End of History and the Last Man*, New York: Free Press, 1992.

33 Panitch and Gindin, *The Making of Global Capitalism*, p. 277.

34 Ibid., p. 330.

35 Ibid., p. 336.

36 James Kynge, Richard McGregor, Daniel Dombey, Martin Arnold, Helen Warrell and Cynthia O'Murchu, 'The China Syndrome', *Financial Times*, 3 March 2011.

37 US Congress, *Annual Report to Congress*, US-China Economic and Security Review Commission, 1 November 2010.

38 US Congress, *Annual Report to Congress*, US-China Economic and Security Review Commission, 20 November 2013.

39 David Harvey, *The New Imperialism*, Oxford: Oxford University Press, 2003, p. 181.

40 Ibid., pp. 210–11.

41 Harvey does not discuss this in his 2003 'dispossession' book, or in his major work, *The Limits to Capital* (London: Verso, 2006).

42 François Chesnais, 'The Economic Foundations of Contemporary Imperialism', *Historical Materialism*, Vol. 15, No. 3, 2007, pp. 121–42 (pp. 122–4).

43   Ibid., pp. 131–2.

44   Maria Ivanova has also clearly set out the links between the expansion of the financial system and the worldwide problems of capital accumulation, something ignored by many others who instead see the growth of finance as driven by a financial elite that controls government policy. (See Maria Ivanova, 'Money, Housing and the World Market: The Dialectic of Globalised Production', *Cambridge Journal of Economics*, Vol. 35, No. 5, 2011, pp. 853–71; 'The Dollar as World Money', *Science & Society*, Vol. 77, No. 1, 2013, pp. 44–71; 'Marx, Minsky and the Great Recession', *Review of Radical Political Economics*, Vol. 45, No. 1, 2013, pp. 59–75.) The latter view naturally leads to calls for government policies to regulate finance, often contrasting the (potentially) good productive capitalists to the bad, irresponsible financiers. An example of this view can be found in Costas Lapavitsas, *Profiting Without Producing: How Finance Exploits Us All*, London: Verso, 2013, p. 324.

45   I consider the term 'financialisation' to be, at best, a very superficial description of capitalist reality rather than a concept that helps to explain it. A useful article discussing the limitations of the concept is Brett Christophers, 'The Limits to Financialisation', *Dialogues in Human Geography*, Vol. 5, No. 2, 2015, pp. 183–200.

2. The Anglo-American System

1   See R. S. Sayers, 'The Return to Gold', in Sidney Pollard (ed.), *The Gold Standard and Employment Policies Between the Wars*, London: Methuen, 1970, for an enlightening analysis, on which some of the following details are based.

2   Robert Skidelsky, *John Maynard Keynes: A Biography, Volume 2: The Economist as Saviour*, London: Macmillan, 1992, p. 200. It is ironic that Skidelsky, Keynes's biographer, notes this important imperial dimension when his subject does not.

3   House of Commons Debate, 'Return to Gold Standard', *Hansard*, Vol. 183, cc 52–8, 28 April 1925, available at hansard.millbanksystems.com.

4   Cited in Steil, *The Battle of Bretton Woods*, p. 224.

5   Keith Kyle, *Suez: Britain's End of Empire in the Middle East*, London: Weidenfeld & Nicolson, 1991.

6   Clive Ponting, *Churchill*, London: Sinclair-Stevenson, 1994, p. 734.

7   Britain's concern about rising US power was also an important factor in the

government's decision to return to the Gold Standard in 1925, as previously noted.

8   Clive Ponting, *1940: Myth and Reality*, London: Cardinal, 1990, pp. 202–4.

9   Steil, *The Battle of Bretton Woods*.

10   Christopher Bayly and Tim Harper, *Forgotten Wars*, London: Allen Lane, 2007.

11   Cain and Hopkins, *British Imperialism, 1688–2000*, p. 625.

12   The $4.03 exchange rate per one pound sterling applied only for a relatively short period. But in the UK up to the 1960s, the sum of five shillings (in the pre-decimal currency, a quarter of one pound) was commonly referred to as a 'dollar'.

13   This 1958 sterling convertibility (into US dollars, etc.) was for sterling held by *non-UK* residents, and only for banks acting on their behalf, which usually meant the British Overseas and Commonwealth Banks, and foreign banks that, in practice, were mainly US banks. Other foreign exchange transactions were still restricted. Only in 1979 were all UK exchange controls abolished, allowing UK tourists, for example, to take more than a minimal amount of sterling out of the UK.

14   A good review of the system in the late 1940s is D. K. Fieldhouse, 'The Labour Governments and the Empire-Commonwealth, 1945–51', in Ritchie Ovendale (ed), *The Foreign Policy of the British Labour Governments, 1945–51*, Leicester: Leicester University Press, 1984.

15   House of Commons, 'A Bill Presented on West African Marketing Boards', 1951, at theyworkforyou.com.

16   House of Commons, 'Discussion on the Commonwealth Economic Conference', 1953, at theyworkforyou.com.

17   Partha Sarathi Gupta, *Imperialism and the British Labour Movement, 1914–1964*, London: Macmillan Press, 1975, p. 376.

18   Gupta's 1975 book is a rare academic study of Labour Party imperialist policy. This rarity reflects a self-censorship among many British historians. Exceptions are Bayly and Harper's *Forgotten Wars*, covering the post-1945 British wars in Asia, and more general surveys by Curtis, *Web of Deceit: Britain's Real Role in the World*, and Newsinger, *The Blood Never Dried*. See also my article 'Labour's Colonial Policy', 7 December 2014, at economicsofimperialism.blogspot.co.uk.

19   Cain and Hopkins, *British Imperialism, 1688–2000*, p. 636. Susan Strange's *Sterling and British Policy: A Political Study of an International Currency in Decline*, London: Oxford University Press, 1971, is a valuable study of the international role of British finance to the end of the 1960s.

20   J. O. N. Perkins, *The Sterling Area, the Commonwealth and World Economic Growth*, 2nd edition, University of Cambridge Department of Applied Economics, Occasional Papers 11, 1970, Table 6.1, p. 62.

21   Radcliffe, *Committee on the Working of the Monetary System: Report*, Cmnd 827, August 1959, London: HMSO 1959, para. 633, p. 233.

22   Cain and Hopkins, *British Imperialism, 1688–2000*, Table 5.8, p. 165.

23   Michie, *The City of London*, p. 134.

24   Ibid., p. 137.

25   Radcliffe, *Committee on the Working of the Monetary System: Report*, para. 626, p. 230.

26   Ibid., para. 659, p. 241. The Radcliffe Report was prepared over the period from May 1957 to August 1959, and these comments would have been made either before or just after sterling was made convertible in 1958.

27   Paul Langley, *World Financial Orders: An Historical International Political Economy*, London: Routledge, 2002, p. 66.

28   Ibid., pp. 66–7.

29   Gary Burn, *The Re-Emergence of Global Finance*, Basingstoke: Palgrave Macmillan, 2006, p. 26.

30   See, for example, ibid., p. 101; BoE, 'London as an International Financial Centre', *Bank of England Quarterly Bulletin*, Q4, 1989, pp. 516–28 (pp. 521–3).

31   Konings, 'American Finance and Empire in Historical Perspective', pp. 58–9.

32   Eichengreen, *Exorbitant Privilege*, p. 50.

33   After a series of increasingly desperate international attempts to shore up the system from the mid-1960s, including the devaluation of sterling and the French franc and the revaluation of the Deutsche mark versus the US dollar in 1967–8, it collapsed in 1971 when the US government unilaterally ended gold convertibility for the dollar. Eichengreen, in *Exorbitant Privilege*, gives a concise summary of these events.

34   Catherine R. Schenk, 'International Financial Centres, 1958–1971: Competitiveness and Complementarity', in Stefano Battilossi and Youssef Cassis (eds), *European Banks and the American Challenge: Competition and Cooperation in International Banking Under Bretton Woods*, Oxford: Oxford University Press, 2002, p. 90.

35   Joshua Feinman, 'Reserve Requirements: History, Current Practice, and Potential Reform', *Federal Reserve Bulletin*, June 1993, p. 576.

36   Dong He and Robert McCauley review the mechanisms involved in 'Eurodollar Banking and Currency Internationalisation', Bank for International Settlements, *Quarterly Review*, June 2012, pp. 33–46.

37 Note that *interbank* deposit interest is always paid gross, i.e. with no tax deduction.

38 Feinman, 'Reserve Requirements: History, Current Practice, and Potential Reform', p. 575; Federal Reserve, 'Credit and Liquidity Programs and the Balance Sheet', 2013, at federalreserve.gov. In his otherwise thorough analysis of the development of the euromarkets, Gary Burn does not mention this in his 2006 book, *The Re-Emergence of Global Finance*.

39 The removal of controls on capital movements by major capitalist countries in recent decades, and a reduction of the differences in bank regulation, means that little distinction can now be made between 'euro' and domestic currencies. Where there are still controls on the movement of capital or significant differences in regulation, as in Brazil or China, the terms 'onshore' and 'offshore' are most commonly used to describe the different markets in which funds are borrowed or lent.

40 BEA, 'International Transactions, 2011', Table 1, line 51, at bea.gov.

41 BoE, 'Extract from a Speech by the Governor Delivered to the Bankers' Club of Chicago', 27 April 1971, *Bank of England Quarterly Bulletin*, Q2, 1971, pp. 224–31 (pp. 224–5).

42 BoE, 'The Eurocurrency Business of Banks in London', *Bank of England Quarterly Bulletin*, Q1, 1970, pp. 31–49 (p. 37).

43 Burn, *The Re-Emergence of Global Finance*, p. 17.

44 Bank credit creation is explained in Chapter 4.

45 Burn, *The Re-Emergence of Global Finance*, p. 187.

46 Ibid., p. 10.

47 BoE, 'Extract from a Speech by the Governor Delivered to the Overseas Bankers' Club at Guildhall', 1 February 1971, *Bank of England Quarterly Bulletin*, Q1, 1971, pp. 83–4 (p. 83).

48 For example, Ingham, *Capitalism Divided?*; Helleiner, *States and the Re-Emergence of Global Finance*; and Burn, *The Re-Emergence of Global Finance*. Lapavitsas's *Profiting Without Producing* offers a more recent argument along the same lines, reviewed in Norfield, 'Capitalist Production Good, Capitalist Finance Bad', 6 January 2014, economicsofimperialism.blogspot.com.

49 BoE, 'Extract from a Speech by the Governor Delivered to the Bankers' Club of Chicago', 1971, pp. 225–6.

50 BoE, 'The Eurocurrency Business of Banks in London', 1970, pp. 31–49 (p. 36). Accepting houses were institutions that specialised in 'accepting' bills of exchange issued by other companies, which meant that they guaranteed that the bill would be paid at maturity. For this they received a commission, and this function helped the flow of funds in the money market.

51   BoE, 'Overseas and Foreign Banks in London: 1962–68', *Bank of England Quarterly Bulletin*, Q2, 1968, pp. 156–65 (p. 156).

52   BoE, 'Extract from a Speech by the Governor Delivered to the Bankers' Club of Chicago', 1971, p. 83.

53   Burn, *The Re-Emergence of Global Finance*, p. 24.

54   E. R. Shaw, *The London Money Market*, London: Heinemann, 1981, 3rd edition, Chapter 7, especially pp. 104–5.

55   Ibid., Table 29, pp. 138–9.

56   The *official* UK LIBOR fixing dates from 1986. There are '-IBORs' in many countries where there is an active interbank unsecured loan market. PIBOR (Paris) and others disappeared with the birth of the euro, to be replaced by a system-wide EURIBOR. However, there is a CIBOR (Copenhagen), a TIBOR (Tokyo) and now even a SHIBOR (Shanghai). In this respect, the US money market is still an anomaly.

57   Schenk, 'International Financial Centres, 1958–1971', pp. 86–97; Ranald C. Michie, *The Global Securities Market: A History*, Oxford: Oxford University Press, 2006, pp. 249–50.

58   BoE, 'London as an International Financial Centre', 1989, p. 521.

59   BoE, 'The Bank of England: How the Pieces Fit Together', *Bank of England Quarterly Bulletin*, Q1, 1996, pp. 91–6 (p. 92), emphasis added.

60   Although there have been reports of establishment moves against Labour Prime Minister Harold Wilson in the 1960s and 1970s, and BBC television made a programme about this in 2006. See 'The Plot Against Harold Wilson', YouTube.com.

61   Helleiner, *States and the Re-Emergence of Global Finance*, p. 84.

62   Ibid., pp. 85–6.

63   Schenk, 'International Financial Centres, 1958–1971', p. 87.

64   Michie, *The City of London*, p. 146.

65   Michie, *The Global Securities Market*, p. 247.

66   Ibid., p. 310.

67   TheCityUK, 'Global bond market up 5% in 2010 to record $95 trillion: more than two-thirds the size of equity market', 4 July 2011, p. 2, at thecityuk .com. In 2010, the global bond market (measured by the value of bonds outstanding) was valued at $95 trillion, and government bonds had a 43 per cent share of this. The international bond market makes up 30 per cent of the total. The global bond market is nearly twice as big as the global equity market, and the latter's capitalisation value was $55 trillion in 2010.

68   Calculated from BoE, 'London as an International Financial Centre', Table E, p. 518.

69   BoE, 'Japanese Banks in London', *Bank of England Quarterly Bulletin*, Q4, 1987, pp. 518–24 (p. 518).

70   Japanese banks regularly paid a premium over interbank lending rates in all major currencies compared to their counterparts from other major countries, so much so that they came to be excluded from panels to determine the official LIBOR fixings.

71   Peter Rodgers, 'Dresdner Chooses London as Centre for Eurobond Dealings', *Independent*, 16 October 1996, at independent.co.uk.

3. Finance and the Major Powers

1   Getting UK unemployment to below two million is seen as progress today! Official definitions of unemployment have changed over time, but, under any definition, the percentage of the workforce that is unemployed has grown dramatically since the 1960s. A rough indication would be from around 2 per cent in the 1960s to around 6 per cent in 2014, when 2014 was an economic 'recovery' year.

2   Philip Armstrong, Andrew Glyn and John Harrison, *Capitalism Since World War II: The Making and Breakup of the Great Boom*, London: Fontana, 1984, p. 320.

3   Barry Eichengreen, 'Sterling's Past, Dollar's Future: Historical Perspectives on Reserve Currency Competition', text of the Tawney Lecture delivered to the Economic History Society, Leicester, 10 April 2005, Table 2, p. 29, at emlab.berkeley.edu.

4   Svante Karlsson, *Oil and the World Order: American Foreign Oil Policy*, UK: Berg Publishers Limited, 1986, p. 249.

5   David E. Spiro, *The Hidden Hand of American Hegemony: Petrodollar Recycling and International Markets*, New York: Cornell University Press, 1999, pp. 107–9.

6   Ibid., p. 148. This 'special relationship' between the US and Saudi Arabia – and the US military role in the Gulf – increased 'after Britain announced that its protective role in the Gulf would end in 1971' (Karlsson, *Oil and the World Order*, p. 256).

7   Spiro, *The Hidden Hand of American Hegemony*, pp. 104–5.

8   BoE, 'The Surpluses of the Oil Exporters', *Bank of England Quarterly Bulletin*, Q2, 1980, pp. 154–9 (p. 154).

9   Ibid., Table D and p. 159.

10   Denis Healey, *The Time of My Life*, London: Penguin Books, 1990, pp.

428–32; Alan Moran, 'Defining Moment: Denis Healey Agrees to the Demands of the IMF', *Financial Times*, 4 September 2010.

11   See John Darwin, *The Empire Project: The Rise and Fall of the British World-System, 1830–1970*, Cambridge: Cambridge University Press, 2009, for an interesting historical study of Britain's links with the 'Anglo-Saxon' world.

12   This UK opt out was agreed in a deal whereby UK prime minister Major gave Germany's Chancellor Kohl clearance for the EU's recognition of Croatia, a German area of interest in the former Yugoslavia. This was one of the factors helping provoke the savage conflict between Serbs and Croats in Yugoslavia as that country broke up. Croatia joined the EU in July 2013.

13   See Bernard Connolly, *The Rotten Heart of Europe: The Dirty War for Europe's Money*, London: Faber and Faber, 1995, for a depiction of the politics of European monetary relations during this period.

14   John Redwood, *Our Currency, Our Country: The Dangers of European Monetary Union*, London: Penguin Books, 1997.

15   The Maastricht rules for EMU do not even have a procedure for leaving the system after a country becomes a member, pretending that membership is 'irrevocable'. This has been sorely tested with the crisis in Greece, which has led the German Council of Economic Experts to suggest that countries that cannot manage their debts should leave the system (German Council of Economic Experts, *Special Report of the Council*, 28 July 2015, at sachverstaendigenrat-wirtschaft.de).

16   Cabinet Office, 'German Unification: No10 Memorandum of Conversation (MT & President Mitterrand) [Prospect of Unification Had Turned Them Into "The 'Bad' Germans They Used To Be"] [declassified 2010]' (1990), at margaretthatcher.org/document/113883.

17   Ed Balls, then a Treasury adviser to Labour Chancellor Gordon Brown, constructed the five tests in 1997. Scepticism as to whether they should be taken as the result of a profound economic analysis is reinforced by the story that they were written on the back of an envelope while Balls was travelling in a taxi to a political meeting. The tests are no longer UK government policy and are not on the UK Treasury's website, but they are listed at Europa, 'United Kingdom: EMU Opt-Out Clause, including the Labour Government's "5 Economic Tests"', at europa.eu.

18   Tony Blair, *A Journey*, London: Arrow, 2011, pp. 318–19.

19   Europa, 'United Kingdom: EMU Opt-Out Clause'.

20   BoE, 'Quantitative Easing Explained', 2012, at bankofengland.co.uk.

21   Helleiner, *States and the Re-Emergence of Global Finance*, p. 111.

22   A financial futures contract has a price that is related to the expected future

exchange rate of a currency, a money-market interest rate or the price of a government security on a particular date. Trading in these contracts is undertaken for hedging financial risks and for speculation on price moves.

23   Geoffrey Howe, *Conflict of Loyalty*, London: Pan Books, 1995, pp. 140–1.

24   Helleiner, *States and the Re-Emergence of Global Finance*, pp. 142–3.

25   Federal Reserve Bank of New York, 'International Banking Facilities', April 2007, at newyorkfed.org/aboutthefed.

26   Adrian Blundell-Wignall and Frank Browne, 'Increasing Financial Market Integration, Real Exchange Rates and Macroeconomic Adjustment', OECD Department of Economics and Statistics, Working Papers No. 96, February 1991, Chart 1, p. 36.

27   Michie, *The Global Securities Market*, pp. 292–4.

28   Coakley and Harris, *The City of Capital*, p. 45.

29   Michie, *The Global Securities Market*, p. 277.

30   Coakley and Harris, *The City of Capital*.

31   TheCityUK, *Key Facts About EU Financial and Related Professional Services*, August 2013, pp. 11, 13, at thecityuk.com.

32   Helleiner, *States and the Re-Emergence of Global Finance*, pp. 167, 202.

33   Gillian Tett, 'Beware Hidden Costs as Banks Eye "Grexit"', *Financial Times*, 24 May 2012.

34   Geoff Dyer and George Parker, 'US Accuses UK over China Stance', *Financial Times*, 12 March 2015.

35   Burn, *The Re-Emergence of Global Finance*, pp. 9–10.

4. Power and Parasitism

1   Arash Massoudi, Michael Stothard and Anne-Sylvaine Chassany, 'Holcim and Lafarge Cement Deal to Salvage €41bn Merger', *Financial Times*, 20 March 2015.

2   Karl Marx, *Capital*, Volume 3, London: Lawrence & Wishart, 1974, p. 343. In *The City of London*, Michie discusses the history and development of the City and implicitly endorses Marx's analysis of this transition from commerce and money dealing to credit and interest-bearing capital, although he makes no reference to Marx in this work.

3   Jill Treanor and Dominic Rushe, 'HSBC Pays Record $1.9bn Fine to Settle US Money-Laundering Accusations', *Guardian*, 11 December 2012.

4   Karl Marx, *Theories of Surplus Value: Part Three*, London: Lawrence & Wishart, 1972, pp. 357–8.

5   Laurence Harris, 'On Interest, Credit and Capital', *Economy and Society*, Vol. 5, No. 2, 1976, pp. 145–77 (pp. 165, 170).

6   Tony Norfield, 'Derivatives and Capitalist Markets: The Speculative Heart of Capital', *Historical Materialism*, Vol. 20, No. 1, 2012, pp. 103–32 (pp. 118–20).

7   Marx's discussion of banking and credit recognises the fictitious nature of some bank assets, for example in his comments on how banks could issue notes not backed by capital they actually possessed (*Capital*, Volume 3, pp. 541–2). He also remarks on how a bank can open a credit account for a customer and how cheques, not even bank notes, may be used to settle payments in a clearing house system (p. 457). However, these are incomplete observations, and the impression is given elsewhere that the credit system plays the role of gathering up existing surplus funds (e.g., Karl Marx, *Capital*, Volume 1, London: Lawrence & Wishart, 1974, p. 587). Suzanne de Brunhoff has offered the most systematic account of Marx's views on bank credit creation, something rarely discussed. See her *Marx on Money*, New York: Urizen Books, 1976, especially p. 94. Money creation is specifically a banking operation. Non-bank financial companies cannot create deposits. Mike Hall has an interesting critique of the Marxist literature for ignoring bank credit creation in his essay 'On the Creation of Money and the Accumulation of Bank-Capital', *Capital & Class*, 48, Autumn 1992.

8   There are often several ways of organising transfers of funds between accounts, but this is the basic mechanism.

9   The Bank of England has produced a very helpful explanation of credit creation in the modern economy, one that notes how economics textbooks are misleading when they give the example of a bank lending out 90 per cent of an original deposit and keeping back 10 per cent as a reserve, etc. BoE, 'Money Creation in the Modern Economy', *Bank of England Quarterly Bulletin*, Q1, 2014. Another BoE article describes the different interbank payments systems: 'The Bank of England's Real-Time Gross Settlement infrastructure', *Bank of England Quarterly Bulletin*, Q3, 2012.

10   On this point, see Chapter 8 especially.

11   Marx, *Capital*, Volume 3, Chapter 29.

12   It is also possible for some capitalists to get securities as a form of indirect payment for services to a company, as with some start-up ventures. Or equity securities may be given to favoured individuals or company managers, without them necessarily having advanced any of their own funds to invest in the company.

13   Marx, *Capital*, Volume 3, Chapter 27, pp. 436–8.

14 Lee Spears and Sarah Frier, 'Facebook Stalls in Public Debut After Record $16B in IPO', Bloomberg News, 18 May 2012.

15 James Surowiecki, 'Unequal Shares', *The New Yorker*, 28 May 2012. This control-ownership trick via different classes of shares is not unusual. For example, the Murdoch family owns only 14 per cent of the shares in News Corp, but controls 39.4 per cent of the voting rights (Matthew Garrahan et al., 'Murdoch Loses Saudi Ally at News Corp', *Financial Times*, 4 February 2015).

16 Felix Salmon, 'No Need for Banks in an Era of Intellectual Capital', *Financial Times*, 21 August 2014; Hannah Kuchler, 'Facebook Warns New Buys Will Hurt Margins', *Financial Times*, 20 October 2014.

17 Rudolph Hilferding, *Finance Capital: A Study in the Latest Phase of Capitalist Development*, London: Routledge & Kegan Paul, 1981 (1910), p. 225.

18 Ibid.

19 Privately owned companies do not have publicly quoted securities, but they are usually much smaller enterprises than the monopolistic companies Hilferding focused upon.

20 Hilferding, *Finance Capital*, p. 368.

21 Ingham, *Capitalism Divided?*, pp. 33–5.

22 V. I. Lenin, 'Notebooks on Imperialism', in *Collected Works*, Vol. 39, Moscow: Progress Publishers, 1976, p. 202.

23 Hilferding, *Finance Capital*, pp. 334–5.

24 Partha Sarathi Gupta, *Power, Politics and the People: Studies in British Imperialism and Indian Nationalism*, ed. Sabayasachi Bhattacharya, London: Anthem Press, 2002, pp. 75–6.

25 Later, in 1941 after escaping Nazi Germany, Hilferding was killed by the Gestapo in Paris.

26 V. I. Lenin, 'Imperialism, the Highest Stage of Capitalism, a Popular Outline', in *Selected Works in Three Volumes*, Volume 1, Moscow: Progress Publishers, 1976, Chapter 10, pp. 727–8.

27 J. A. Hobson, *Imperialism: A Study*, Nottingham: Spokesman, 2011, Part I, Chapter IV. Hobson's book was first published in 1902. It is a striking text, and was among the first comprehensive analyses of imperialism. However, like others at the time, Hobson's analysis was 'underconsumptionist', seeing the driving force of foreign investment as being a lack of demand at home. His critique of foreign expansion also focused on the 'dangerous' special interests of the financiers and was laced with anti-Semitism. He argued that in Europe financial businesses were run 'chiefly by men of a single and peculiar race, who have behind them many centuries of financial experience' (p. 86).

28 Cain and Hopkins, *British Imperialism, 1688–2000*, Table 5.8, p. 165.

29 I will not cover this issue further, but the following are useful references: John Smith, 'The GDP Illusion: Value Added versus Value Capture', *Monthly Review*, Vol. 64, No. 3, July–August 2012; John Smith, 'Southern Labour – "Peripheral" No Longer: A Reply to Jane Hardy', *International Socialism*, Vol. 140, 2013; William Milberg and Deborah Winkler, 'Trade, Crisis, and Recovery: Restructuring Global Value Chains', in *Global Value Chains in a Postcrisis World: A Development Perspective*, Washington: World Bank, 2012; Norfield, 'Capitalist Production Good, Capitalist Finance Bad' and 'Labour's Colonial Policy', both at economicsofimperialism.blogspot.com.

30 Credit Suisse Research Institute, *Global Wealth Report 2014*, October 2014, p. 25.

31 Michie, *The City of London*, pp. 70, 76–8.

32 Federal Reserve, *2013 Survey of Consumer Finances*, September 2014, pp. 510–11, at federalreserve.gov. The median value of equities *directly held* by the top families was $110,200, so the remainder was in the form of investment fund holdings. Seven per cent of these top families *also* directly held bond securities, with a median value of $400,000.

33 Paul A. Grout, William L. Megginson and Anna Zalewska, 'One Half-Billion Shareholders and Counting: Determinants of Individual Share Ownership around the World', Preliminary Draft, Centre for Market and Public Organisation and Department of Economics, University of Bristol, September 2009, Table 1, p. 9.

34 UK Office for National Statistics (ONS), 'UK Ownership of Quoted Shares, 2010', Tables A and B, p. 21, at ons.gov.uk.

35 Figures calculated from ONS, 'Chapter 5: Financial Wealth, Wealth in Great Britain 2010–12', 15 May 2014, Figure 5.15, p. 19, at ons.gov.uk.

36 For example, one must distinguish between the larger 'defined benefit' and the smaller 'defined contribution' pension assets. In the former, a company invests pension contributions in financial assets, but the pension fund stock of assets attributed to the individual is valued by calculating the sum of assets needed to provide the pension income he or she is contractually due. As yields fall, the size of the required assets rises, and this has resulted in pension fund deficits. The 'defined contribution' assets are, in contrast, valued at the market prices of the assets.

5. The World Hierarchy

1 There are 155 countries included in the calculation below. Those with a population of less than some 200,000 are excluded because several items of data do not exist for them.

2 IMF, *World Economic Outlook Database, 2015*, April 2015, at imf.org.

3 This is not to confuse GDP and GNP (Gross National Product). GNP includes the net income from external sources. The point being made is that GDP 'value added' data for a particular country may include an element of value created in other countries (see Smith, 'The GDP Illusion').

4 I discuss this question in relation to Bangladeshi T-shirt production in 'T-Shirt Economics: Labour in the Imperialist World Economy', in Nicolas Pons-Vignon and Mbuso Nkosi (eds), *Struggle in a Time of Crisis*, London: Pluto Press, 2015.

5 I use nominal (money) GDP in current exchange rate terms. Other figures, such as 'purchasing power parity' GDP, might give a better measure of relative national welfare, but my focus is on how much a country is 'worth' in the world economy, and this implies measuring output in current money.

6 UNCTAD, *World Investment Report 2014, Investing in the SDGs: An Action Plan*, United Nations Conference on Trade & Development, June 2014, Annex Table 4.

7 Bank for International Settlements (BIS), *Quarterly Review*, June 2015, Table 2A. These data cover forty-three countries. The BIS also gives figures for bank assets and liabilities by the *nationality* of the bank, not just by the country in which its operations are located, but only for nine countries. The latter figures show a similar rank order to the bank-location data.

8 Note that since two currencies are involved in any foreign exchange deal, the total percentages will add up to 200 per cent.

9 The different forms of this are covered in Chapter 8.

10 SIPRI, 'Military Expenditure Database', data for 2014, at sipri.org.

11 Adam Hanieh makes a convincing case for the emergence of a strong Saudi ruling class, despite its clear reliance on US military protection. See his *Lineages of Revolt: Issues of Contemporary Capitalism in the Middle East*, Chicago: Haymarket, 2013. Saudi Arabia has also played an active role undermining protests in the Middle East, not only in Bahrain and Yemen, but also in Egypt. On the general index measure explained below, Saudi Arabia ranks number 21.

12 In order to compare the index of power results, I have given the country with the highest value under each of the five headings the number 20. This

means that if a country has the highest GDP then its value is 20. Other countries with smaller GDPs are then shown as a proportion of that number, for example, as 10 for a country with half the biggest GDP. The five measures used are given equal weights, and the total index is the sum of the individual values. If a particular country happened to have the top score under each heading, it would total 100; if another country had a score that was a quarter of the value of whichever country was top, then it would have a score of 25.

13 Other signs of China's rise to prominence in the world include the new financial institutions it has taken charge of, discussed in Chapter 9.

14 Tom Bower, *The Squeeze: Oil, Money and Greed in the 21st Century*, London: Harper, 2010, pp. 142, 224.

15 The figure for UK resident ownership of UK quoted shares was 47 per cent (ONS, 'UK Ownership of Quoted Shares, 2012', 25 September 2013, ons .gov.uk). This was down sharply from 69 per cent in 1998. British capitalists also increased their ownership of shares on foreign stock exchanges.

16 Wellington Nyangoni, *Africa in the United Nations System*, New Jersey: Fairleigh Dickinson University Press, 1985, p. 128.

17 Thomas Friedman, 'A Manifesto for the Fast World', *New York Times*, 28 March 1999.

18 P. L. Pham, *Ending 'East of Suez': The British Decision to Withdraw from Malaysia and Singapore 1964–1968*, Oxford: Oxford University Press, 2010.

19 Central bank and regulatory authorities nowadays distinguish 'systemically important financial institutions' from others.

20 Given the movements towards independence in many countries from the late 1940s onwards, it is common for people to think that colonial rule no longer exists. Among other examples, this ignores Britain's continued rule over Northern Ireland, Gibraltar, the Malvinas and elsewhere.

21 For example, see Harvey, *The New Imperialism*, especially Chapter 4, 'Accumulation by Dispossession'.

22 Lenin, 'Imperialism, the Highest Stage of Capitalism, a Popular Outline', *Selected Works in Three Volumes*, p. 700.

23 Gartner Research, 'Gartner Says Smartphone Sales Surpassed One Billion Units in 2014', March 2015, at gartner.com.

24 UNCTAD, *World Investment Report 2013, Global Value Chains: Investment and Trade for Development*, United Nations Conference on Trade & Development, June 2013.

25 Milberg and Winkler, 'Trade, Crisis, and Recovery', p. 29.

26 Marx had already noted in *Capital* that the establishment of monopolies

in certain spheres had provoked 'state interference' (*Capital*, Volume 3, Chapter 27, p. 438).

27   Daniel Yergin, *The Prize: The Epic Quest for Oil, Money and Power*, New York: Free Press, 1990, pp. 107–10.

28   Estes Kefauver, *In a Few Hands: Monopoly Power in America*, London: Pelican, 1966.

29   Chico Harlan, 'In South Korea, the Republic of Samsung', *Washington Post*, 10 December 2012.

30   Joseph E. Harrington, Jnr, 'How Do Cartels Operate?', *Foundations and Trends in Microeconomics*, Vol. 2, No. 1, 2006.

31   Calculated from OICA, 'World Motor Vehicle Production by Manufacturer: World Ranking of Manufacturers, 2011', 2012, at oica.net.

32   'Johnson Controls Earnings: Weak Europe Could Offset Gains From Asia', *Forbes*, 16 January 2013.

33   *The Barth Report, Hops 2013/2014*, Barth-Haas Group 2014, at barthhaasgroup.com

34   Trefis, 'Otis Worldwide Success In Emerging Markets Will Lift United Technologies's Stock', 10 April 2013, at trefis.com.

35   Gartner Research, 'Worldwide Mobile Phone Sales to End Users by Vendor in 2012', February 2013, at gartner.com.

36   Ken Silverstein, 'A Giant Among Giants', *Foreign Policy*, May–June 2012.

37   Interesting details of Rich's links to the Clintons and to Israel are available on the Wikipedia page for Marc Rich.

38   Andrew G. Haldane, 'On Being the Right Size', speech given on 25 October 2012, at bankofengland.co.uk.

39   Euromoney, 'Euromoney's Annual FX Market Ranking', 2013, at euromoney.com.

40   UNCTAD, *World Investment Report 2014*, Annex Table 28.

41   S. Vitali, J. B. Glattfelder, S. Battiston, 'The Network of Global Corporate Control', 2011, at plosone.org.

42   Hank Paulson, *On the Brink: Inside the Race to Stop the Collapse of the Global Financial System*, London: Headline Publishing, 2010, p. 214.

43   Alistair Darling, *Back from the Brink: 1000 Days at Number 11*, London: Atlantic Books, 2011, pp. 120–6.

6. Profit and Finance

1   Tax revenues on people's incomes or from sales taxes like VAT are much higher than the taxes directly taken from company profits. However, *all* taxation is essentially a deduction from the surplus value created by the productive sector.

2   Here I have not included formulae for different types of profitability. For a fuller discussion of capitalist profit rates, see my 'Value Theory and Finance', *Research in Political Economy*, Vol. 28, 2013, pp. 161–95.

3   This ratio can be expressed as either borrowing/equity or equity/borrowing, which give inverse numbers. So 2000/100 = 20 can also be reported as 100/2000 = 5 per cent. Here I use the first ratio, of borrowing/equity, so a bigger number means more relative borrowing.

4   US Census Bureau, *The 2012 Statistical Abstract*, Table 794, at census.gov.

5   CFA Institute, *Derivatives and Portfolio Management, Level II 2012*, Boston: Pearson, 2012, pp. 408–9.

6   Andrew G. Haldane, 'Risk Off', speech given on 18 August 2011, at bankofengland.co.uk.

7   Federal Reserve, 'Profits and Balance Sheet Developments at US Commercial Banks in 2008', *Federal Reserve Bulletin*, Vol. 95, 2 June 2009, p. A76.

8   Norfield, 'Derivatives and Capitalist Markets', pp. 116–18.

9   Patricia Hurtado, 'The London Whale', Bloomberg, 23 April 2015, at bloombergview.com.

10   Hilferding, *Finance Capital*, p. 172.

11   Ibid., p. 180.

12   Daniel E. Saros, in 'The Circulation of Bank Capital and the General Rate of Interest', *Review of Radical Political Economics*, Vol. 45, No. 2, 2013, pp. 149–61 (p. 154), and Lapavitsas in *Profiting Without Producing* (p. 127, n. 45), also assume, with Hilferding, that the rate of profit for the financial sector will tend to equal the average rate of profit in the industrial and commercial sectors.

13   Ben Fine, 'Banking Capital and the Theory of Interest', *Science & Society*, Vol. 49, No. 4, Winter 1985–86, pp. 387–413 (p. 399).

14   I developed the following points through useful discussions with Ben Fine.

15   As in Gérard Duménil and Dominique Lévy, 'The Real and Financial Components of Profitability (United States, 1952–2000)', *Review of Radical Political Economics*, Vol. 36, 2004, pp. 82–110 (p. 104).

16   For example, ONS, 'Profitability of UK Companies, 3rd Quarter 2010', 5 January 2011, at ons.gov.uk. The UK's official 'capital employed' measure

is based on the value of inventories and fixed assets, including buildings, plant, machinery and software.

17 Wayne Roberts, statistics official at the UK Office of National Statistics, email to the author in response to a query on ONS data for UK non-financial and financial corporate assets and profits, 19 February 2014.

18 Harry Wallop, 'Metro Bank Granted FSA licence', *Daily Telegraph*, 5 March 2010.

19 SIFMA, Excel sheet on 'Global CDO Issuance and Outstanding', updated 4 April 2012, at sifma.org.

20 See BoE, 'DQ Definitions', 16 April 2008, p. 1, at bankofengland.co.uk, for the Bank of England's instructions to banks for completing the statistical returns for financial derivatives positions. These are internationally agreed rules.

21 Alan Freeman argues that this is not double counting because the banks' loans are a form of invested money-capital. See his 'The Profit Rate in the Presence of Financial Markets: A Necessary Correction', *Journal of Australian Political Economy*, Vol. 70, 2012. But this also ignores the fact that the loans are largely the result of bank credit creation processes and so should not be seen as representing an independent sum of value.

22 Bank of England data show £504bn of UK bank outstanding loans to non-financial businesses at end-2011, just 14.6 per cent of the total loans of £3,443bn in Table 7.1.

23 It does not follow that the financial sector is 'unprofitable' in the sense of not managing to secure an income in excess of its costs, or that it cannot bring revenues into the country in which it is based. Chapter 7 gives further examples of how the financial sector assists the appropriation of surplus value from the rest of the world economy.

24 Lapavitsas makes some useful points on these questions, but from a different perspective and with a view, which I do not share, that 'financial profits' can also be seen as 'ultimately deriving from future wage payments' (*Profiting Without Producing*, Chapter 6 and p. 167). Also, he does not properly distinguish transaction revenues from capital gains.

25 Other forms of financial revenue, including fees and commissions, also usually depend on the size of the transaction undertaken.

26 Note that, as a financial client, if you want to buy or sell a security or currency, or to borrow or lend, you have to take the financial market maker's (higher) selling price if you want to buy or borrow and the (lower) buying price if you want to sell or lend.

27 The argument here concerns financial securities and interest-bearing

capital. In the case of the money-dealing aspects of financial operations, as with some foreign exchange dealing, the transaction revenues should be seen as deductions from the surplus value contained in the commodities being produced.

28   Marx, *Capital*, Volume 3, p. 213.

29   Karl Marx, *Grundrisse: Foundations of the Critique of Political Economy (Rough Draft)*, Harmondsworth: Penguin, 1973, p. 748.

30   Kathrin Hille, 'Foxconn to Increase Robot Usage 100-Fold', *Financial Times*, 1 August 2011.

31   ONS, 'Contracts with No Guaranteed Hours, Zero Hour Contracts, 2014', 25 February 2015, at ons.gov.uk.

32   For example: Alan Freeman, 'What Makes the US Profit Rate Fall?', *Munich Personal RePEc Archive*, 17 March 2009, available at mpra.ub.uni-muenchen .de; Andrew Kliman, *The Failure of Capitalist Production: Underlying Causes of the Great Recession*, London: Pluto Press, 2012; and Fred Moseley, *The Falling Rate of Profit in the Post-War United States Economy*, London: Macmillan, 1991. Michael Roberts has also done some interesting work on trying to produce a *world* rate of profit, using international data. See his article 'A World Rate of Profit: Globalisation and the World Economy', July 2012, at thenextrecession.files.wordpress.com.

33   Armstrong et al., *Capitalism Since World War II*.

34   However, the view of many authors, including those of the Armstrong et al. book, was that the fall in profit rates into the 1970s was due to wage militancy rather than a rising organic composition of capital. That analysis is wrong, as well as blaming the working class for the capitalist crisis.

35   John Smith's article 'The GDP Illusion' is useful on this point.

7. The Imperial Web

1   Matt Taibbi, 'The Great American Bubble Machine', *Rolling Stone*, 9–23 July 2009. It is worth noting that investment banks in the US are not directly regulated by the US Federal Reserve and have more freedom of manoeuvre in their business. However, in 2008, at the height of the financial crisis, both Goldman Sachs and Morgan Stanley converted themselves from investment banks into bank holding companies. The risk they faced of greater Fed supervision was offset by the benefit of their greater access to central bank funds as the financial crisis continued.

2   Bank for International Settlements, 'Triennial Central Bank Survey: Foreign

Exchange Turnover in April 2013, Preliminary Global Results', Table 2, p. 10, September 2013. Note again that the market shares of all currencies would add up to 200 per cent, since there are two currencies involved in any foreign exchange transaction. The GDP of euro member countries is not far behind that of the US, emphasising the much bigger international role of the US dollar.

3   Exceptions occur, as in the case of BP plc, the UK oil major. Its annual accounts are reported in US dollars, given the dollar pricing of energy products in global markets. However, other big UK corporations, such as Vodafone, BAE Systems and GlaxoSmithKline, report in terms of sterling.

4   European Commission, *One Currency for One Europe: The Road to the Euro*, 2007, p. 17, at ec.europa.eu.

5   Linda Goldberg and Cedric Tille, 'The International Role of the Dollar and Trade Balance Adjustment', *Occasional Paper*, No. 71, 2006, Group of 30, Table 1, p. 15.

6   European Central Bank, *The International Role of the Euro*, Table A11, p. 77, July 2014.

7   IMF, *Annual Report on Exchange Arrangements and Exchange Restrictions*, International Monetary Fund, October 2012, Table 1, p. 5, at imf.org.

8   Federal Reserve Bank of New York, 'How Currency Gets into Circulation', June 2008, at newyorkfed.org.

9   Bo Nielsen and Adriana Brasileiro, 'Supermodel Bündchen Joins Hedge Funds Dumping Dollars', Bloomberg News, 5 November 2007.

10   ECB, *The International Role of the Euro*, January 2005, p. 58; ECB, *The International Role of the Euro*, July 2014, p. 23.

11   '500 Euro Notes Withdrawn Over Organised Crime Fears', *Telegraph*, 13 May 2010.

12   A note to the reader, and to border officials: I have not actually done this, but curiosity led me to check the measurements.

13   The Bank of England reports the net income from assets bought with its issuance of sterling banknotes, but this is not the type of seigniorage used here, and neither does it relate to the international dimension (BoE, *Annual Report 2012*, p. 97).

14   However, holding a bank account (in Swiss francs or Japanese yen, for example) outside the relevant country does not mean that any notes actually leave the national territory and are physically held in the foreign country. Modern seigniorage refers to individuals and companies holding currency *notes*.

15   The term originates from French government criticism of the dollar's role in the 1960s, and was coined by de Gaulle's finance minister, Valéry Giscard d'Estaing, who used it to refer to the US ability to fund its current account deficit by issuing dollars at low rates of interest (Eichengreen, *Exorbitant Privilege*, p. 4).

16   In *Exorbitant Privilege* Eichengreen mainly refers to the former while Maurizio Michael Habib focuses on the latter in his 'Excess Returns on Net Foreign Assets: The Exorbitant Privilege from a Global Perspective', *ECB Working Paper Series*, No. 1158, February 2010.

17   Matthew Higgins and Thomas Klitgaard, 'Reserve Accumulation: Implications for Global Capital Flows and Financial Markets', *Current Issues in Economics and Finance*, Vol. 10, No. 10, September/October 2004.

18   US current account data are from the regular reports of the Bureau of Economic Analysis. China's FX reserve data are taken from Pitchan Arunachalam, 'Foreign Exchange Reserves in India and China', *African Journal of Marketing Management*, Vol. 2, No. 4, April 2010, pp. 69–79 (Table 3, pp. 76–7).

19   Francis E. Warnock and Veronica C. Warnock, 'International Capital Flows and US Interest Rates', *Journal of International Money and Finance*, No. 28, 2009.

20   Even if the foreign purchases were only of US *government* securities, the lower yields would have had an impact on the credit system. Other bond and longer-term loan interest rates are based upon the benchmark rate for government securities.

21   A useful recent book on international finance is Brett Christophers, *Banking Across Boundaries: Placing Finance in Capitalism*, Chichester: Wiley-Blackwell, 2013.

22   Ricardo Hausmann, 'Good Credit Ratios, Bad Credit Ratings: The Role of Debt Structure', third draft of a paper prepared for the Conference on Rules-Based Fiscal Policy in Emerging Market economies, Oaxaca, Mexico, 14 to 16 February 2002.

23   BEA, 'US International Transactions, 1960–present', 2014, Table 1.1, lines 6 and 14, at bea.gov.

24   Ricardo Hausmann and Federico Sturzenegger, 'Global Imbalances or Bad Accounting? The Missing Dark Matter in the Wealth of Nations', Centre for International Development at Harvard University, Working Paper No. 124, January 2006, pp. 3–8, at hks.harvard.edu.

25   Panitch and Gindin, *The Making of Global Capitalism*.

26   The 'offshore' Chinese renminbi currency has the ISO code CNH, and this might be used instead of the 'onshore' CNY. To avoid a proliferation

of codes, I will use CNY whenever I refer to China's currency.

27   Camilla Hall, 'Dubai Jittery over Business with Iran', *Financial Times*, 12 August 2012.

28   Shannon Bond, 'BTMU Fined $250m over US Sanctions Breaches', *Financial Times*, 20 June 2013.

29   Jack Ewing and Stephen Castle, '5 Central Banks Move to Supply Cash to Europe', *New York Times*, 15 September 2011.

30   The largest portion of total financial services revenues for the US comes from 'management' fees, which amounted to $20.6bn in 2011. These include charges for the use of the headquarters' IT systems. Securities lending, electronic funds transfer and other financial services revenues amounted to another $15bn, while $14.2bn came from brokerage fees (BEA, *Survey of Current Business*, July 2013, Table G, at bea.gov).

31   BEA, 'US International Services, Table G, Other Private Services Receipts', at bea.gov.

32   BEA, 'Gross-Domestic-Product-(GDP)-by-Industry Data, US Bureau of Economic Analysis, Data file: GDPbyInd_VA_NAICS, Excel Tab 02 NAICS _VA, GO, II', at bea.gov.

33   Calculated from ONS, 'United Kingdom National Accounts – The Blue Book, 2013', 22 November 2013, Table 1.7.1, at ons.gov.uk.

34   *Factsheet: Luxembourg Financial Centre 2013*, at luxembourgforfinance.lu.

35   The apparent discrepancy between financial services activity accounting for a quarter of Luxembourg's GDP and financial services export revenues amounting to three-quarters is because export revenues are not measured on a 'value-added' basis.

36   Swiss Bankers' Association, *The Economic Significance of the Swiss Financial Centre*, 2013, at swissbanking.org.

37   Nicholas Shaxson, *Treasure Islands: Tax Havens and the Men Who Stole the World*, London: The Bodley Head, 2011, p. 53.

38   For a concise article on the links between opium smuggling and British finance and commerce in Hong Kong, including the role of HSBC, see Jean-Louis Conne, 'HSBC: Chinese for Making Money', *Le Monde Diplomatique*, English Edition, February 2010.

39   'The Financial Services Sector in Hong Kong', *Hong Kong Monthly Digest of Statistics*, April 2012, pp. FB2–3, at censtatd.gov.hk.

40   Bank for International Settlements, 'Triennial Central Bank Survey: Global Foreign Exchange Market Turnover in 2013', February 2014, p. 72.

41   Monetary Authority of Singapore, 'Recent Economic Developments in Singapore', 11 June 2013, p. 19.

42   Calculated from Central Statistics Office Ireland, 'National Accounts Output and Value Added by Activity, 2002–2009', 29 November 2012, Table 2.

43   Michael Lewis has given an excellent analysis of the Irish property disaster. He noted how the Irish government's decision to guarantee not only bank deposits (a reasonable policy to prevent a bank run), but also bank-issued bonds, lumbered taxpayers with the losses that would otherwise have been borne by the bond investors. Michael Lewis, 'When Irish Eyes Are Crying', *Vanity Fair*, 8 February 2011.

44   Calculated from Central Statistics Office Ireland, 'National Accounts Output and Value Added by Activity, 2002–2009', 29 November 2012.

45   An enlightening discussion of Switzerland in this respect, although now somewhat dated, is Jean Ziegler, *Switzerland Exposed*, trans. Rosemary Sheed Middleton, London: Allison and Busby, 1978.

46   ONS, 'United Kingdom National Accounts – The Blue Book, 2012', 15 August 2012, Table 1.2, p. 58, at ons.gov.uk; plus the author's calculations from London Stock Exchange, 'New Issue and IPO Summary' and 'Further Issues Summary', at londonstockexchange.com.

47   BBC News, 'Vodafone Seals Mannesmann Deal', 11 February 2000, at news .bbc.co.uk.

48   Bank for International Settlements, 'Triennial Central Bank Survey: Report on Global Foreign Exchange Market Activity in 2010', December 2010, Table B.6, p. 15.

49   Market observers question how far the Chinese stock market numbers can be compared with those for the US and other countries, because of the strong influence of the Chinese state and the relatively small percentage of a large company's equity that is actively traded (for example, Carl E. Walter and Fraser T. Howie, *Red Capitalism: The Fragile Financial Foundation of China's Extraordinary Rise*, Singapore: John Wiley & Sons, 2011). However, that observation leaves aside the not too dissimilar distortions of a 'free market' occurring in other exchanges, particularly those resulting from prolonged low central bank interest rates.

8. Inside the Machine

1   For the data cited here, see TheCityUK, *Key Facts about EU Financial and Related Professional Services*, August 2013, and *Key Facts about UK Financial and Professional Services*, January 2013, at thecityuk.com.

2   Darling, *Back from the Brink*, p. 310.

3   Cain and Hopkins, *British Imperialism, 1688–2000*, Table 5.8, p. 165.

4   Office for Budget Responsibility, *Economic and Fiscal Outlook*, March 2015, p. 82, at cdn.budgetresponsibility.independent.gov.uk.

5   Chapter 4 discussed the different types of financial institution and the particular roles they play in the capitalist system. Measuring the 'value' of financial services is beset by many problems and the methods used by official statistics are questionable. For a discussion of these points, see Brett Christophers, 'Making Finance Productive', *Economy and Society*, Vol. 40, No. 1, 2011, pp. 112–40, and Andrew G. Haldane, 'The Contribution of the Financial Sector: Miracle or Mirage?', speech given on 14 July 2010, at bankofengland.co.uk.

6   Data for the revenue from dealing spreads should be based on the difference between buying and selling prices, but it is difficult, if not impossible, to separate this revenue from that which dealers make in profitable bets on a move up or down in market prices.

7   These asset plus liability numbers for end-2014 were: US, $8,766bn; Japan, $7,249bn, and the UK, $7,158bn (BIS, *Quarterly Review*, June 2015, Table 8A and author's calculations).

8   Vanessa Houlder, 'Tax Havens Told to Drop Opposition to UK Call for Central Register', *Financial Times*, 27 March 2015.

9   These offshore centres are discussed below.

10 BoE, 'The Foreign Exchange and Over-the-Counter Interest Rate Derivatives Market in the United Kingdom', *Bank of England Quarterly Bulletin*, Q4, 2013, pp. 394–404 (Table A, p. 397).

11 The standard divisions in the balance of payments data are: the current account, the financial account, the 'capital' account and 'errors and omissions'. The capital account includes 'capital transfers and the net acquisition or disposal of non-produced, non-financial assets'. The largest single item, one that largely explains the steady net surplus of around £1bn to £4bn in the past decade, is net migrants' transfers into the UK. These figures are too small to warrant further investigation here. It is also worth noting that some people use the term 'capital flows' to describe investment flows. However, investment flows do not appear in the capital account, they are in the 'financial account'.

12 These inflows can result from not rolling over a deposit or loan once it has matured. The data cited in this paragraph are from ONS, 'United Kingdom Balance of Payments – The Pink Book, 2013', Tables 7.1 to 7.7, 31 July 2013.

13 Some goods may arrive at a port and then be reshipped somewhere else, but these goods will not registered as imports if they do not clear customs.

Usually imports are refined or changed in some way before being re-exported, as in the case of crude oil or other raw materials.

14   The UK's total net asset position here and below excludes derivative assets and liabilities. A high proportion of derivatives positions are offsetting or matching trades that boost *both* the asset *and* liability totals dramatically, usually without changing the net position by very much. Also, I want to examine the investment returns on assets and liabilities, and no investment income is recorded as coming from derivatives positions. The gains/losses from derivatives are reflected in current account financial transactions commission and spread income, and in the valuation of the derivatives positions. Derivatives are also discussed in Chapter 6.

15   One of the idiocies of mainstream economics is to assume that rates of return on all types of investment will tend to equalise, despite a mountain of evidence to the contrary. Chart 8.3 indicates a marked difference between FDI and other returns, but mainstream economic theory suggests that the rate of profit on productive investment will tend to equal the rate of interest. Chapter 6 explains that each rate is determined differently and is based on different types of capital.

16   Tony Norfield, 'UK Foreign Direct Investment Profits', 22 March 2013, at economicsofimperialism.blogspot.com.

17   This results from a myriad of different financial deals of different maturities in different currencies. It does not necessarily show that British-based capitalists must pay more for their liabilities than the return they could get on the same kinds of assets in the same currency, for the same maturity, etc.

18   BBC News, 'Fitch Downgrades UK Credit Rating to AA+', 19 April 2013, at news.bbc.co.uk.

19   See Shaxson, *Treasure Islands*, especially Chapter 6.

20   ONS, 'Foreign Direct Investment Involving UK Companies, 2013', 20 January 2015, calculated from Table 3.3, at ons.gov.uk.

21   Goetz von Peter, 'International Banking Centres: A Network Perspective', BIS *Quarterly Review*, December 2007, p. 37.

22   BoE data include the asset and liability positions of UK-based banks in deposits and loans, their issuance and purchase of bonds, notes and various money-market instruments, but they exclude direct investments, equity and derivatives positions.

23   Shaxson, in *Treasure Islands*, gives a useful survey of these centres, mainly focused on tax avoidance. Palan offers another perspective, but one that greatly exaggerates their political and economic independence, arguing, absurdly, that they indicate the 'demise of the nation state'. Ronen Palan, *The*

Offshore World: Sovereign Markets, Virtual Places and Nomad Millionaires, New York: Cornell University Press, 2003, especially chapters 6 and 7.

24   Funds from these tax havens are in addition to those received more directly by the City from a variety of criminals, and presumably also at relatively low cost. See Leila Simona Talani, *Globalization, Hegemony and the Future of the City of London*, Basingstoke: Palgrave Macmillan, 2010, where Chapter 6 is a good review of London as a money-laundering centre.

25   BEA, *Survey of Current Business*, July 2012, Tables K, L and M, pp. 14–15, at bea.gov.

26   'The Rt Hon Gordon Brown Officially Opens Lehman Brothers' New European Headquarters', Lehman Brothers Press Release, 5 April 2004.

27   Martin Wolf, 'The Case of Brussels and Banker Bonuses', *Financial Times*, 1 March 2013.

9. Eternal Interests, Temporary Allies

1   BoE, 'The UK at the Heart of a Renewed Globalisation', speech given by Mark Carney, Governor of the Bank of England, at an event to celebrate the 125th anniversary of the *Financial Times*, 24 October 2013, p. 7, at bankofengland.co.uk.

2   Ibid. p. 4.

3   A Canadian with strong British links, Carney was formerly the governor of the Bank of Canada and is yet another official financial alumnus of Goldman Sachs. He was taken on to replace Mervyn King, who had fallen out of favour, not least for his critical comments on British banks.

4   Martin Wolf, 'Bank of England's Mark Carney Places a Bet on Big Finance', *Financial Times*, 29 October 2013.

5   Other examples include new Basel rules for the required levels of bank capital and proposals from the UK's Vickers Commission on Banking to 'ring fence' retail banking from what was considered to be more risky wholesale market activities. See BIS, 'The Basel III Capital Framework: A Decisive Breakthrough', speech by Hervé Hannoun, Deputy General Manager of the Bank for International Settlements, 22 November 2010; Patrick Jenkins, 'HSBC Prepares to Leap the Vickers Ringfence', *Financial Times*, 8 December 2013; 'The Independent Commission on Banking: The Vickers Report', House of Commons Library Standard Note SNBT 6171, by Timothy Edmonds, 3 January 2013.

6   Oxfam, 'Financial Transaction Tax', 2014, at oxfam.org.

7   Thomas Richter, 'Financial Transaction Tax Will Damage Economy', *Financial Times*, 8 September 2013.

8   Joshua Smith, 'Update on the EU's Proposed Financial Transactions Tax', 24 June 2014, available at lexology.com.

9   Philip Stafford and Brooke Masters, 'Libor Deal Commences Rehabilitation of Benchmark', *Financial Times*, 9 July 2013.

10   Mark Hollingsworth and Stewart Lansley, *Londongrad: From Russia with Cash. The Inside Story of the Oligarchs*, London: Fourth Estate Ltd, 2010.

11   Nicholas Watt, 'UK Seeking to Ensure Russia Sanctions Do Not Harm City of London', *Guardian*, 3 March 2014.

12   Partick Jenkins and Camilla Hall, 'Sheikh in Barclays Rescue Sells Stake', *Financial Times*, 18 July 2013.

13   Owen Jones, 'The Left Must Put Britain's EU Withdrawal on the Agenda', *Guardian*, 14 July 2015.

14   BBC News, 'Cameron Unveils Islamic Bond Plan', 29 October 2013, at news .bbc.co.uk.

15   Elaine Moore and Thomas Hale, 'UK Sukuk Bond Sale Attracts £2bn in Orders', *Financial Times*, 25 June 2014.

16   TheCityUK, *UK: the Leading Western Centre for Islamic Finance*, October 2013, at thecityuk.com.

17   BEA, 'US International Transactions Tables', 2014, pp. 2, 79–81, at bea.gov.

18   Walter and Howie, *Red Capitalism*, p. 163.

19   BBC News, 'BRICS Nations to Create $100bn Development Bank', 15 July 2014, at news.bbc.co.uk.

20   Josh Noble, 'Renminbi Joins Top Five Most-Used Currencies', *Financial Times*, 28 January 2015.

21   Josh Noble, 'UK and China Establish Currency Swap Line', *Financial Times*, 23 June 2013.

22   Lucy Hornby and Patrick Jenkins 2013, 'Chancellor George Osborne Cements London as Renminbi Hub', *Financial Times*, 15 October 2013.

23   Simon Rabinovitch and James Fontanella-Khan, 'London to Dominate Rmb? Not So Fast, Says Luxembourg', *Financial Times*, 31 October 2013.

24   HM Treasury, 'Britain Issues Western World's First Sovereign RMB Bond, Largest Ever RMB Bond by Non-Chinese Issuer', 14 September 2014, at gov .uk.

25   Geoff Dyer and George Parker, 'US Accuses UK over China Stance', *Financial Times*, 12 March 2015.

26   George Parker, Anne-Sylvaine Chassany and Geoff Dyer, 'Europeans Defy US to Join China-Led Development Bank', *Financial Times*, 16 March 2015.

27 Jamie Smyth, 'Australia to Join China-led Bank Despite US Opposition', *Financial Times*, 28 March 2015.

28 Simon Mundy, 'South Korea to Join China-led Development Bank', *Financial Times*, 27 March 2015.

29 Gerald F. Seib, 'Obama Presses Case for Asia Trade Deal, Warns Failure Would Benefit China', *Wall Street Journal*, 27 April 2015.

30 Marx, *Capital*, Volume 1, Chapter 10, p. 224.

Select Bibliography

Below are some books and articles the reader may find useful to follow up, listed under headings that correspond to themes raised in this book. Otherwise, detailed references to works I have cited, and sources of data, are given in the footnotes to the main text.

The world monetary system

Eichengreen, Barry 2011, *Exorbitant Privilege: The Rise and Fall of the Dollar*, Oxford: Oxford University Press

Konings, Martijn 2009, 'American Finance and Empire in Historical Perspective', in Panitch, Leo and Martijn Konings (eds) 2009, *American Empire and the Political Economy of Global Finance*, Hampshire: Palgrave Macmillan

Michie, Ranald C. 1992, *The City of London: Continuity and Change, 1850–1990*, London: Macmillan

Norfield, Tony 2014, 'Capitalist Production Good, Capitalist Finance Bad', 6 January 2014, economicsofimperialism.blogspot.com

Spiro, David E. 1999, *The Hidden Hand of American Hegemony: Petrodollar Recycling and International Markets*, New York: Cornell University Press

Steil, Benn 2013, *The Battle of Bretton Woods: John Maynard Keynes, Harry Dexter White, and the Making of a New World Order*, Council on Foreign Relations Books, New Jersey: Princeton University Press

Contemporary economic and financial developments

Christophers, Brett 2013, *Banking Across Boundaries: Placing Finance in Capitalism*, Chichester: Wiley-Blackwell

Lewis, Michael 2011, 'When Irish Eyes Are Crying', *Vanity Fair*, 8 February 2011

Milberg, William and Deborah Winkler 2012, 'Trade, Crisis, and Recovery: Restructuring Global Value Chains' in *Global Value Chains in a Postcrisis World, A Development Perspective*, Washington: World Bank

Norfield, Tony 2012, 'Derivatives and Capitalist Markets: the Speculative Heart of Capital', *Historical Materialism*, Vol. 20 No. 1, 2012

No.rfield, Tony 2013, 'Derivatives, Money, Finance and Imperialism: A Response to Bryan and Rafferty', *Historical Materialism*, Vol. 21 No. 2, 2012

Shaxson, Nicholas 2011, *Treasure Islands: Tax Havens and the Men Who Stole the World*, London: The Bodley Head

Smith, John 2013, 'Southern Labour – "Peripheral" No Longer: A Reply to Jane Hardy', *International Socialism*, 140, isj.org.uk

Vitali, S, Glattfelder J. B., Battiston S 2011, 'The Network of Global Corporate Control', available at: plosone.org

Reviews of British imperialism

Bayly, Christopher and Tim Harper 2007, *Forgotten Wars*, London: Allen Lane

Cain, P. J. and A. G. Hopkins 2002, *British Imperialism, 1688–2000*, London: Longman

Curtis, Mark 2003, *Web of Deceit: Britain's Real Role in the World*, London: Vintage

Darwin, John 2009, *The Empire Project: The Rise and Fall of the British World-System, 1830–1970*, Cambridge: Cambridge University Press

Fieldhouse, 'The Labour Governments and the Empire-Commonwealth, 1945–51', in Ritchie Ovendale (ed), *The Foreign Policy of the British Labour Governments, 1945–51*, Leicester: Leicester University Press, 1984.

Gupta, Partha Sarathi 1975, *Imperialism and the British Labour Movement, 1914–1964*, London: Macmillan Press

Newsinger, John 2006, *The Blood Never Dried: A People's History of the British Empire*, London: Bookmarks

Index